INDIA AND THE MIDDLE EAST

INDIA AND THE MIDDLE EAST

Prithvi Ram Mudiam

British Academic Press
An Imprint of I.B.Tauris
London · New York

To my Father and Mother

Published in 1994 by
British Academic Press
45 Bloomsbury Square
London WC1A 2HY

An imprint of I.B.Tauris & Co Ltd

In the United States of America
and Canada distributed by
St Martin's Press
175 Fifth Avenue
New York
NY 10010

ISBN 1 85043 703 3

A CIP record for this book is available from the British Library.

Library of Congress Catalog card number: 93–60685
A full CIP record is available from the Library of Congress

Typeset by Philip Armstrong, Oxford
Printed and bound in Great Britain by
WBC Ltd, Bridgend, Mid Glamorgan

Contents

Preface

This book is a modified version of my doctoral thesis submitted to the University of London in May 1991. The substantial part of the thesis was completed by the end of 1990. As such, the events of 1991 and 1992 either in the Middle East or in the superpower relations had very little bearing on its contents or conclusions. And hence, it was a conscious and deliberate decision on my part not to update the thesis. Nothing that has happened in the Middle East since the completion of my work has, in any substantial way, disproved or invalidated any of my major arguments or conclusions. In a sense the dramatic developments after 1991 were a truly different trajectory which has only tenuous causal connection with the previous era, although they now provide a new contextual perspective.

No doubt the Iraqi occupation of Kuwait and its subsequent liberation by the US-sponsored and -led international coalition under the auspices of the UN have changed the tenor and content of Middle Eastern politics dramatically. But the Indian response to this major crisis in the Middle East was (not surprisingly) confused, ad hoc and ineffectual. India, having conveniently and smugly reduced Middle Eastern politics to the Arab-Israeli dispute over the decades, has found herself in a political and diplomatic quandary. No wonder the Indian leadership simply did not know how to react to a situation wherein an inter-Arab dispute saw the majority of the Arab countries arrayed on the same side as the superpowers and Israel against a fellow Arab country. Similarly, the recent establishment of full diplomatic relations with Israel (which I advocated in my thesis) in no way either explains or justifies India's attitude to the Jewish state over the years; nor does it detract from the criticisms which I put forward in relation to India's earlier treatment of Israel. In short, it is my considered opinion that the book has lost very little in terms of argument or perspective because of my decision not to update it.

This study seeks to examine critically India's relations with the Middle East in terms of India's political, security and economic interests in the region between 1947 and 1986. It tries to define India's general foreign policy objectives and the means and strategies she adopted to realize them in relation to the Middle East. The study focuses on the misperceptions and fallacies that governed India's interaction with the region, which over the years artificially restricted India's manoeuvrability and policy options in the region.

The introductory chapter provides a historical backdrop of independent India's foreign policy with special reference to the Middle East. The first and second chapters focus on India's politico-diplomatic interests in the region by examining India's bilateral ties with the four most important states in the region, namely Egypt, Iraq, Iran and Saudi Arabia. The third chapter critically evaluates India's security concerns in the region with special emphasis on developments in the 1970s and 80s and India's responses to them. The fourth chapter seeks to quantify India's economic interaction with the region and endeavours to put India's economic stake in the region in perspective. Chapters five and six concentrate on India's relations with Israel and the PLO respectively and emphasize the need for India to take a fresh look at the problem in the light of new and far-reaching developments in the region.

This study takes the view that the constancy of India's Middle Eastern policy is more an outcome of lack of imagination and an absence of subtlety and sensitivity on the part of the Indian political elite than any unwavering commitment on its part to any high principles and ideals. It also underlines the untenability of such a policy in future in the context of the rapidly changing political and strategic landscape of the Middle East.

Academic research is a demanding but rather lonely occupation. Many individuals and institutions have helped me in various ways to steer my research endeavours to a successful conclusion. To start with, I would like to express my grateful thanks to my supervisor, Dr. Gautam Sen, for reposing so much faith in me and for his constant support and encouragement. No words can adequately express my sense of gratitude and indebtedness to my "friend, philosopher and guide" at the LSE, Prof. T.J. Nossiter. He was a source of great encouragement and inspiration to me throughout and helped me in innumerable ways, not only in the completion of my thesis but also in its publication. I thank him from the bottom of my heart.

I am extremely grateful to the London School of Economics for awarding me a Studentship, without which neither my PhD nor book would have been possible, and to the Committee of Vice-Chancellors and Principals (CVCP) for granting me an Overseas Research Students Award (ORS) which covered a substantial part of my tuition fee. My thanks are also due to the Central Research Fund (CRF), University of London, for awarding me a travel grant for my study tour to Washington D.C. I am indebted to Prof. Avi Shalaim of St Antony's College, Oxford, for reading my chapter on Indo-Israeli relations and making valuable suggestions. I also take this opportunity to express my sincere and heartfelt thanks to Prof. G. Ram Reddy, the then Vice-Chancellor of the Indira Gandhi National Open University (IGNOU), whose help and generosity made my field trip to New Delhi both successful and comfortable.

I acknowledge with gratitude the assistance I received from the staff of various libraries: the British Library of Economic and Political Science, the School of Oriental and African Studies, Chatham House, the International Institute for Strategic Studies in London, Sapru House, Patiala House, Jawaharlal Nehru University (JNU), the Federation of Indian Chambers of Commerce and Industry, the Institute of Defence Studies and Analysis and the Indian Institute of Foreign Trade in New Delhi, and the Library of Congress and the Woodrow Wilson Center for Advanced International Studies in Washington D.C.

I also thank all the academics, diplomats, bureaucrats and journalists - particularly Messrs. A.P. Venkateswaran, A.K. Damodaran, Girilal Jain, H.K. Dua, Sridhar, Prof. M.S. Agwani and Dr. Girijesh Pant - who were kind enough to share with me their views which no doubt went a long way in enhancing my own understanding of the intricacies of India's interaction with the Middle East.

I simply cannot thank adequately Ms. Alma Gibbons (Word Processing Advisor - LSE), for being instrumental in preparing the Camera Ready Copy (CRC) for the publishers.

It is with great pleasure that I acknowledge my friends Prabhakar, Stelios, Kirti, Subbu, Partho, Bayjool, John, Bello, Pradhip, Rajiv, Damayanti, Mr. Sinha and Dr. Pramod for their companionship and consideration. Finally, I thank my publishers I.B.Tauris, particularly Dr. Lester Crook, for their courtesy and cooperation.

Needless to say that while this book owes its existence to the help, intellectual and otherwise, that I received from many quarters, I alone am responsible for its contents.

Prithvi Ram Mudiam
September, 1993

Introduction

The foreign policy of India, like that of any other country, has sought to maintain, since independence, a balance between its long-term goals and short-term objectives through a variety of means, political, diplomatic, economic and military, either separately or in combination, depending on their appropriateness for the occasion and the existing national capabilities. A detailed discussion of India's foreign policy objectives in general, and the emphasis placed on the means to obtain them, would throw considerable light on the question of where the Middle East is perceived to stand in the eyes of the policy-makers in Delhi in terms of its importance *vis-à-vis* India's politico-strategic, diplomatic and economic goals.

However, the general objectives of India's foreign policy and their orientation towards the Middle East are best analysed in the context of the perspectives and attitudes that developed during the freedom struggle, along with the geopolitical situation obtaining in the world at the time of independence.

The contacts between the Indian subcontinent and the Middle East date back almost to the beginnings of recorded history, and there have been extensive political, commercial and cultural ties between the two regions over the centuries.[1] The great ancient civilizations of the Nile, Mesopotamia and the Indus valley were not only contemporaneous but also interacted with each other. The extensive trade relations between the two regions led to the establishment of Arab settlements on the western and southern coasts of India and that of the Indians along the Gulf, as well as in Alexandria in Egypt.

The advent of Islam and subsequent penetration of the subcontinent by successive Muslim adventurers from the Middle East reached its apogee with the establishment of the Mughal empire in India in the 16th century, and brought the two regions closer than ever before in political and cultural spheres, leading to the conversion of a large native population to Islam.

From the time of the first sustained Muslim influences in the eleventh century, the models for political structures and processes, as well as religious inspiration for an important segment of the subcontinental population and cultural influences, came from Iran and the Arab Middle East.[2]

The onset of the Industrial Revolution in Europe marked the beginning of a new era in human history. The new and superior European technology and organization led to the gradual penetration and conquest of Afro-Asian societies by the Europeans. The Middle Eastern land mass now constituted a crucial link between the continents of Asia, Africa and Europe and was called the "gateway of Asia and Africa". It was this unhappy but common experience of European imperial domination that has brought the two regions together since the 18th century.

Common historical experience of imperial domination
Though the process of European domination, first commercial and later political, of the Indian subcontinent and the Middle East started more or less simultaneously, it was not until the end of World War I that the entire Middle Eastern region came under European tutelage. The consolidation of the British rule in India sealed the fate of the Middle East as well, for the latter commanded the imperial communication lines to India. The opening of the Suez Canal in 1869, linking the Mediterranean and the Red Sea, made the region a virtual nerve-centre of international communications both over land and sea. Till the First World War, Britain sought to protect its lines of communication to India through the Middle East by supporting the Ottoman empire in order to prevent the other European powers from getting a foothold in the region, and by establishing a series of protectorates in the Persian Gulf during the 19th century. However, towards the end of the 19th century, Britain recognized France as the dominant power in Algeria, Morocco and Tunisia, and Libya came under Italian control. After the First World War, following the collapse of the Ottoman empire, Britain and France divided the Fertile Crescent consisting of Palestine, Lebanon, Syria and Iraq between themselves under the Mandates System.

However, the interwar period witnessed the rise of strong nationalistic sentiments in both the regions and helped to forge new bonds of camaraderie.

While the nationalist movement in India sympathised with the national aspirations of the Arabs, the latter realised that their own emancipation was tied up with the outcome of the Indian struggle.[3]

Such sentiments were readily reciprocated by many of the Middle Eastern freedom fighters. An Iraqi statesman, Kamil al-Chadirchi, wrote to Jawaharlal Nehru in 1938:

We wholeheartedly appreciate your struggle, and wish we had the opportunity to share in it though in a small measure, for we both are in the same boat. True endeavour in the campaign against imperialism and exploitation must not be considered in separate units, but rather that neither geographical frontiers nor political obstacles can suppress it.[4]

Jawaharlal Nehru, who always considered India's struggle for freedom as part of a larger world drama, wrote to his daughter Indira in 1933:

The Nationalist movements of India and Egypt have adopted different methods but fundamentally the urge for national freedom is the same. And the way imperialism functions in its efforts to suppress these nationalist movements is also much the same. So each one of us can learn much from the other's experiences.[5]

The Congress of Oppressed Nationalities held in Brussels in 1927 was a momentous event in the struggle against imperialism, because for the first time an attempt was made to coordinate the freedom movements in various parts of the world and to create an institutional framework for such coordination. Jawaharlal Nehru, who attended the Congress of Oppressed Nationalities in Brussels as the official representative of the Indian National Congress (INC), took a very active and enthusiastic part in the proceedings of the Congress and was also made a member of the Presidium. The general agenda of the Brussels Congress included, inter alia:

Co-operation between the national liberation movements in oppressed countries and the labour and anti-imperialist movements in imperialist countries [and] Establishment of a permanent world-wide organization linking up all forces against imperialism and colonial oppression.[6]

Egypt, Persia, Syria, Morocco, French North Africa, the Dutch East Indies, Korea, Mexico and the states of Central and South America were among the participants. The Brussels Congress enabled Nehru to develop personal contacts with leaders of freedom movements from different parts of the world, particularly from Asia, which left a deep and lasting impression on him.

A permanent organization, "the League against Imperialism", was formed to provide a sense of unity and solidarity to freedom struggles all over the world, and Nehru was made an honorary president of the League as well as a member of the Executive Committee. In his report to the All India Congress Committee (AICC) on the Brussels Congress, Nehru urged that India should develop close and direct contacts with various nationalist organizations in Asia, not only to publicize India's own struggle but also to broaden its outlook on foreign affairs.

The INC responded by proposing a session of the Pan-Asiatic Federation in India some time in 1930 which, however, failed to materialize for various reasons. It also sent out letters of invitation to nationalist organizations in Egypt, Palestine and Tunisia inviting "fraternal" delegations to annual Congress sessions, and many such delegations from various countries attended the annual sessions of the INC in the 1930s and '40s. Moreover, the 1928 annual session of the INC adopted a resolution declaring that the Indian struggle for freedom was part of the general world struggle against imperialism, and that India should develop contacts with freedom struggles elsewhere. Nehru's passion for Asian resurgence in world affairs, which almost bordered on the romantic, inevitably led to close personal rapport and friendship with leaders such as Mustafa Nahas of Egypt, Faris al-Khuri of Syria and Iraq's Kamil al-Chadirchi.[7]

The British policy of divide and rule

The British policy of "divide and rule" was one of the most significant factors that made the Middle East loom large in the perceptions and calculations of the Indian leaders even during the freedom struggle. This was not a policy devised exclusively for India by the British. They found it both expedient and effective to use such tactics by pitting one community against another or one tribe against another whenever such an opportunity presented itself anywhere in their vast empire in order to cling on to their imperial possessions.

The Muslims, who constituted a substantial minority in India, were particularly vulnerable to such tactics for certain historical reasons. The

Muslim invaders from the Middle East were different from the earlier invaders of the Indian subcontinent in the sense that the former brought with them a new, vigorous and proselytizing religion, Islam, which was fundamentally at variance with Hinduism, the predominant religion of the subcontinent. As a result, the Muslim community in the subcontinent successfully resisted the all-absorbing and integrating progress of Hinduism and to a large measure retained its distinct identity. Though the two communities interacted with each other at a political and social level, there was very little meeting ground between the two, and the accent over the years was on coexistence rather than integration.

The arrival of the British introduced a new element into the picture. The British held the Indian Muslims largely responsible for the 1857 revolt and made a conscious attempt to sideline the community thereafter. The Muslims themselves, shattered by the failure of the revolt and the subsequent British oppression, withdrew into their shell.

When Sir Syed Ahmad Khan started the "Muslim Renaissance" in the 1870s, he was a nationalist to begin with.[8] The fact that he sought to achieve a rapprochement between the British and the Muslim communities in India by stressing the loyalty of the latter to the British rule somewhat diluted his nationalist sentiments. However, the prospect of progressive introduction of representative institutions in India by the British made him positively hostile to the idea of Indian nationalism.

He wrote to Badruddin Tyabji in 1888:

I do not understand what the words "national congress" mean. Is it supposed that the different castes and creeds living in India belong to one nation, or can become one nation; and their aims and aspirations be one and the same? I think it is quite impossible and when it is impossible there can be no such thing as a National Congress, nor can it be of equal benefit to all peoples.[9]

Referring to the logic of electoral politics in India he said:

It is certain the Hindu members will have four times as many [votes] because their population is four times as numerous. Therefore, we can prove by mathematics that there will be four votes for the Hindu to every one vote for the Mahomedan. And now how can the Mahomedan guard his interests? It would be like a game of dice, in which one man had four dice and the other only one.[10]

The fear of being reduced from proud overlordship to the status of a permanent minority haunted the Indian Muslims and found expression in their representation to Lord Minto in 1906 which urged that

> ... the position accorded to the Mahomedan community in any kind of representation, direct or indirect, ... should be commensurate not merely with their numerical strength but also with their political importance ... [and to] give due consideration to the position which they occupied in India a little more than a hundred years ago ...[11]

The founding of the All-India Muslim League in 1906 was the logical consequence of such fears and aspirations and came as a godsend to the British administration in India which was confronted with the increasingly militant tide of secular nationalism of the Indian National Congress. This development also sensitized the INC to the fears, aspirations and sensibilities of the Indian Muslims, and it started taking an active interest even in issues that affected the Indian Muslims exclusively. This period also witnessed the INC's increasing interest in and attention to the Muslim states of the Middle East. While this could be partly explained in terms of the necessity of solidarity among anti-imperialist movements the world over, it was also partly aimed at the domestic Muslim constituency in India, which was increasingly being used by the British to counter the growing popularity and strength of the INC.

The Khilafat issue

The arrival of Gandhi on the Indian political horizon heralded the dawn of mass-based politics. His basic strategy was to transform the INC into a political institution which would represent and reconcile the interests of the divergent religious, ethnic and ideological groups so that it could present a united front to British imperialism. When the Khilafat issue came to the forefront in 1920, Gandhi grabbed it with both hands as a golden opportunity to forge Hindu-Muslim unity. He, in fact, considered it as providing such an opportunity of uniting Hindus and Muhammadans as would not arise in a hundred years.

The issue itself was fairly simple.[12] The Sultan of Turkey, known as Caliph or Khalifa, was considered by Muslims all over the world as their spiritual head. However, the First World War saw Turkey join the side of Germany in fighting Britain. This placed the Indian Muslims in a real predicament, as they were torn between their fears about the fate of the Khalifate and their loyalty to the British. Since the British Indian Army included many Muslims, the British government took pains to assure the Indian Muslims that Turkey would get a fair deal in any post-war settlement. However, the armistice which ended the war not only deprived Turkey of its lands but also put the Sultan under the control of the allied powers. The Khilafat movement was aimed at defending the Khalifate. In a nutshell, it sought "Muslim control over every portion of the Jazirat-ul-Arab, the Khilafa's wardenship of the Holy Places, and the integrity of the Ottoman empire".[13]

The Indian National Congress had been sensitive to the feelings of Indian Muslims towards the fate of Turkey from the beginning. At the annual session of the Congress in 1912, its President R.N. Mudholkar referred to the profound sorrow and sympathy which all non-Muslim Indians felt for their Muslim countrymen because of the misfortunes of the Caliphate. He hoped that it might be possible to meet the legitimate aspirations of the Christian provinces of the Ottoman empire without destroying the latter or making it powerless.[14] At the next session of the Congress in 1913, the President Nawab Syed Mohammad made further reference to the troubles of the Islamic world outside India and the anxiety they caused among Indian Muslims.[15]

However, with the advent of Gandhi, the entire complexion of the Congress started changing rapidly. The Congress was no longer content with passing resolutions. These resolutions had to be supported by mass action in order to put pressure on the government. Gandhi found the time opportune for such movement following the Jallianwala Bagh massacre, which shocked the whole country, and the Khilafat issue, which greatly agitated the Indian Muslims for a long time. In his letter to the Viceroy, Gandhi averred

that the Imperial Government have acted in the Khilafat matter in an unscrupulous, immoral and unjust manner and have been moving from wrong to wrong in order to defend their immorality ...[16]

The Non-Cooperation Resolution adopted by the INC at its Calcutta session in 1920 emphasized the importance of the Khilafat issue to the Indian Muslims, and called upon the non-Muslim Indians to support their Muslim brethren in their hour of trial and tribulation.

In view of the fact that on the Khilafat question both the Indian and Imperial Governments have signally failed in their duty towards the Musalmans of India and the Prime Minister has deliberately

broken his pledge word given to them, and that it is the duty of
every non-Moslem Indian in every legitimate manner to assist his
Musalman brother in his attempt to remove the religious calamity
that has overtaken him.[17]

The Hindu-Muslim unity which Gandhi desperately tried to promote by
making the Congress adopt the Khilafat issue proved to be extremely short-
lived, because it had very little to do with the real issue that haunted the
Indian Muslims, i.e. their position in the post-British political dispensation
in India. As long as this issue remained unsolved, no amount of support
to pan-Islamic issues was going to win the confidence of the Indian
Muslims. As one writer points out,

... it [Khilafat] was a movement which might have taken the road
towards some form of Muslim nationalism if it had not started on
the wrong - i.e. Pan-Islamic - foot.[18]

Nehru made a very accurate assessment of the Non-Cooperation
Movement.

Looking at this question from the point of religious groups, the
Muslims had joined the movement, as a body, chiefly because of the
Khilafat. This was a purely religious question affecting the Muslims
only, and non-Muslims had nothing to do with it. Gandhi, however,
adopted it and encouraged others to do so, because he felt it his
duty to help a brother in distress. He also hoped in this way to bring
the Hindus and Muslims nearer each other. The general Muslim
outlook was thus one of Muslim nationalism or Muslim inter-
nationalism and not of true nationalism. For the moment the conflict
between the two was not apparent.[19]

Moreover, the shallowness of the Khilafat issue became quite clear when
the Turks themselves, under Kemal Pasha, abolished the Caliphate and
declared Turkey a Republic in 1923.

This approach of the INC to win the approval and confidence of the
Indian Muslims by strongly supporting pan-Islamic issues which had little
more than an emotional appeal to them, which were essentially external
in nature and had no relevance or bearing on the real issues confronting
the Indian Muslims, spilled over into the thinking of the post-independence
India as well, and influenced its policy towards the Middle East, as we
shall see later.

The Palestine problem

The Palestine problem, which came to the forefront following the Balfour Declaration in 1917, was another issue related to the Middle East which caught the attention of Indian leaders during the freedom struggle. The attitude of the Indian leaders towards this issue was of considerable importance, for the perceptions and predilections that evolved in relation to this issue have had an important bearing on the policies of free India towards the region.

As Turkey joined World War I on the side of Germany and Austro-Hungary against Britain, France and Russia, the Sultan of Turkey, who was considered the spiritual head of Muslims the world over, issued an appeal to all Muslims for loyalty in a jihad. This made the British jittery, because they feared that this appeal might touch a responsive chord among Muslims in the Middle East and even in British India. At about the same time, Arab nationalists sent feelers to the British to gauge their war aims. In 1915, an agreement was reached between the British representative, Sir Henry McMahon, and the Arab leader Hussain who was the Sheriff of Mecca, under which Hussain was to call an Arab revolt against Turkey with the help of British funds, arms and advisors, while the British government committed itself in writing that once the Turks were defeated it would recognize one independent Arab state all over Syria (which then included Palestine and Transjordan) and Iraq.

However, in 1916, Britain and France signed a secret agreement known as the Sykes-Picot agreement which sought to divide the Eastern Arab World into British and French spheres of influence, partly under Arab suzerainty but subordinate to and subserving the dominant power concerned.

Britain also sought to woo the Jews to the allied cause, because they were sympathetic to Germany out of their hatred for the anti-Semitic Czarist Russia. It was felt that the pacifist tendencies of American Jews who played a crucial role in American industry had to be overcome. It was further argued that American entry into the war, or at least American financial help, would be encouraged by some promise to Zionism.

On 2 November 1917, Lord Balfour, the Foreign Secretary of Britain, made an official statement in relation to the Jewish demand for a homeland, popularly known as the "Balfour Declaration". It stated that

> His Majesty's Government view with favour the establishment in Palestine of a national home for the Jewish people and will use their best endeavours to facilitate the achievement of this object, it being

clearly understood that nothing shall be done which may prejudice the civil and religious rights of the existing non-Jewish Communities in Palestine ...[20]

The multiplicity of contradictory promises made to different parties by the allied powers in order to gain their support for the war effort was not meant to be kept. Without even waiting for the formal convening of the League of Nations which was supposed to bestow the mandates, the allied powers shared the mandates amongst themselves. Two independent states of Syria and Lebanon were created, to be under French influence. Iraq and Palestine were to be under British mandate, with a special clause provided for giving effect to the Balfour Declaration.

However as Nehru points out, "Palestine was not a wilderness or an empty, uninhabited place. It was already somebody else's home."[21] While expressing "sympathy for the Jews in the terrible trials they are passing through in Europe", Nehru did not lose sight of the basic fact that "Palestine is essentially an Arab country, and must remain so, and the Arabs must not be crushed and suppressed in their own homelands."[22] Nehru was also quite convinced that the real issue in Palestine was not religion but imperialism. "... England pits Jewish religious nationalism against Arab nationalism and makes it appear that her presence is necessary to act as an arbitrator and to keep the peace between the two."[23] The future of Palestine could be secured only "on the stable foundation of Arab-Jew cooperation and the elimination of imperialism".[24]

Like Nehru, Mahatma Gandhi also had nothing but sympathy for the age-old persecution of the Jews whom he described as the "untouchables of Christianity". However, this sympathy he had for Jews, he said, should not obscure the requirements of justice. His reasoning was clear, simple and logical.

> Palestine belongs to the Arabs in the same sense that England belongs to the English or France to the French. It is wrong and inhuman to impose the Jews on the Arabs .... Surely it would be a crime against humanity to reduce the proud Arabs so that Palestine can be restored to the Jews partly or wholly as their national home.
>
> The nobler course would be to insist on a just treatment of the Jews wherever they are born and live. The Jews born in France are French in precisely the same sense that Christians born in France are French. If the Jews have no home but Palestine, will they relish the idea of being forced to leave the other parts of the world in which

they are settled? Or do they want a double home where they can remain at will? This cry for a national home affords a colourable justification for the German expulsion of the Jews.[25]

It was expected that the Indian National Congress would reflect the views of its two most important leaders, Gandhi and Nehru. As early as 1921, the Congress Working Committee passed a resolution "to assure the Musalman States, that when India has attained self-government her foreign policy will naturally be always guided so as to respect the religious obligations imposed upon Musalmans by Islam".[26] In 1922, the INC asserted that unless "the Jazirat-el-Arab [the Arab World] were freed from all non-Muslim control there cannot be peace and contentment in India".[27] The Congress session in Madras in 1927 asked for the withdrawal of Indian troops from Mesopotamia (Iraq) and Persia (Iran) and from all other countries.[28] In 1928, sympathy was extended to Egypt, Syria, Palestine and Iraq in their struggle against Western imperialism.[29]

In 1936, the Congress Working Committee sent its greetings to the Arabs in Palestine and expressed its sympathy for their struggle for freedom. At its insistence, 27 September 1936 was observed as "Palestine Day" and meetings and demonstrations were organized all over the country. In 1937, the AICC protested vigorously against the reign of terror in Palestine and strongly supported the Arab opposition to the proposed partition of Palestine.[30] In 1938, it appealed "to the Jews not to seek the shelter of the British Mandatory and not to allow themselves to be exploited in the interests of British imperialism".[31] Again, in 1939 the Congress, in its annual session, adopted a resolution on Palestine expressing its sympathy with the Arabs, and looking forward to the emergence of an independent democratic state in Palestine with adequate provision for the protection of Jewish rights. In the same year, it adopted another resolution condemning Hitler's pogroms against Jews and offered them asylum in India, but criticized Jews for relying on "British armed forces to advance their special privileges in Palestine and thus aligned themselves on the side of the British imperialism".[32]

While the consistent support of the INC for the Arab cause in general and the Palestine issue in particular can be explained in terms of anti-imperialism, a growing sense of Asian solidarity and the innate justness of the issues involved, it must be noted that there were more mundane and less altruistic motives behind this support. The political stalemate between the INC and the Muslim League over the issue of the status of the Muslims in post-British India, and the skilful exploitation of this stalemate by the

British in order to perpetuate their increasingly tenuous hold over the subcontinent necessitated such support. Gandhi himself made it very clear when he said the following with reference to the Khilafat movement.

> If I were not interested in the Indian Mohammedans, I would not interest myself in the welfare of the Turks any more than I am in that of the Austrians or the Palestinians. But by helping the Mohammedans of India at a critical moment in their history, I want to buy their friendship.[33]

Similarly, leaders like Gandhi and Nehru and the Indian National Congress could never have agreed to the partition of Palestine on the basis of religion while repudiating and resisting such a demand from Indian Muslims.

It should suffice to say that there was as much pragmatism involved in this approach as principle, and it was one of those rare occasions when policy coincided with precept. However, the more the Congress tried to win over the support of Indian Muslims by supporting pan-Islamic issues, the less it addressed itself to the domestic issues that affected them. It was this stalemate which eventually led to the partition of the subcontinent and the creation of Pakistan.

The creation of Pakistan

The question of relative status between the Hindu majority and Muslim minority has always been an underlying current of the Muslim separatist tendencies in the Indian subcontinent. Muslim separatism and the subsequent demand for Pakistan was essentially a quest for parity on the part of Indian Muslims *vis-à-vis* Hindus who were numerically in a majority. Sir Syed Ahmad Khan broached this question as early as 1888.

> Is it possible that under these circumstances two nations - the Mohammedan and Hindu - could sit on the same throne and remain equal in power? Most certainly not. It is necessary that one of them should conquer the other and thrust it down. To hope that both could remain equal is to desire the impossible and the inconceivable.[34]

This claim and clamour for parity on the part of the Muslims was based on certain historical grounds - of course, as seen by the Muslims themselves. Firstly, the Muslims conquered India from the Hindus despite the latter's numerical superiority. So, minority status which would have implied permanent political subordination and inferiority to the Hindus was not acceptable. As Sisir Gupta observes,

> It ought to be remembered that the demand for Pakistan and the two-nation theory was advanced by the Muslim League as a culmination of its demand for parity, essentially parity of status between the 25 per cent Muslims and the rest in India. It is because of the impossibility of solving the status problem in terms of majority and minority, which almost by definition determines the status of the two groups, that the two-nation theory was advanced.[35]

Secondly, since the English conquered India from the Muslims, it was incumbent upon the former to ensure that the Muslims got an equal share of the power which would befit and be commensurate with their status as the erstwhile rulers of India. Thus, the partition of India on the basis of religion did not solve the problem of relative status of the two communities but only institutionalized it.[36]

Another factor that complicates Indo-Pakistani relations is the divergent ideological foundations of the two states. While India proclaimed itself as a liberal secular state, Pakistan declared itself to be an Islamic country.[37] In a nutshell, the two states represented irreconcilable ideological conflict between secularism and theocracy.

Prima facie, each country has a vested interest in the collapse of the other. If India's secularism is successful, given its large Muslim minority even after partition, the *raison d'être* for the very creation of Pakistan is undermined. Further fragmentation of Pakistan along regional or linguistic lines would also dilute the two-nation theory. On the other hand, if India's experiment with secularism fails, it would only validate and strengthen the two-nation theory.

In other words, if secular nationalism is an essential prerequisite for the survival of India's unity and integrity, religion is an inseparable part of Pakistani nationalism. This ideological antagonism would remain more or less a permanent feature in Indo-Pakistani relations.

Moreover, the bloodbath that accompanied partition and the mass exodus that took place across the border in both directions made it almost impossible to establish normal relations between the two countries.

The Kashmir issue

The Kashmir issue[38] which closely followed on the heels of partition, more or less symbolized the underlying conflict between the two countries and buried any hopes of rapprochement in the foreseeable future. At the time of Indian independence, the Princely states, which enjoyed nominal independence under British rule, were given the freedom of choice to join either India or Pakistan or remain independent.

However, problems arose only in relation to three Princely states, namely Junagadh, Hyderabad and Kashmir. In case of Junagadh and Hyderabad, though the rulers were Muslim, both states were predominantly Hindu and neither had geographical contiguity with Pakistan. Hence their secession to India, though causing tension and acrimony, did not poison Indo-Pakistani relations as Kashmir did.

The case of Kashmir was unique. It was the only Princely state which was geographically contiguous to both India and Pakistan and had a Muslim majority with a Hindu ruler. The situation was further complicated by the existence of a popular movement, National Conference, led by Sheik Abdullah, which fought the autocratic and oppressive Dogra ruler Hari Singh for decades. Sheik Abdullah was a secular nationalist who refused to subscribe to the two-nation theory of Jinnah and was a close associate of Nehru and a sympathizer with the goals and values of the Indian National Congress.[39]

Hari Singh, who initially toyed with the idea of independence, sought to buy time by signing a "Standstill agreement" with both India and Pakistan. While Pakistan agreed to the proposal, there was no response from the Indian government because there was a delay in communicating the proposal. According to Mountbatten, it was this initial reluctance of Hari Singh to secede either to India or to Pakistan that lay at the root of the problem of Kashmir as it unfolded later.

Suspicious of India's intentions and not trusting Sheik Abdullah, Pakistani leaders tried to force the events by encouraging if not abetting a tribal invasion of Kashmir.[40] When the tribesmen were knocking on the doors of Srinagar, Hari Singh panicked and sought India's military assistance. India insisted on formal secession before any help could be rendered and Hari Singh had little choice but to sign on the dotted line, though the secession was to be confirmed later by a plebiscite, after law and order had been restored in the state. Indian troops who were air-lifted to Srinagar saved the city in the nick of time and cleared three-fourths of Kashmir of raiders[41] before Nehru sought UN arbitration to settle the dispute, primarily at the instance of Mountbatten, a decision which he regretted later.

The battle over Kashmir was as much ideological as it was over material gains in terms of security and economic advantage. As Josef Korbel sums up:

The real cause of all the bitterness and bloodshed, the recalcitrance and the suspicion that have characterised the Kashmir dispute is the uncompromising and perhaps uncompromisable struggle of two ways of life, two concepts of political organisation, two scales of values, two spiritual attitudes, that find themselves locked in deadly conflict, a conflict in which Kashmir has become both symbol and battleground.[42]

Pakistani leaders considered it almost axiomatic that Kashmir should join Pakistan, without which the latter would be incomplete both ideologically and geographically. For Nehru, Kashmir would "give a demonstration to all India and to the world how we can function unitedly and in a non-communal way in Kashmir. In this way this terrible crisis in Kashmir may well lead to a healing of the deep wounds which India has suffered in recent months."[43] India and Nehru had never accepted partition along religious lines in 1947 but only as an established fact. They, therefore, did not allow religious concerns to guide their actions over Kashmir.

The issue was further complicated by the fact that it became enmeshed in power politics once it was referred to the UN for arbitration. Nehru was furious that the "fundamental issue", i.e. the Pakistani aggression, "has been slurred over and bypassed and passed over". He was convinced that "The United States and Britain have played a dirty role, Britain probably being the chief actor behind the scenes."[44] The general feeling in India was that the British support to Pakistan was a continuation of British support to the Muslim League in pre-independence days, and was at least partly aimed at winning back the support of the Muslim world which was alienated by the British policy in Palestine.[45]

More importantly, what enabled India to take such a firm stand over Kashmir in defiance of Britain and the USA was the fact that the state power was securely in the hands of Indians, and Britain could no longer act as an arbitrator between the Indian National Congress and the Muslim League as it had before independence.

India's general foreign policy objectives

At this juncture, it is essential to dwell at some length on two general tendencies which seem to permeate the whole gamut of India's foreign relations. The first is the status that was envisaged for India in the comity of nations by its leaders at the time of independence, and the second is the centrality of security considerations to India's foreign policy endeavours from the very beginning.

Firstly, the Indian elite, either before the attainment of independence or after it, were anything but modest about India's future status as a great power.[46] They were aware of India's potential as a great power and were determined to attain such status for India in right earnest.

Nehru also believed that India had the wherewithal to become the fourth most important power in the world. In his own words, "Leaving aside for a moment these three countries, the United States, the Soviet Union and China, if you look at the world there are other great countries, very advanced countries, but if you peep into the future and if nothing goes wrong, wars and the like, then obviously the fourth great country in the world is India."[47]

Secondly, it is no exaggeration to say that the overriding consideration of India's foreign policy has been the security of the nation, in both internal and external terms. This is but natural for a country which has experienced colonial domination for almost two centuries, and whose servitude was at least partly due to its perennial and endemic lack of internal cohesion. Nehru conceived India's security interests in very broad and comprehensive terms. For him, defence meant much more than mere military preparedness. His security perceptions were largely, as we will see, a product of India's freedom movement.

It was Nehru's firm conviction that the greatest danger to the stability and security of the infant Indian state came from within and not without. He saw the danger on two fronts. First, he realized that India's groaning poverty made it a fertile ground for internal communist subversion, and the most effective way of countering this threat was rapid economic development coupled with distributive justice. For him, this was essentially a political battle to be won or lost on the political plane. Hence, he considered India's economic development as an integral part of India's security in the long run.

Nehru also conceived India's development as a genuinely secular entity as an essential prerequisite for its long-term viability as a strong and stable state. In a multi-religious country like India, only a secular framework could ensure national unity, integrity and solidarity. The partition of the country on the basis of religion only confirmed Nehru's worst fears. For him, it opened the Pandora's box which might result in the Balkanization of India.

Secessionist voices were heard at the time of independence in different parts of the country, particularly among the Tamils in the south, the Akali Sikhs in the Punjab and in the tribal north-east. Both Nehru and Congress adamantly refused to accept the thesis that accepting the creation of

Pakistan was tantamount to accepting the two-nation theory. They knew full well that once the two-nation theory was accepted, it would be illogical and untenable not to accept, at least in theory, a 20-nation theory or whatever the number. For them, partition was the price the country had to pay to get rid of both the imperialist British and the intransigent Muslim League, but certainly not the Muslims. This was the reason why they pooh-poohed any idea of exchange of populations as suggested by people like Rajagopalachari.

It is quite revealing that Nehru once told Chester Bowles, the then US Ambassador to India, that he personally considered the establishment of a secular state in India as his greatest contribution.[48] However, by failing to act decisively in this regard, particularly in relation to the Muslim community in India, Nehru left the job only half done. This created problems for his successors in continuing with the process of political integration and modernization of the Indian state, as we shall see later.

Nonalignment: rationale and resilience

Very few concepts in international relations have, in recent times, evoked so much comment, controversy and confusion as that of nonalignment. From being labelled as "immoral" to the present status of "respectability", nonalignment has passed from its uncertain youth to enter a more mature middle age. India, apart from being one of the founding members of the nonaligned group, has always been in the forefront of the movement.

Nonalignment, in simple terms, is an assertion of India's independence and sovereignty, of its ability and desire to guide its destiny according to its own free will without outside influence or intervention, both in external as well as internal affairs.

Nehru was aware that the technological revolution of the 20th century had made the world rather small and interdependent. Hence, isolation of any kind was neither feasible nor desirable. Moreover, Nehru, being aware of India's great potential, sought to place India in the thick of things by deliberately adopting a high profile in international affairs, in order to develop a positive and profitable relationship with the rest of the world.

For Nehru, alignment was "war-time psychology" and he saw no reason why it should be imported into times of relative peace. States have no permanent friends but only permanent interests. Hence, it would be diplomatically imprudent to foreclose one's options with regard to matters as serious as war. Thus there was a degree of opportunism in India's nonaligned stance. As Nehru himself put it, "We are not going to join a war if we can help it. We are going to join the side which is to our interest when the time comes to make the choice."[49] For Nehru, while non-alignment was a basic policy, "its application to a particular circumstance or resolution is a matter of judgement".[50]

There are also strong psychological reasons beneath India's nonaligned stance. Nehru "perceived in alignment the danger of psychological return to deep-rooted feelings of dependence and inferiority that he saw still lurking beneath the surface of the Indian national consciousness after the trauma of imperialism. Should India ever lose its sense of a great national destiny, Nehru reflected, it could all too easily succumb once again to divisive centrifugal stresses."[51]

It is for these reasons that Nehru called nonalignment the "natural policy" for India. Nehru saw India as a great power in the making because of its history, civilization, size, population and resources. He simply could not envisage India playing anything less than an independent and assertive role in world affairs. It was her right and destiny. Nonalignment symbolized and epitomized this urge and aspiration.

It is in this sense, not in any ethical sense, that he once remarked that it would be a "terrible moral failure" on the part of India if it ever gave up its nonaligned policy. To him, it was tantamount to admitting India's failure to live up to her potential and destiny which should be hers as a matter of right. However, it must be noted that while Nehru's insistence on nonalignment for India was understandable and justified, his political and probably intellectual aversion to aligned nations did adversely affect India's relations with important Middle Eastern countries like Iran and Saudi Arabia, which were otherwise well disposed towards India. Nehru also seemed to have made a distinction between radical and conservative states in relation to the Middle East, which was unwarranted.

Consequently, Indian policy lost some of its flexibility and adaptability, which in turn circumscribed India's already limited options in the region, as we shall see later.

Nonalignment and balance of power

At this juncture, it is essential to explain at some length the relationship between nonalignment and the theory of balance of power. However, this will be done in two stages. First, we will consider the linkage between nonalignment and the theory of balance of power in general, and later we will discuss the balance of power theory in specific relation to India which, of course, is our main interest.

Nonalignment is neither an abstention from nor an alternative to the theory of balance of power, but an integral part of it.

The doctrine and practice of nonalignment suggests that it is a form of power politics - albeit a form that is suitable for a weaker state that, either by inclination or compulsion, must be externally involved if it is to shape its immediate external environment and if it is to direct internal economic and social change through peaceful means.[52]

However, the modern theory of balance of power is different from its classical version in so far as it takes into account three important new variables of the post-war era, namely the emergence of the superpowers, the advent of nuclear weapons and the crystallization of a Third World consisting of newly independent Afro-Asian nations, all of which make it a different sort of game altogether in the second half of the 20th century.

A preliminary explanation ... may best start by considering the position of the statesmen entrusted with the conduct of foreign affairs in any independent State. Obviously, their first concern must be the survival of the State and the preservation of its independence ... . In meeting these responsibilities statesmen are obliged to take account of the distribution of power in mind. They must strive to establish such relations with other countries as will ensure that no preponderance of power among the latter, singly or collectively, will threaten their independence or encompass their downfall. In the pursuit of this defensive aim they may decide, from time to time, to enter into or form alliances with other Powers, particularly when those countries whose designs they fear are linked by treaty engagements. In other circumstances they may eschew all alliances, fearing that by entering into one they would provoke a hostility of a rival group and be drawn into conflicts which they might avoid by remaining dissociated from either group. Much depends upon the geographical position and natural resources of the State in question: each State is unique in size, however defined in resources and in geographical position in relation to other States. Consequently the precise measures appropriate to the maintenance of a defensive balance of power differ in different countries. What is common is the aim of survival.[53]

There can be very little doubt that the nonaligned countries as a group sought to exploit the rough balance of power that emerged in the world after the Second World War, between the Western countries led by the USA and the Socialist bloc under Soviet auspices. The material and military weakness of the nonaligned made it impossible for them to adopt a confrontationist attitude towards the power blocs. On the other hand, it was neither possible nor desirable for them to remain aloof from them, for they needed the goodwill and the assistance of both in the modernization of their nations. In other words, nonalignment made it both possible and feasible for the Third World countries to combine simultaneously their contradictory yearnings for strategic isolation and an active role in international affairs.

The Afro-Asian countries which had just become free from colonial control were in no mood to brook any interference in their affairs. The nonaligned stance enabled them to insulate themselves from Cold War politics by minimizing opportunities for outside intervention. It also enabled them to shift the focus from power politics, i.e. Cold War issues, to issues which were more important and urgent to the Third World countries, i.e. economic and social issues.

The nonaligned also facilitated the trend towards loosening of blocs and towards multi-polarity by providing an alternative to bloc politics through the formation of what is termed "the area of peace". The nonaligned were never peace-makers in the conventional sense. They only facilitated it. The major powers knew the consequences of a global conflict, and were as much interested as the nonaligned in de-escalating and localizing conflicts so that they could stop short of reaching a point of no return without complete loss of face. And therein lay the strength, utility and relevance of the nonaligned.

Nehru was both annoyed and puzzled that the powers-that-were either failed or refused to take notice of the changing power equation between the Western world and the newly emerged Afro-Asian world. He bemoaned that "... the countries which enjoyed the privileged position in that 19th century set-up, many of them have lost their position. It is not easy for them to adjust themselves to the new thinking, the new balance in the world ...".[54]

The real "significance of nonalignment ... lies in the fact that it announced the desire of the Asian and African States to enter the balance of power struggle in their own right. Not all the Afro-Asian States had the geographical and other advantages to realize this aim. It was, therefore, fitting that those who had the advantage took the lead".[55]

It was in the fitness of things that India, potentially the most powerful and important of the nonaligned countries, was the torch-bearer of this struggle of the Afro-Asian countries to redefine and refashion their relationship with the West.

It goes without saying that Nehru was, from the beginning, acutely aware of and alive to the realities and requirements of the balance of power game. "India talked about the undesirability of power politics during the 1950s, but in practice it did not try to exempt itself from the opportunities and obligations of power politics."[56]

Ironically, India's nonaligned stance, which sought to diminish and de-escalate the intense Cold War tensions of the years immediately following World War II, found sustenance and gained in importance and stature from the same Cold War tensions.

> The unique configuration of world politics after the Second World War admirably suited the establishment of India's nonalignment and gave it greater significance than it would have had in other circumstances ... . India would have pursued nonalignment *vis-à-vis* any greater powers as an assertion of its true independence, but when that posture was proclaimed, and later achieved, with respect to the two coalitions dominating the global arena, India's uniqueness gained for it a special kind of influence or power.[57]

Thus, the Cold War was not one of the fundamental stimuli for India's nonaligned stance; it merely acted as a catalyst and brought nonalignment into sharp focus. India insisted upon each state actor, particularly the newly independent Afro-Asian countries, participating in the balancing process in its own right as independent and sovereign nations rather than taking shelter behind other powers.

India's balance of power policy operated on three broad planes: subcontinental, regional and global. It suited India to be nonaligned on all three planes for different reasons.

Global balance

Nehru was aware that India was protected by a global balance of power, if only she took advantage of it and played her cards shrewdly. He implicitly acknowledged the existence of a rough but uneasy balance in the global context. "As things are today, we have reached a certain kind of balance - it may be a very unstable balance, but it is still some kind of balance - when any kind of major aggression is likely to lead to a world war. That itself is a restraining factor."[58]

It was Nehru's understanding that such an unstable balance could easily be disturbed, with grave consequences for the world at large. He was also aware that this acted as a restraining factor on all the major powers in general and on the superpowers in particular. Hence, he sought to take advantage of the nuclear paralysis of the superpowers, to carve out a niche for India and the materially weak Third World by creating and enlarging what he called an "area of peace", not geographically but "politically, diplomatically, morally". Superpowers themselves took notice of and availed themselves of the "cushioning effect" that the nonaligned produced and paraded.

Nehru was only too well aware of India's great potential. He also appreciated the fact that it really did not require great weight to tilt the scales in the unstable balance that existed in the world. For these two reasons, India counted, despite its material and military weaknesses.

Regional balance

China has always been India's principal rival for regional influence and leadership. Nehru saw this much earlier than others. He realized quite early that, in military terms at least, the regional balance between India and China was adverse to India.

He had two options before him for responding to this potential threat to India's security, physical as well as ideological. The first was to join the Western alliance aimed at containing China. This option had two serious shortcomings. Firstly, joining any such alliance, apart from incurring the immediate wrath of China, would inevitably alienate the USSR, and that was the last thing that Nehru wanted. In fact, he anticipated the Sino-Soviet schism much earlier than many, and joining the Western alliance would have meant that India foreclosed the option of exploiting Sino-Soviet differences to its advantage.

Secondly, he was also aware that any alliance would entail mutual obligations, which would inevitably lead to a dilution of India's independence of action. Neither India nor Nehru, just free from Western colonial domination, was prepared for such a possibility.

Nehru, however, reasoned that China, despite its current military superiority, could not pose an immediate threat to India. "He staked his hopes for a peaceful relationship, not on Chinese goodwill, but on the assumption that the Chinese leaders needed a period of peace in which to solidify their revolution."[59]

Nehru's strategy was to buy time for India so that India would be able to take on the Chinese challenge on its own when the time came.[60] Hence, he made an unceasing and unabashed effort to cultivate and woo China without losing sight of India's primary interests. So nonalignment became India's first line of defence against China.

However, the regional plane proved to be the most tricky ground for the operational efficacy of nonalignment for it "was powerless against such states as Pakistan and China whose interests *vis-à-vis* India would have been constant regardless of New Delhi's diplomatic stance".[61]

Subcontinental balance

India always considered the subcontinental sphere as its own backyard. It has always been the predominant power in this sphere from the beginning and it could pursue and protect its interests on its own without any alignment. In fact, its endeavour has been to keep the subcontinent free from outside influence, so that outside powers could neither restrict nor restrain India's freedom of action nor bolster other powers in the subcontinent against India. India also had the material and military strength to back up its policies in this sphere, and it never shirked or shied away from doing so when the occasion demanded it.

Since independence, it has been India's endeavour to preserve the balance that existed in its favour in the subcontinent, and to increase it progressively with the passage of time. It is in this context that Indo-Pakistani relations acquire significance, for Pakistan almost has a mirror-image of India's perceptions, policies and interests.

This three-fold division of India's balance of power approach is not rigid and in fact, there is, of necessity, much overlapping and interaction. Nevertheless, it serves as a useful analytical framework. Nor should it be forgotten that India also shifted its emphasis on nonalignment on the three planes, depending on the exigencies of the situation.

In other words, by insulating the subcontinent from outside intervention or influence, India sought to take advantage of the existence of rough global and regional balance to preserve and promote the subcontinental balance which was in its favour.

India's approach to the concept of balance of power can be summed up in the words of G.S. Bajpai:

India ... has to develop her strength to support her foreign policy. The inherent goodness of that policy is insufficient to sustain or further it. On this view the inference that politics cannot be divorced from power holds true also for India... . Today, India is the major stabilising factor for peace in Asia; the measure of stability that she can impart to this part of the world is not a matter of good intentions but of power... . It is not power but its misuse or abuse which is morally reprehensible.... . Thus viewed the idea of balance of power is nothing evil or incompatible with India's highest ideals.[62]

It goes without saying that Pakistan and the Middle East constituted important factors in India's balance of power calculations at the subcontinental, regional and global levels. Indian policy-makers perceived that Pakistan had a direct and the Middle East a derivative bearing on India's internal cohesion and regional aspirations. Hence, this had a more direct impact on India's foreign policy than its more general nonaligned stance because of the immediacy of its consequences. India's contest with Pakistan also had an effect on her relations with China. Both China and Pakistan considered India's nonaligned stance to have no bearing on their respective interests *vis-à-vis* India. It was this basic community of interests between Pakistan and China that alerted India to a potential adverse balance of power at the regional level.

Pakistan and the Middle East were also factors in India's global balance of power concerns. Pakistan joining the Western alliance in the 1950s and its close relations with Middle Eastern states such as Iran (which were part of the Western alliance system) alerted Indian policy-makers to a possible adverse global balance and the problems that a nonaligned India might face in countering such adverse balance. It is in this three-fold balance of power framework that we shall examine India's relations with the superpowers, China and Pakistan, respectively, in order to explain and appreciate India's interactions in these spheres in the context of its overall foreign policy objectives.

India and the superpowers

India's relations with the two superpowers, the USA and the USSR, more or less epitomized India's great power aspirations and also throw considerable light on India's preferred means of achieving them.

As we have already seen, Nehru saw India's opportunity in the rough global balance that existed between the two power blocs at the time of Indian independence. Nehru was quite convinced that the Cold War primarily represented the conflict of geopolitical interests between the United States and the Soviet Union, with ideological divergence only adding a sharp edge to it. Nehru saw quite early the awesome potential of the United States and its implications for the rest of the world. He wondered whether "the great problem of the near future will be American imperialism, even more than British imperialism, which appears to have had its day and is crumbling fast. Or, it may be, that the two will unite together in an endeavour to create a powerful Anglo-Saxon bloc to dominate the world."[63]

Nehru no doubt saw the Soviet Union as the only credible and effective countervailing force to the ever-increasing and all-pervading power and influence of the United States. His instructions to the Indian Ambassadors to the USA and China about sum up India's approach to the two power blocs. "Both America and Russia are extraordinarily suspicious of each other as well as of other countries. This makes our path difficult and we may well be suspected by each of leaning towards the other. This cannot be helped ... ." India needs America because "There is much goodwill for America and expectation of help from her in many fields, especially technical." Nor could India afford to antagonize the Russians. "The Soviet Union being our neighbour, we shall inevitably develop closer relations with it. We cannot afford to antagonise Russia merely because we think that this may irritate someone else."[64]

Explaining the geopolitics of India's approach to superpowers, Nehru said, "Situated between the vast Communist land mass of Eurasia and the Indian Ocean controlled by the West we had to cooperate with both."[65]

However, the fact remains that Nehru generally displayed a greater sensitivity to Russian sensibilities than to those of the Americans. The reasons for this are not far to seek.

First, Nehru considered the United States "too far away for effective action". The Americans on the other hand felt that their interests in South Asia were only marginal. It would follow from the above that the incentive for the United States to intervene in the region on behalf of or against India would also be limited.

The USSR, however, was a different kettle of fish. Nehru was aware of the proximity of the USSR to India and realized that it could easily be a thorn in India's side if relations became strained. In 1940, Nehru surmised that the Russians "were not likely to ignore India which touched their frontiers in Asia". If Russia had a greater stake in South Asia than the USA, then it follows that the Russian need to intervene in the region either on behalf of or against India was also greater to that extent.

Hence the need not to antagonize the USSR; this, at least partly, explains India's rather mild and muted criticism of the USSR when it chose to intervene militarily in Hungary in 1956 and Czechoslovakia in 1968. Nehru, at least from the mid-50s, began to consider the USSR as the most effective counter against the growing Chinese pressure on India; because of both Chinese dependence on the USSR and the ability of the USSR to intervene physically in any future Sino–Indian conflict to the advantage of India, if the USSR so desired.

At the height of the Cold War, India along with the other nonaligned countries tried to act as a "bridge" between the USA and the USSR. The existence of a rough global balance and the advent of nuclear weapons both necessitated and facilitated such a role.

Nehru was quite aware of the similarity of interests between the USA and the USSR. Hence, once détente, however limited, was achieved between the two superpowers, India manoeuvred to become an area of agreement between them. This process was facilitated by two factors: the acceptance by the superpowers of India's middle path, based on ideological as well as methodological moderation; and the rise of China as an independent factor in international politics.

Explaining the international significance of India's internal experiment, Nehru said:

> ... today there is almost universal understanding and appreciation of what we are trying to do on the economic plane - that is, planning under a democratic pattern of socialism. This has set a new pattern for Asian and African development and it is significant that economists and other experts from both the worlds ... are extremely interested in our development plans and progress. This makes of India itself a kind of an area of agreement between the opposing ideological forces.[66]

Consequently, both the superpowers developed a stake in the stability and security of India and sought its cooperation in countering China on two planes. Firstly, both the superpowers sought to cultivate India's active cooperation in moderating the Third World's political and economic demands and keeping the radical elements within the movement under check. India too became a willing partner, for it eminently suited India's interests. India herself, given her nonaligned stance, needed to maintain a working and workable relationship with both the superpowers and to continue to be an area of superpower agreement to the extent possible. This would not have been possible if Third World countries, of which India was the unofficial spokesman and leader, overtly showed a tilt in favour of one superpower or the other. Secondly, the advent of nuclear weapons, according to Indian perceptions, had changed the rules of the game, which the nations of the world could ignore only at great peril to themselves. The most important issue confronting mankind was the threat of a nuclear holocaust. And if it was expected of the USA and the USSR that they ought to come to some sort of understanding in order to avoid nuclear catastrophe, Third World countries should also moderate their demands and the means of achieving them, however justified and urgent they may be, in order to avoid disaster. As Nehru argued, "The only way to avoid conflicts is to accept things more or less as they are. No doubt, many things require to be changed, but you must not think of changing them by war."[67]

There were at least two occasions when the nonaligned movement appeared to have confronted the problem of divisions between radical and confrontationist elements on the one hand and moderate and reformist elements on the other.

The first occasion was in the early 1960s, when Indonesia's Sukarno, under Chinese influence and inspiration, sought to persuade the Third World to adopt a more militant and confrontationist attitude towards the developed countries in making its demands, and tried to wrest the leadership of the Third World from its moderate and reformist leadership. Addressing the Nonaligned Conference at Cairo in October 1964, he made it clear that he saw no special need for the Third World to strive for better understanding between the two superpowers. He also saw nothing evil or unnatural in the Third World adopting a confrontationist approach. Sukarno, as if to prove his point, later withdrew Indonesia from the United Nations.

However, the ascendancy of the radical elements in the Third World movement proved to be short-lived. Firstly, the radical approach did not find favour with most Third World leaders. The fall of Sukarno was also a great blow to the radical elements. More importantly, moderate countries like India seized this opportunity to assert themselves and bring the movement back under their control.

In 1966, as if to make a formal assertion of their ascendancy, the moderate elements within the Third World saw to it that "an explicit declaration was made by the developing countries in their meeting at Algiers that there was no need for a confrontation between the developed and the developing countries for the creating of what was called a just economic order".[68]

The second occasion was when the nonaligned movement showed a slight drift to the left under the chairmanship of Cuba, based on the argument that the Socialist bloc was the "natural ally" of the Third World. India was not amused. As soon as India took over the chairmanship from Cuba, she made an assiduous and persistent effort to restore balance to the movement and put it firmly on the middle path once again. Thus, whatever may be their differences with India, neither the USA nor the

USSR could afford to ignore the moderating role that India had played in the politics of the Third World.

Secondly, both the superpowers at one time or the other wanted India to play a more active regional role in opposition to China. The USA from the beginning wanted India to take Southeast Asia under its wing against a possible Chinese threat. In 1969, after serious clashes between Russian and Chinese forces along the Ussuri river, the Soviet Union proposed what it termed the Asian Collective Security as a counter to China, and tried to involve India.

On both occasions, India shied away from the responsibility. India, perhaps, did not want to enter into any overt anti-Chinese alliance sponsored by either superpower, for this could have restricted its own diplomatic options in relation to China. India also possibly did not want to get entangled in regional issues which could be a drain on scarce resources and distract attention from domestic reconstruction, which remained her top priority. India may also have been unwilling to alienate China since the border issue was still unsettled and the Sino-Pakistani collusion was causing considerable concern. It may be that India discounted China as a real threat to Southeast Asia under the changed circumstances of the 1970s.

Though India resisted the overtures of both the USA and the USSR to enter into any formal alliance with either of them to protect Southeast Asia from a possible Chinese threat, the fact remained that both the USA and the USSR had a stake in the stability and security of Southeast Asia and hence this made it another important area of agreement between them with regard to India.

While India certainly desired and worked to remain an area of agreement between the superpowers and sought to solve its own problems as well as those of the Third World in concurrence rather than in confrontation with them, the last thing it ever wanted was a superpower condominium. Hence it always stoutly resisted any such tendencies, however incipient, on the part of the superpowers.

India's policies, both individually and in concert with other Third World countries, have been geared to check and curtail the power and influence of the superpowers, and to ease gradually their stranglehold over the international system. In fact, "... military defense, aspirations for regional and global influence, leadership in the building of a new international economic order, and the gradual curtailment of superpower dominance over world affairs have been the central policies of the Government of India since its founding in 1947".[69]

Another important area where India had serious disagreements with both the superpowers and stubbornly and persistently refused to yield to their pressures and blandishments is on the issue of nuclear technology. India has pursued a zealously independent line with regard to the nuclear issue ever since independence, and has defied both superpowers in refusing to sign the Nuclear Nonproliferation Treaty (NPT) which it branded as discriminatory. India's approach to the issue can be summed up in the words of V.C. Trivedi:

> The problem of negotiating a treaty on nonproliferation has implications far beyond the realm of proliferation of nuclear weapons or even of general and complete disarmament. The attitudes that we take and the approaches we adopt on this will reflect our attitudes and approaches on international relations in general. It is therefore imperative that we take a global approach on this issue, take into account the needs and requirements of all members of the international community and follow an approach which reflects our firm adherence to the sovereign equality of all nations and to the principles of equality and mutual benefit.[70]

India's approach to the issue of the Indian Ocean is yet another example of India's ability and willingness to differ from and oppose both the superpowers wherever and whenever she considered her own vital interests to be at stake. India looked upon the Indian Ocean as her own lake and considered any intrusions from outside as unwarranted and undesirable. Since she would not possess the naval strength to dominate the Indian Ocean in the near future, India utilized diplomatic means to persuade the UN General Assembly to pass a resolution declaring the Indian Ocean to be a "Zone of Peace". Though India had been putting a lot of diplomatic pressure on both the superpowers to leave the Indian Ocean alone, she was particularly worried about the American base at Diego Garcia. Apart from its proximity to India, such a long-term and sophisticated base could make it much more difficult for India to nudge the USA out of the Indian Ocean in the future when India would be in a position to extend her sway in the Indian Ocean.

India has also been fairly ambivalent to the superpowers, particularly the United States, in relation to two issues. The first issue is India's desire to evolve as an independent and autonomous power centre and the response of the USA and the USSR to such a desire. It has been India's experience that the USSR rather than the USA has appeared to be much more sympathetic and helpful in assisting India achieve this goal. The United States, in the 1950s and 60s, refused to help India in setting up basic industries like steel mills, and refused to transfer technology for the establishment of an indigenous arms industry, whereas the Russians helped India on both these counts.[71]

The second issue is the attitude of the superpowers to Pakistan in relation to India. While both the USA and the Soviet Union at some time or another tried to follow an even-handed policy with regard to India and Pakistan and used economic aid and arms sales for this purpose, it was the USA again that the Indians suspected of shoring up Pakistan under the illusion of maintaining parity between the two countries and, what was worse, of trying to build up Pakistan as a counter to India.[72]

These are very sensitive issues and the attitude of the superpowers to them would significantly determine the nature and content of future interaction between the USA and the USSR on the one hand and India on the other. However, generally speaking, for most Indians "an appropriate environment for India's strategic interaction with the great powers is one that simultaneously precludes their country from being ignored or coerced".[73]

India and China

As we have already stated, China has always been India's rival for regional leadership, and nonalignment was most vulnerable and least effective against China in a diplomatic sense, hence the policy of deliberate friendship.

It appears that, at least initially, Nehru considered China to be a counter to Russia and not vice versa. Nehru reasoned that China was beset with internal problems and would need time to consolidate its revolution, whereas Russia, which was already a superpower, appeared to be potentially a greater threat to India.[74] Hence, cultivating China would be a useful counter to any possible Russian threat.

Nehru was also swayed by his strong sense of Asian solidarity. He was piqued by the fact that Asia's viewpoint was not being given the attention that it deserved. For him, the treatment being meted out to China was at least partly due to the arrogance and ignorance of the Western powers with regard to problems relating to the independent and resurgent Asia.

Nehru did envisage some sort of Sino–Indian coalition as a counter to the West, in a political and diplomatic if not military sense. However, being conscious of potential Sino-Indian regional rivalry, Nehru must have been aware of the serious limitations of such a coalition if ever it materialized.

India's championing of China's case in international forums has a less noble and more pragmatic side to it. Nehru foresaw the Sino-Soviet rift, and was keen on facilitating if not hastening it. The best way to do this, as he saw it, was to reduce China's exclusive dependence on the Soviet Union for political and diplomatic support. The first step towards a friendly relationship with China was India's immediate recognition of the Communist regime.

When the Chinese armed forces marched into Tibet in 1950, there was very little that India could have done to stop it. India refused to represent Tibet in the United Nations and discouraged it from taking the issue to the UN. She did, however, mediate a 17-point agreement, which envisaged a large degree of autonomy for Tibet, coupled with an assurance to preserve the distinct culture and traditions of the Tibetans. In other words, the Tibet episode was deliberately played down in order not to alienate China.[75]

Nevertheless, the Indian government was quite alive to the changed strategic situation on its northern borders and "responded to the altered Himalayan situation in a manner that must be described as politically discreet, diplomatically cautious, economical of financial and material resources and projected over a long time".[76]

The outbreak of the Korean War and China's involvement in it also gave Nehru an opportunity to demonstrate his goodwill towards China. He refused to brand China as an aggressor and was critical of the USA for bringing the Seventh Fleet into the Taiwan straits. He was also opposed to American policy in Indo-China. This was not exactly designed to please the Chinese but it couldn't have failed to go down well with them as they were actively involved in the region.

The Panch Sheel which was signed in 1954 was the high water mark of the "Hindi-Chini Bhai Bhai era". Nehru seemed to have been quite keen on committing the Chinese formally to these principles which he thought might act as a restraint on future Chinese behaviour. Explaining the significance of Panch Sheel, he said that it was "a question of following a policy which ... makes it more and more difficult progressively for the other country to break trust".[77] However, it is difficult to assess the extent to which Nehru considered the Panch Sheel effective in moderating the Chinese behaviour.

India also adopted a deliberately low-key approach to Southeast Asian security problems, at least partly not to offend China. The United States was quite keen on India taking Southeast Asia under its wing in order to protect it from any possible Chinese threat. Though Nehru was aware of India's need to protect its flanks, he was convinced that China posed no immediate threat to the region. Nor was he prepared to take on new responsibilities which had no direct or immediate relevance to India and which would distract attention from the more pressing needs of economic development.

The general policy of deliberate friendship with China was also greatly responsible for India's low-key and ostrich-like approach to the border question, which led to disastrous consequences later.[78] When India protested to the Chinese about maps showing large tracts of territory claimed by India as its own, the non-committal Chinese reply was that they were published by the previous government and that the Communist government did not revise them for want of time. On another occasion, the Chinese expressed the opinion that the time was not yet "ripe" to settle the border issue. But the Chinese gave the impression that they accepted the McMahon line as the boundary in general.[79]

It was not until September 1957 that the Indian government came to know about the existence of the Karakoram highway linking Tibet with Sinkiang, which ran through Aksai Chin area of Ladakh which India claimed to be its own territory. In October 1958, India protested against the Chinese "violation of its territorial sovereignty". In March 1959, "a full-scale popular uprising" in Tibet followed a high-handed Chinese attempt at the "Sinicization" of Tibet. The subsequent flight of the Dalai Lama to India vitiated the atmosphere further. Chou En-lai's visit to Delhi in April 1960 failed to break the deadlock. In the meantime, public opinion in India hardened against the Chinese, and criticism in Parliament of Nehru's China policy became virulent, leaving him with little elbow room.

The more extravagant the Chinese claims became, the more difficult it became for Nehru to keep incensed Indian public opinion in check. The Chinese were in possession of more or less all the territory they claimed in Ladakh, and made wild claims in the eastern sector as a sort of bargaining chip.

In other words, they presented Nehru with a *fait accompli*, and made it clear that any attempt on the part of India to change the *status quo* would be met with force. They did not appear to be keen on even going through the motions of a compromise based on a give-and-take approach. It is clear that the Chinese wanted a settlement on their terms and also wanted the world to know that it was so.[80]

Why, then, were the Chinese so implacable and intransigent? By 1962 the Sino-Indian border issue had advanced well beyond a bilateral territorial dispute between the two countries, and had become enmeshed in the quagmire of international politics. With the thaw in the Cold War in Europe and a limited détente between the USA and the USSR, the focus of attention shifted to Asia and Africa. In order to insulate the region, which provided many an opportunity for the superpowers to fish in troubled waters, the nonaligned declared the Third World as an area of peace on the basis of a superpower agreement which was fairly *status quo*-oriented. China, fearing a superpower condominium and having failed to convince the Third World that it was one of them, proved a new threat to the idea of the Third World as an area of peace, which was, generally speaking, acceptable to the USA and the Soviet Union. There were also countries within the Third World such as Indonesia which accepte the Chinese line. Here again India played a moderating role and checked the radical elements within the Third World movement. This was one of the reasons for Chinese wrath against India, for it left China rather isolated. Once moderation and accommodation became the watchwords for the Capitalist, the Soviet Communist and the Third Worlds, led by the USA, the USSR and India respectively, China could not fit into any of these categories.

While joining the Capitalist bloc was out of the question for obvious reasons, sticking to the Communist bloc meant playing second fiddle to the Soviet Union, which was not acceptable to China. Nor could China sell itself as a developing country to the Third World and replace India as its leading light because of its ideological militancy and its clamour for major power status, which was confirmed when it accepted with alacrity the permanent membership of the Security Council.

The emerging order was anathema to China, for it tended to push it into political, diplomatic and military isolation. What it feared was a superpower condominium, with India lending a helping hand to the exercise on behalf of the Third World. So China chose to strike against India, the weakest link in the chain, in order to demonstrate its ability to act independently of both the superpowers, to expose the hollowness of India's claim as a rival to China and to undermine India's status in the Third World by exposing its nonalignment to be in reality bialignment.[81]

The serious military reverses that India suffered at the hands of the Chinese in the winter of 1962 were the result of a combination of factors. Nehru and Menon refused to believe till the very end that there could be a large-scale conflict with China. Hence, precious little was done by way of strategic thinking and tactical refinement in case of a general war with China.[82] Nehru also placed too much faith in the Russian ability to restrain China. The more he flaunted the Indo-Soviet friendship to deter China, the more the Chinese felt compelled to put India, and through her the

Soviet Union, in her place.[83] The emphasis on self-reliance, though justified in the long run, was taken to such absurd limits that it ruled out the buying of weapons and equipment abroad to meet a possible emergency in the short run.[84]

India's military debacle on the Himalayan frontier brought India's nonalignment and Nehru's China policy under close scrutiny and review. Nehru vigorously defended both, and reiterated their continued utility and relevance for India.[85] The Sino-Indian conflict, if anything, strengthened India's nonaligned stance in the sense that India could now depend on both the United States and the Soviet Union to come to its aid in case of a massive Chinese attack. Exclusive alignment with either one of them would needlessly alienate the other.

India resumed diplomatic relations with China in 1976, and intermittent talks have been going on between the two countries over the border issue, with no solution in sight. In the light of Sino-Indian rivalry for regional influence, it is difficult to see how even a satisfactory solution to the border issue can really give a big boost to the relations between the two countries. More than the border issue, the Chinese attitude to Southeast Asia and internal developments within China are likely to influence the future relations between the two Asian giants.

Self-sufficiency
Perhaps the most crucial segment of India's nonalignment policy has been her passionate search for self-sufficiency. Self-sufficiency constitutes an integral part of India's nonaligned stance and is its very core and essence.

India's search for self-sufficiency can be broadly divided into three categories: economic, technological and military. It goes without saying that these three categories are not mutually exclusive. They are, in fact, so closely interrelated and interwoven that it is almost impossible to discuss any of these categories without a reference to or implications for the others. Moreover, there has been in India over the years a deliberate, conscious and systematic attempt to integrate these categories into a comprehensive and compact whole. At this stage, it would suffice to state that India's Five-Year "Economic" Plans were supplemented and supplanted by Five-Year "Technological" and Five-Year "Military" Plans.

However, it must be noted that India's goal of self-sufficiency is only a relative one. No country in history has ever been able to achieve absolute self-sufficiency and no country is likely to achieve it in future either. Hence, India's endeavour has been to achieve self-reliance at least in those critical areas where dependence on foreign assistance is neither possible nor desirable.

Another interesting element in India's approach to the issue of self-sufficiency is the principle of diversification. India, ever since independence, sought to diversify its sources of economic assistance, technological transfer and military hardware in order to overcome the problem of dependence in the short run. Though this created problems in terms of integration and maintenance, this was considered a relatively small price to pay for the relative autonomy that India gained which would not otherwise be available to her.

The philosophy behind India's crusade for self-sufficiency and self-reliance can be best summed up in the words of an "Indian official". India, at any rate, is too conscious of her responsibilities, and of the need to preserve and develop the innate strength and self-reliance of her people, to participate in any arrangement that might induce a sense of dependence or compromise her freedom of action.

> It is time for a wider recognition in the west that we have come to the end of an historical epoch. The eclipse of India in the eighteenth century was not an isolated phenomenon; it was part of the world movement by which the science and technology of Europe captured Asia and turned it, under different forms, into an appendage of the west. India's re-emergence is likewise related to the revival of the entire continent ... . Its ultimate result must necessarily be to transform the politico-economic map of the world, and establish a new relationship between east and west.[86]

Bilateralism

Bilateralism is another important and striking feature of India's political and diplomatic stance over the years, which has its roots in her non-alignment or policy of independence. It is but another facet of India's nonalignment and represents her desire to emerge as an independent and autonomous actor in international politics who could hold her own in matters that are of relevance and significance to her.

However, India's application of the principle of bilateralism lacked conviction and verve in relation to the Middle Eastern states. The exaggerated fears of an Islamic bloc and an overemphasis on Pakistan and Islam as factors in India's interaction with the Middle East made Indian policy-makers place too much premium on anti-imperialist rhetoric, and on extending vociferous support to general Arab causes such as Palestine. This, in turn, resulted in India paying less than adequate attention to cultivating the Middle Eastern states on a more durable bilateral basis, as we shall see in subsequent chapters.

It is against this general framework of India's foreign relations since independence that we need to evaluate India's policies and postures towards the Middle East, the motives and assumptions that prompted them and how realistic and effective these policies were in serving India's perceived interests in the region.

1. India's Politico-diplomatic Interests in the Middle East: Egypt and Iraq

The fact that India had substantial and enduring politico-diplomatic interests in the Middle East has been recognized by the Indian political leadership from the early days of independence in 1947. The Indian subcontinent and the Middle East had experienced centuries of imperial domination which created an emotional bond between the leaders of the two regions, and fostered a certain similarity in their political outlook and orientation after they attained their independence from colonial rule. This, in turn, provided opportunities as well as challenges for the Indian leadership towards the region in the post-independence era. How well and how effectively India seized these opportunities and tried to counter and overcome these challenges constitutes the main theme of this chapter.

The Pakistan factor

Pakistan or no Pakistan, the Middle East would have been an extremely important and crucial region for India in politico-diplomatic terms. It constituted about a dozen independent states of varying sizes and potential, occupied some five million square miles (or one-tenth of the earth's land surface) and was inhabited by about a hundred million people.[1]

However, the creation of an avowedly Islamic state in the Indian subcontinent and the fact that a large number of Muslims remained in India after partition added a sharp edge to Indo-Pakistani rivalry, and made it almost imperative for them to vie with each other to cultivate the states of the Middle East. This, in turn, put Indian policy makers on the defensive from the outset and made them extremely sensitive and cautious in their dealings with the Middle East.

Pakistan, of course, enjoyed a natural advantage over India in wooing a predominantly Muslim Middle East because, in a manner of speaking, the creation of Pakistan "undercut the most obvious basis for unity between post-independence India and the Muslim states of West Asia: a continuous land bridge and a common religion. Pakistan inherited the advantages of both and used them for its own benefit".[2]

Hence, one of the overriding objectives of India's foreign policy in the Middle East from the outset has been to counter and neutralize the sympathy and support that Pakistan was likely to evoke as a Muslim country. India also had to safeguard its secular credentials against the Pakistani "propaganda" onslaughts of ill-treatment of the Muslim minority in India.

According to K.M. Panikkar, this propaganda did have some effect in the region initially and, as a result, Arab governments were suspicious of, and the Arab public antipathetic to, India. However, general Indian support for Arab causes in due course changed their attitude to India.[3]

India's fears of an Islamic bloc

The Indian government also conjured up visions of the entire Muslim Middle East, including Pakistan, acting as one single bloc to the disadvantage and detriment of India. Nehru expressed such fears to veteran journalist Durga Das. Eminent Muslim leaders like Chagla and Ali Yavar Jung were critical of Nehru for supporting progressive Muslims among the Arabs while he chose to lend his ear to conservative Muslims in India.

Nehru defended this dichotomy in his approach by explaining to Durga Das that his friendship with Nasser and other progressive Arab leaders was "designed to counterbalance the conservative Muslim bloc, which stretched from Pakistan to Jordan and posed a threat to India's security and secularism".[4] However, he was hesitant to attempt any reforms in the domestic sphere because of his fear that Muslim obscurantists would rise the cry "Islam in danger".

It should, however, be admitted that Pakistan did make a strenuous and persistent effort to forge an alliance with the Muslim countries of the Middle East in order to bolster its own political and diplomatic strength *vis-à-vis* India, which was much bigger and enjoyed considerable prestige and goodwill under the premiership of Nehru.

Between the years 1947 and 1954, Pakistan tried to bring various Muslim countries of the Middle East and beyond together on the basis of religious solidarity by playing host to various conferences.

While Pakistan did enjoy considerable sympathy and goodwill in the Middle East because it was a predominantly Muslim country, its efforts to forge an alliance on the basis of religion in the region were bound to fail for various reasons.

Firstly, the imperial rule that preceded the independence of the countries of the region over a period of time resulted in strong nationalistic sentiments based on anti-imperialist and territorial loyalties.[5] The disappearance of the Ottoman empire and the abolition of the Caliphate by the Turkish nationalist Kemal Pasha was ample proof of this. The first Arab regional organization, which was formed in 1945, was called the "Arab League" not "Muslim League". Azzam Pasha, the first Secretary General of the Arab League, who was an Egyptian, declared, "We are Egyptians first, Arabs second and Muslims third." President Nasser too made his priorities clear when he placed the Islamic brotherhood in the third and last circle after the Arab circle and the African Continent circle. "The Arab world experienced a sharp clash between territorial and pan-Arab loyalties, but Islam as a basis of regional or international political alliance had clearly receded into the background." [6] Hence, in such a political environment, Pakistani efforts to cultivate Middle Eastern countries on the basis of religion were overly optimistic and, not surprisingly, unsuccessful.

Secondly, the Muslim League's demand for Pakistan did not find much support in the Middle East, for it conjured up the examples of the partition of Ireland, the proposed partition of Palestine and the separation of Sudan from Egypt. For the Arabs, the partition of India was "yet another manifestation of the same imperialistic strategy of divide and rule".[7] Many of them believed that the Muslim League, by demanding Pakistan, "was playing into the hands of British imperialism, while the Congress Party was putting up a genuine fight for freedom, just as they themselves were doing".[8]

Thirdly, Middle Eastern countries saw in Pakistani efforts to forge an Islamic alliance a thinly disguised attempt at the leadership of the Islamic world. Some Pakistanis referred to Pakistan as the "biggest Muslim country" and the "natural leader" of the Muslim nations. This naturally did not go down well with many Middle Eastern countries which themselves entertained leadership ambitions. King Farouq ridiculed Pakistan's overzealous devotion to Islamic causes when he told his courtiers, "Don't you know that Islam was born on 14 August 1947?" Thus, Pakistan's ambition to the leadership of the Muslim world was "wholly unrealistic and ... tactics manifestly amateurish" and did precious little to improve its image and standing in the Middle East.[9]

Finally, the countries of the region were far too seasoned politically to be unaware of the power realities of the subcontinent. Unfortunately for Pakistan, the general impression in the early days of its creation was that

"India was going to be a world power while Pakistan might very well be a transitory phenomenon ...".[10] Hence, most of these countries were reluctant to make an absolute choice between the friendships of India and Pakistan. However, if a choice were to be made, "India as more powerful, more stable and more influential was likely to have the advantage".[11]

Besides, Pakistan had to contend with a bitter border dispute with Muslim Afghanistan, which exposed the chinks in the Islamic solidarity which Pakistan was trying to propagate. Indonesia, the largest Muslim country in the world, found itself more in tune with India politically in the 1950s because it made secularism, socialism and nonalignment the pillars of its own policy.

The Arab world itself was a divided house with Arab-Non-Arab, Shia-Sunni and Progressive-Conservative divides and power rivalries cutting across the apparent unifying force of Islam.[12]

Against this backdrop, it is amazing, at least in retrospect, that India's leaders entertained fears of a unified Islamic bloc siding with Pakistan in its bilateral disputes with India, primarily on the basis of religious solidarity. Such fears were greatly exaggerated and misplaced because, realistically, the Muslim Middle East could never attain the sort of unity that Indian policy makers feared; nor were Middle Eastern countries so naive or romantic as to side automatically with Pakistan in her rivalry with India, just because Pakistan happened to be an Islamic state.[13] "Curiously, there was a tendency both in Pakistan and in India to rate the political efficacy of pan-Islamism higher than was warranted by empirical realities."[14]

However, Pakistan was the first to realize the limitations of pan-Islamism as a political force and started looking for an alternative source of support in its dealings with India. Pakistan's joining of the Western alliance in the mid-50s was the clearest proof, if any were needed, of its disillusionment with pan-Islamism as a means of achieving political objectives.

But it was India's fears of Pakistan making use of the "Islamic card" which persisted much longer than they should have. While India's initial misgivings were understandable, its persistence in this folly to this day is as incomprehensible as it was then.

What is worse is that these unwarranted and far-fetched fears not only led to a distorted and self-conscious policy towards the region, but also introduced an element of inflexibility to it.

In order to counteract the threat of being completely isolated from the Islamic world, India opposed the mixture of religion with politics, publicised its secular state doctrine, and deplored international ties based on religion alone. But at the same time, it tried to project the image of India as the third most populous Muslim country, thereby courting the approval of traditional Islamic leaders.[15]

India's attempt to have it both ways was neither practicable nor desirable. There was no way India could have convinced anyone that it was as Islamic as Pakistan, if not more. Playing the Islamic card would only mean playing into Pakistan's hands, for that was its trump card. Nor was it necessary. It may be politically expedient to refer to India as the second or third largest Muslim state in the world, but "How much violence it tended to do to its secular character, which was the real strength of India, is another matter."[16]

It was this rather curious and naive logic that led India to seek representation at the Islamic Conference held in Rabat in 1969. "In the misplaced fear of isolation among the Muslim countries and an unfriendly resolution on the Kashmir issue, the External Affairs Ministry energetically pursued the chimera of an invitation to participate."[17] Pakistan firmly opposed India's participation and threatened to boycott the conference if India was allowed to participate. Pakistan's viewpoint finally prevailed and India was kept out, cutting a rather sorry figure.

The Indian government, in its anxiety to forestall any Pakistani attempt to score diplomatic points over India at Rabat, failed to take note of the significant fact that quite a few important Muslim countries declined the invitation to the Rabat Conference. Nasser could not attend the conference because of "influenza". Iraq and Syria too absented themselves from the conference. The Presidents of Turkey and Indonesia declined to attend on the ground that they were secular states. Against this background, India's clamour to attend an Islamic Conference on overtly religious lines was a "disgrace".[18]

Secondly, these Islamic Conferences in reality were anything but "Islamic". "The game was being played in international forums with an air of urgency and an eye on the political advantages to be gained for the delegates' own nation."[19] The Rabat Conference itself was plagued by the rivalry between King Feisal of Saudi Arabia and King Hassan of Morocco.[20]

Moreover, the whole exercise was the brainchild of politically conservative states like Saudi Arabia and Iran, which found it politically convenient to use the Islamic card to counter the growing influence of radical pan-Arab ideology represented by Egypt, Syria and Iraq. Indian policy makers, however, betrayed a pathetic lack of appreciation of inter-Arab rivalries and jealousies and hence failed to overcome the outdated and worn-out assumptions of their predecessors. This was borne out by the fact that even though the later Islamic groupings attracted more countries, their "net impact on world developments has been politically nil".[21]

Lastly, the Indian government, in its indecent haste to secure an invitation to Rabat in this game of political one-upmanship with Pakistan, ignored a very practical and realistic approach that Nehru laid down for India in relation to attending Muslim Conferences of pan-Islamic nature. In a directive issued in 1955, Nehru emphasized that while India should oppose any Islamic grouping, it could send non-official delegations to such conferences.[22] Such an approach would have at once emphasized the secular credentials of the Indian state, would have been politically consistent with India's opposition to mixing religion with politics and would have given an opportunity to Indian Muslims to renew their emotional and cultural bonds with fellow Muslims elsewhere, without such occasions acquiring significant political overtones.

It is easy to describe the Rabat episode as an "aberration". While the incident itself is not very significant, the misplaced fears and assumptions which prompted such an attitude on the part of the Indian government are. If anything, the Rabat episode demonstrated that Indian policy makers, even with the passage of time, failed to absorb and assimilate the realities of Arab politics and continued to allow imaginary fears and anxieties to distort and debase their approach to the region.

Kashmir

Another issue that made the Indian political leadership tread gingerly in relation to the Middle East was the problem of Kashmir, the outlines of which have already been mentioned in the first chapter. Three elements in relation to the Kashmir dispute made it difficult for India to treat the issue either as her own internal affair or even as a bilateral dispute between India and Pakistan, and so led to its internationalization. This, in turn, made it imperative for India to solicit at best the support, and at the least the neutrality, of the Middle Eastern countries in relation to Kashmir.

Firstly, Kashmir has always been portrayed as a religious issue between Hindu India and Islamic Pakistan by the latter. The partition of India on the basis of religion, the fact of Kashmir being predominantly Muslim and its geographical contiguity with Pakistan give some substance to such claims. Pakistan's use of Islam in supporting Kashmir's right to self-determination was designed to make it a pan-Islamic issue and thereby internationalize it. Such tactics are understandable in view of India's superior size and resources (and thus power) in relation to Pakistan.

Consequently, "Kashmir as an ideological obsession will remain an obstacle not only in Indo-Pakistani relations but also more generally in Pakistan's aim to achieve a flexible foreign policy."[23]

Thus, Indian policy makers, in addition to dealing with Kashmir as an ideological battle, had to contend with the rigidity that the Kashmir issue had introduced into the foreign policies of the two countries. Since both countries saw it as a zero-sum game, they saw no alternative to drumming up support for their respective stands on the issue in the world in general and the Middle East in particular. The fear that Pakistan would score over India in such endeavours in a predominantly Muslim Middle East made Indian policy makers extremely touchy in their dealings with the region.

Secondly, India's decision to take the Kashmir issue to the UN gave a legal basis to the internationalization of the Kashmir issue. Once the issue got enmeshed in power politics at the UN, it became imperative for both India and Pakistan to cultivate member countries for voting purposes. Under the circumstances, the 12 or so votes that the Arab countries possessed at the UN became crucial for both countries. These votes became particularly important for India in view of the unsympathetic attitude of the Western powers, particularly the USA and the UK, to the Indian position.

Thirdly, the very division of Kashmir, with India in possession of three-fourths of it and Pakistan the rest, kept the issue alive for various reasons. Firstly, the line of control that divided Kashmir is arbitrary and hence quite porous and not easily defensible. Secondly, the line of control separates families and friends from each other in their own land. The human tragedy that resulted as a consequence kept the issue boiling and attracted international attention.

India sought to counter Pakistani attempts to gain the support of the Muslim Middle East in its dealings with India in general, and in relation to the Kashmir issue in particular, by extending vigorous support to Arab causes in general and to the Palestinian issue in particular.

Apart from sustained support for the just rights of Palestinians, India tried to neutralize at best and minimize at the least Arab support to Pakistan by using its nascent relationship with Israel as a bargaining chip. Upgrading relations with Israel has always been an implicit threat in India's posture towards the region, if Arab support to Pakistan extended beyond what India might consider as tolerable or acceptable.

Nevertheless, India failed to obtain such a *quid pro quo* from the Arabs over the years, either in relation to Kashmir or in relation to Indo-Pakistani disputes in general.[24] Most of the Arab states, generally speaking, either supported the Pakistani position or tried to take a sort of neutral stance whose only virtue, from the Indian point of view, was that it was not anti-Indian. This was true even of Egypt, which was considered a close friend of India under Nasser. Even during the Sino-Indian war of 1962 when Pakistan was not a direct factor, most Arab countries, including Egypt, adopted a more or less neutral stance.[25]

> That the twin obsession with Pakistan and Kashmir prevailed and Pakistani influence in Arab circles was thus sought to be neutralised during Nehru's tenure is not as surprising as the fact that having found this *quid pro quo* arrangement with the Arabs to be a failure, later Indian leaders persisted in it.[26]

While Kashmir has been an important foreign policy issue for India over the decades, and while it is quite understandable that it sought to gain the support or at least the neutrality of Muslim countries of the Middle East over the issue, it is difficult to fathom why Indian policy makers adopted such a defensive posture in relation to Kashmir.

India has had considerable advantage over Pakistan with regard to Kashmir. First, the word, partition, was anathema to the Arabs because they had opposed it vehemently in Palestine. India, therefore, should have made more effective use of this Arab opposition to the "divide and rule" policy of Britain by drawing an analogy between Kashmir and Palestine. That would have made the Arab countries think twice before lining up behind Pakistan.

India was also in effective physical control of three-fourths of Kashmir, and Pakistan was in no position militarily to wrest it from India. This ground reality gave India a tremendous advantage which any number of unfavourable UN resolutions could not neutralize.

More importantly, the change in the Soviet attitude towards India and subsequently to Kashmir in the early 1950s strengthened the Indian position substantially. Till 1952, the Soviet participation in the Security Council debates over Kashmir was not extensive and generally remained non-committal. The Soviet representative occasionally used the opportunity to question the motives of the USA and the UK as they wrestled with the problem and tried to score points over them.

However, in 1952, the Soviet representative openly alleged that "... the purpose of these plans in connexion with Kashmir is to secure the introduction of Anglo-American troops into the territory of Kashmir and to convert Kashmir into an Anglo-American colony and a military and strategic base".[27]

Thus, the Soviet Union perceived a strategic advantage in Kashmir remaining in Indian hands, and started supporting the Indian stand. In 1957, the Soviet representative extended total support to the changed Indian position on Kashmir, that the elections held in the Indian part of Kashmir were an expression of the will of Kashmiri people to stay with India, when he stated that "the Kashmir question has in actual fact already been settled in essence by the people of Kashmir themselves, who consider their territory an integral part of the Republic of India".[28]

A couple of days later, the USSR cast the first ever veto of the Kashmir dispute when it vetoed a draft resolution submitted by Australia, Cuba, the UK and the USA. The consistent Soviet support to India over Kashmir since at least the mid-50s should have made Indian policy makers more confident and relaxed in their dealings with the Middle East, but that was not to be.

Even after the dismemberment of Pakistan in 1971, when Pakistan's pretensions to parity with India were finally put to rest, India as the dominant power in South Asia failed to show any flexibility and dynamism in its policy towards the Middle East. All this makes one wonder whether it was really fears over Kashmir which made the Indian policy makers adopt the sort of policy that they actually did. While Kashmir could have been a contributory factor, it alone cannot explain the whole rationale behind the policy, as we shall see later.

Nonalignment

India, quite predictably, sought to take advantage of the anti-colonial sentiments that existed in both the regions to project the concept of nonalignment to provide community of interests between India on the one hand and the Middle Eastern countries on the other. Externally, nonalignment sought to emphasize the independence of these countries by eschewing military alliances with either of the two superpowers in the context of the Cold War. Internally, it sought to reinforce territorial nationalism in these countries by de-emphasizing religious or political orthodoxy.

In a nutshell, India sought to reinforce secular and nationalistic forces in the region in the political garb of nonalignment in order to counter the possibility of religious resurgence in the region, and to preclude Pakistan from exploiting its religious affinity with the region to its political advantage.

However, it must be admitted that India's propagation of nonalignment did not make much impact on the Arab states in the initial years. But within a decade or so nonalignment made considerable headway in the region, though its acceptance was less than universal.

> After the conclusion of the Baghdad Pact, which deeply embittered Arab nationalist opinion, the concept of nonalignment found vigorous and widespread support in the Arab world. It also helped to create conditions for active cooperation between India and the Arab states in political, economic and commercial spheres.[29]

Be that as it may, nonalignment was essentially India's posture towards the superpowers in the context of the Cold War. India still had to evolve its policy towards the rest of the world on a bilateral basis. It is here that Nehru's penchant for political proselytizing in favour of nonalignment got in the way of India cultivating even a working relationship with the so-called conservative or aligned states in the Middle East.

Nehru's attitude to aligned nations, in the words of the former Foreign Secretary of India, Mr. A.P. Venkateswaran, was "self-righteous".[30] Hence, he failed to appreciate the genuine fears and suspicions of countries like Iran, Turkey and even Saudi Arabia, which prompted them to seek external props for self-defence.

This is not to say that India should have approved or even acquiesced in either the domestic or external policies of these countries. Far from it. However, realism required that India should have tried its utmost to make the best of a bad bargain by trying to cultivate these countries bilaterally by displaying greater accommodation and understanding of the reasons that necessitated their aligned posture without being too moralistic about it. This would have given the Indian political leadership a better chance of keeping in check the support that Pakistan could have managed to obtain from these countries since there were no serious bilateral disputes between India and any of these countries. But that was not to be.

Consequently, India's rather unrealistic policy towards these countries introduced an element of rigidity in her approach and severely restricted her manoeuvrability in the region and foreclosed a number of potentially promising diplomatic openings.

A Cairo-centric policy

As a corollary to the foregoing analysis, Nehru's strong political preference for nonalignment, and his political prejudice against aligned nations, adversely affected the flexibility of the Indian approach to the Middle

East in two ways. Firstly, it made Nehru throw in his entire diplomatic lot with Nasser, whom he once described as "the most prominent symbol of Arab nationalism". This was tantamount to India putting all her political eggs in the Egyptian basket with regard to the Middle East, a folly Nehru sought to avoid in relation to the superpowers by propounding the concept of nonalignment.

Secondly and more importantly, "the close tie with Cairo seemed to hamper New Delhi's interest in cultivating other West Asian states more actively".[31] This led to unnecessary and avoidable complications with a number of other states in the Middle East. India's vocal and personal support for Nasser "was taken amiss by many an Arab state which otherwise swore by Arab unity and neutralism".[32]

To sum up, it goes without saying that Indian policy makers displayed a singular lack of sophistication and finesse in understanding the complexity of the political process in the post-colonial Middle East. India's exaggerated fears of a unified Muslim bloc favouring Pakistan solely on the basis of religious affinity, and Nehru's passion for nonalignment which needlessly alienated the so-called conservative or aligned nations, seriously cramped the style and substance of Indian diplomacy in the region.

It is against this backdrop that we shall now analyse India's bilateral ties with the four most important states in the region, namely Egypt and Iraq (the supposedly radical states) in this chapter, and Iran and Saudi Arabia (the so-called conservative states) in the next. This will establish how India's imaginary fears and anxieties and a rather rigid ideological posture got in the way of her adopting a more flexible and imaginative policy which would have served her politico-diplomatic interests in the region much more effectively than it actually did over the years.

India and Egypt

It is a truism to say that cultivating Egypt was the cornerstone of India's foreign policy pursuits in the Middle East in the 1950s and 60s. The "special relationship" that evolved between Egypt and India in the two decades following India's independence was anything but an accident. It was, in fact, a product of historical circumstances, the political affinity that existed between the leaders of the two countries and the exigencies of the international situation that was obtaining at that time.

The struggle against British colonial role brought the two countries together even before India attained its independence. This common crusade against imperialism gave birth to a similarity of political outlook between the political elites of the two countries which was essentially anti-colonial, anti-racist and which emphasized the solidarity of the newly independent nations.

The advent of the Cold War and the pressures and blandishments that the superpowers applied in the Third World to find converts to their respective causes was seen by the Afro-Asian nations as infringing on their newly won independence. Hence their gravitation to nonalignment was a logical corollary.

> A new core was formed, Nehru, Nasser and Tito. Together they began to provide the political impulse, the elan, the dynamism and the guidance to the nonalignment movement; at once sober but sufficiently radical, for peace as well as for liquidation of colonialism, taking initiatives to assert independence of the newly emerging countries and resolve world tangles but at the same time trying to moderate the cold war and bring great powers in dialogue with each other.[33]

The mutual respect and admiration and the personal friendship that developed between Nehru and Nasser no doubt gave an extra thrust to the relationship between the two countries. Nasser's own outlook on foreign policy and economic planning by his own admission bore the imprint of Nehru.[34] Besides, both India and Egypt saw each other as leading countries in their respective regions, destined to play a positive and progressive role which would be to mutual advantage.

> Egypt, lacking Western support and cautious of a too deep involve-ment with the communist states, relied on India's prestige and support for its own independent foreign policy and its standing in world affairs. It courted India's pro-Arab stance on the Palestine issue. India gained the goodwill of the largest Arab state and thereby undermined any Pakistani plans to promote a pan-Islamic bloc hostile to India.[35]

Nevertheless, at this stage, it is essential to evaluate India's "special relationship" with Egypt in order to assess its advantages and costs for India and to see if India's close ties with Cairo served India's overall and long-term interests in the region.

Egypt's opposition to the formation of an Islamic bloc
The first and foremost gain, it is argued, that accrued to India because of

its close friendship with Egypt was the latter's firm and consistent opposition to the formation of any Islamic bloc for political purposes. It must be granted that Egypt's secular approach to politics acted as a check on Islamic resurgence in the region, and was at least partly responsible for checkmating the persistent Pakistani moves to forge an Islamic alliance with an anti-Indian slant in the region.

However, the secular approach to politics was not the exclusive preserve of Egypt in the Middle East. Countries like Turkey, Iran, Iraq and Syria, despite occasional lip service to Islam, were essentially secular and nationalistic in their outlook. Moreover, the so-called Islamic groupings, as we have already seen, were anything but Islamic. They were mere projections of the rivalries, suspicions and jealousies of various states in the Middle East, with each state trying to promote its own interests in the garb of Islam.

Egyptians were aware and proud of their pre-Islamic civilization, which was one of the most ancient and sophisticated in the world. So they were reluctant to overemphasize the importance of Islam to the point of overshadowing their pre-Islamic cultural heritage. Besides, Egypt considered itself the natural leader of the Arab world because of its size, population and history. Too much accent on Islam might have diluted such leadership ambitions by bringing countries like Saudi Arabia, the custodian of the Muslim Holy Places which had greater claims to Islamic credentials than Egypt, to the forefront of Arab politics. Moreover, Egyptians, because of their geographical location, considered themselves part of both the Asian and African continents. Hence, nonalignment provided them with an opportunity to play a much larger role on the bigger Afro-Asian stage, rather than to tie themselves down to the Middle East in the name of Islamic solidarity.

The idea of an Islamic alliance has been a recurrent theme in Middle Eastern politics. It was first mooted by the British after World War II in order to organize conservative elements in the region to perpetuate their imperial interests, culminating in the Baghdad Pact of 1955. The Pact countries, predictably, opposed Egypt's claim to sovereignty over the Suez Canal and supported the Anglo-French invasion of Suez in 1956. The Iraqi revolution in 1958, however, sounded the death-knell of the Baghdad Pact. Subsequently, the headquarters of the Pact was shifted to Tehran, and the Pact was renamed the Central Treaty Organization (CENTO).

Thereafter, the idea of an Islamic alliance, whenever it was resurrected, acquired a definitely anti-Nasser slant. For instance, in 1965, the idea resurfaced at a conclave in Tehran between the Shah of Iran and King

Feisal of Saudi Arabia. It was stated that Iran and Saudi Arabia would jointly exert themselves to hold a conference of Islamic countries bound together by common interests.[36] When Mrs. Gandhi visited Cairo in July 1966, she reportedly discussed the move to form an Islamic alliance with Nasser and fully appreciated and supported the United Arab Republic's (UAR) opposition to the move.[37]

During a visit to New Delhi in October in the same year, Nasser denounced the move for an Islamic alliance as "a new edition of the Baghdad Pact". He contended that the main purpose behind the move was to use Islam "in the interests of conservatives and reactionaries in collaboration with colonial powers".[38]

Though Nasser's opposition to the so-called Islamic alliance was principally aimed at preserving Egypt's dominance of Arab politics by preventing his opponents in the region from coming together against Egypt, he must have also realized how much such denunciation would please his Indian hosts and earn their goodwill for Egypt at practically no cost.

When an Islamic Conference did finally materialize in Rabat in 1969 in the aftermath of the burning of the Al Aqsa mosque in Jerusalem, Nasser stayed away because of "influenza". It is revealing at this stage to see how seriously and nervously the Indian government reacted to these attempts at forging an Islamic alliance in the Middle East.

The Indian Foreign Minister, addressing the Lok Sabha in April 1970, stated:

It [Pan-Islamism] is one of the most dangerous thoughts that has been prevailing in that part of the world … . It is the mixing up of the religion with politics and the creation of a Pan-Islamic bloc. It constitutes a danger not only for us in India but for other countries in Asia, Africa and the world as a whole.[39]

While it must be admitted that Nasser's opposition to the creation of an Islamic bloc suited India admirably, it should not, however, be forgotten that the stimulus for such a policy came from Egypt's own conception of its national interests and ambitions rather than from any goading or coaxing from India.

Nor should it be forgotten that India did pay a price for closely identifying itself with Nasser by alienating politically conservative states like Iran, Saudi Arabia and Jordan which had no animosity towards India, but felt threatened by the Arab radicalism espoused by Nasser and were loth to accept Nasser's leadership of the region entirely on his terms, which India seemed to endorse unequivocally.

This is borne out by the fact that after the rout of Arab armies by the Israelis in the six-day war in 1967, there was a general realization in Cairo that it was a mistake to seek unity in the region on an ideological basis. The unrelenting hostility towards monarchical regimes only forced them to lean even more heavily than before on Western support for survival. The new strategy was to revolve around a broad Arab nationalist front based on an entente between Nasser, Hussein and even King Feisal. Socialism and the struggle against feudalism were to take a back seat in this new strategy.[40]

The Pakistani-Egyptian equation

Pakistan's less than satisfactory relationship with Egypt in the 1950s and 60s was understandably comforting to India in political terms. However, Nasser's antipathy to Pakistan had much less to do with his aversion to Islamic groupings which Pakistan was trying to promote in those days. His annoyance with Pakistan was primarily the result of the fact that he considered Pakistan's policies and attitudes at that time to be inimical to Egypt's interests and ambitions. India was little more than a marginal factor in this Pakistani-Egyptian equation.

Firstly, the general belief that Pakistan was aspiring to the leadership of the Muslim world irritated Egypt most, because Egypt considered itself the most prominent country in the region and hence its natural leader. "Pakistan with a population five times that of [the] UAR and economic resources more varied and developed than of any of the Arab countries was suspected to be a constant obstacle, if not a possible rival, to Egyptian leadership of the area."[41]

Secondly and more importantly, there was a definite clash of interests between Egypt and Pakistan in the 1950s and 60s, primarily because of Pakistan's alliance with the Western powers. When the proposal for a Middle East Defence Organization was mooted by the British in the early 50s, Egypt demanded the evacuation of the Suez base by Britain and a satisfactory settlement of the Sudanese question as conditions for joining such an alliance. Egypt was anxious that other powers in the region should not join any such alliance until Anglo-Egyptian differences were settled to Egypt's satisfaction. If Western countries were to make progress in forging such an alliance without Egypt, it was feared that there would be less need and incentive for Britain to come to terms with Egypt.

Egypt, therefore, was furious when Turkey and Pakistan announced their intention to join the Baghdad Pact in February 1952 while Britain was still holding the Suez base and Anglo-Egyptian talks were at a critical stage. Cairo Radio described it as a "catastrophe for Islam ... the first stab in our back".[42] Nasser was also furious that during the crisis itself, the Pakistani Foreign Minister Hamidul Huq had gone back on his promise of full support to the Egyptian position. Nasser later complained to Frank Moraes: "Do you know that before the London Conference the Pakistani Foreign Minister, who came to see me, spoke for three hours and he vowed support for Egypt's cause? You know what he did?"[43]

Nasser retaliated by rejecting the Pakistani offer of a contingent for the United Nations Emergency Force (UNEF) while accepting a similar offer from India. A little later, when the Pakistani Prime Minister Suhrawardy was about to leave for Cairo, the Egyptian Ambassador warned him that Nasser did not consider it a suitable time for a visit to Cairo. Later, Nasser "pricked Pakistan's tenderest spot" when he declared, "Suez is as dear to Egypt as Kashmir is to India."[44]

These events generated bitterness and ill-feelings in both countries, and Pakistani-Egyptian relations failed to take off despite a few feeble attempts at reconciliation later. The fact that this suited the Indians was a stroke of political good fortune because Nasser was primarily guided by Egypt's own interests and was not in any sense trying to curry favour with India.

Indo-Egyptian cooperation
Nevertheless, India and Egypt did try to help each other on a number of occasions, though neither side was prepared to go overboard in assisting the other, in spite of the so-called "special relationship" that existed between the two countries.

In 1961, when the Indian Army marched into Goa, the UAR moved a resolution in the UN Security Council supporting the Indian position that the Portuguese enclaves in India came in the way of Indian unity and constituted a threat to international peace and security.

Regarding Kashmir, Egypt, though never totally endorsing India's position, did maintain a discreet neutrality over the issue which itself was not unhelpful to India. Egypt also occasionally tried to block resolutions at the UN which could have caused embarrassment to India. To cite just one example, in June 1962 Egypt refused to sponsor a draft resolution inimical to India and also influenced the other non-permanent members not to press too hard for it. The usefulness of the Egyptian stand from the Indian point of view was highlighted by the reaction of the Pakistani newspaper *Dawn*, which observed that "the UAR's resolve not to go along with the text of the draft which had been agreed to after several weeks of intense discussions has created a critical situation on the eve of the resumption of the debate" and added that "this great Middle East nation has now become a principal obstacle in the way of the Security Council adopting a fairly constructive resolution".[45] Eventually, when the resolution was moved by Ireland, the USSR vetoed it while the UAR abstained from voting on the resolution. It later explained its stand saying that it was a friend of both India and Pakistan, hence its reluctance to side with either.[46]

During the Sino-Indian war of 1962, Nasser offered to mediate between the two warring parties and put forward his own proposals[47] for settling the dispute which were, however, rejected by China. Later, at the Colombo Conference, the UAR was instrumental in preventing the conference from adopting an anti-Indian and pro-Chinese stance. Nevertheless, the Indians were disappointed with the Egyptian stand. They expected Nasser to come out more openly and emphatically on India's side, just as India had supported Egypt in its hour of need. Moreover, many nonaligned Arab states maintained a discreet silence over the issue, possibly taking their cue from Nasser, India's closest friend, who merely offered to mediate.[48]

Again, during the Indo-Pakistani war of 1965 over Kashmir, Egypt maintained a neutral position which was considered helpful by India. At the Casablanca Conference of the Heads of Arab states in September 1965, it was Nasser who played a key role in the conference, issuing a mild and balanced statement which appealed to India and Pakistan "to solve their differences by peaceful means in accordance with the principles and resolutions of the United Nations".[49]

The Indian Foreign Minister acknowledged this in the Lok Sabha in November 1965.

> It is not a secret that in Casablanca, it was mainly his [Nasser's] efforts that resulted in the Arab Conference taking an impartial attitude on this question. Even in the Security Council, [the] UAR's position has always been that this is a matter essentially between Pakistan and India ... and any interference from outside will not lead to any settlement.[50]

India too extended political and diplomatic support to Egypt during this period, though such support was never as complete and as unconditional as was made out in some quarters. Nehru himself, to start with, had some misgivings about the nature of Arab politics and the calibre of Nasser's leadership. After reading Nasser's book *The Philosophy of Revolution*, Nehru wrote to the Indian Ambassador to Egypt, Ali Yavar Jung:

> Egyptian or indeed Arab politics appear to me to be extraordinarily immature and wrapped up in their petty problems with little understanding of what is going on in the world. When I met Nasser, I was attracted to him; he is a likeable person. When I read a little book of his, I felt disappointed, that is, in regard to his intellectual calibre.[51]

Nevertheless, Nehru saw in Nasser a modern, progressive and a nationalist leader who, if cultivated with care, could play a positive and independent role in the Middle East. While the conversion of the largest Arab state to nonalignment would keep superpower meddling in the region in check, encouraging nationalism and secularism would de-emphasize the role of religion in the region and neutralize Pakistani attempts to forge solidarity with the region on the basis of Islam.

The Suez Crisis, 1956

The nationalization of the Suez Canal by Nasser in July 1956 following the decision of the USA and the UK not to assist Egypt in the construction of the Aswan Dam precipitated a major crisis in the Middle East. The fact that Nasser's decision followed closely on the heels of his meetings with Nehru at Brioni and Cairo caused diplomatic embarrassment to India. Nehru made it clear to the Indian Parliament that his discussions with Nasser "did not relate to the Suez Canal or any aspect of Anglo-Egyptian relations".[52]

Though Nehru supported Nasser in public, he tried to restrain him in private. After the nationalization of the Suez Canal, Nehru sent a cable to the Indian Ambassador in Cairo asking him to tell Nasser that "he had acted hastily and that public opinion in India was likely to be unfriendly".[53]

Addressing the Indian Parliament, Nehru conceded that "The suddenness of the nationalization decision and the manner in which it has been implemented may have contributed to the violent reactions. But the very terms of the nationalization under the laws of Egypt are within the province of that Government."[54] He also referred to India's own vital interest in the issue. "India is not a disinterested party. She is a principal user of this waterway, and her economic life and development is not unaffected by the dispute, not to speak of worse developments, in regard to it."[55]

On 24 October, India made its own proposals[56] to solve the Suez issue. The essence of the Indian approach was to negotiate a peaceful solution which would safeguard the legitimate interests of the users of the canal without infringing in any way on the sovereign rights of Egypt. However, when the Israeli invasion of Sinai was followed by an Anglo-French military invasion of the Canal Zone, Nehru reacted quite sharply and described it bluntly as "a flagrant case of aggression" and "a reversion to past colonial methods".[57] Later, India played an active role at the UN in securing the withdrawal of foreign troops from Egyptian soil and in vindicating Egypt's sovereign rights.

The cooling of Indo-Egyptian relations

Though the understanding and rapport that developed between Nehru and Nasser led to political coordination between the two countries' foreign policies in the 1950s and early 60s, the Sino-Indian war and the death of Nehru soon after led to a certain chill in Indo-Egyptian relations. When Shastri visited Cairo in October 1964, a reference to Peking's intransigence in not accepting the Colombo proposals was deleted on Egypt's insistence.[58] The Indians were disappointed by this lack of positive support from Nasser in regard to the vital issues affecting India: Kashmir and the Sino-Indian border dispute.[59] Indians were also piqued by reports in the Egyptian press that India's nonalignment was "in danger of being eroded by American assistance" following the Sino-Indian war.[60]

That the Indians were disenchanted with the attitude of the UAR was confirmed when Mrs. Gandhi deliberately chose to bypass Cairo on her way to Washington and instead spent two days in Paris in May 1966. G.H. Jansen commenting on the episode said: "It came as news to these friends of India that India was tired of being nagged by the Arabs into a position of total hostility towards Israel while the Arabs maintained an equivocal neutrality towards India's antagonists, China and Pakistan."[61]

Though Mrs. Gandhi did visit Cairo in July 1966, there was very little of the old spark in the relations between the two countries. The joint statement that was issued was confined to vague generalities and routine diplomatic niceties. "If the document reflected a measure of icy formality it was because, in the type of relations which now exist between this country and the Arabs, any demonstration of excessive warmth is exceedingly difficult."[62]

Though India extended total and vociferous support to Egypt during the 1967 Arab-Israeli war, the rout of the Arab armies left Nasser a weak and shattered man. The defeat also led to fresh thinking in Cairo; this resulted in a new Arab strategy based on a broad Arab coalition which sought to involve countries like Jordan and even Saudi Arabia, which had hitherto been ignored on ideological grounds. The withdrawal of the Egyptian forces from Yemen eliminated the main source of tension and friction between Cairo and Riyadh and paved the way for a broad Arab coalition. However, the death of Nasser in 1970 and the advent of Anwar Sadat marked a new and more down-to-earth phase in Indo-Egyptian relations.

During the Bangladesh crisis in 1971, Egypt maintained a studied silence which again disappointed the Indians. When Fakhruddin Ali Ahmed met Sadat in Cairo in July 1971, Sadat assured him that he would impress upon Pakistan the need for a political solution to facilitate the return of refugees.[63] However, Egypt continued to maintain a neutral and passive posture on the issue. The Ministry of External Affairs in New Delhi was irked by the fact that there was little to choose between the so-called progressive and conservative Arab states in their approach to an issue which was of critical importance to India.[64]

However, M.H. Haikal, Editor-in-Chief of Egypt's leading daily *Al Ahram* disclosed in New Delhi in February 1973 that Soviet arms and assistance for Bangladesh passed through Egypt.[65] But it is quite possible that the help that Egypt rendered to India was due more to Soviet pressure than to any desire on its part to help an old friend in her hour of peril.

Moreover, Sadat's political priorities and orientation were so different from those of Nasser that the political understanding and affinity that existed between India and Egypt all but ceased to exist in the 1970s. Sadat was a pragmatist and his ambitions for Egypt were rather modest. His first priority was the withdrawal of Israel from Egyptian territory. He also believed in free enterprise and was convinced of the necessity of gaining American support as the only way of breaking Israeli intransigence. Having thrown out the Russians, he launched a major offensive against Israel in coordination with Syria in October 1973. After "unfreezing" the situation, he plumped for the American connection, which eventually led to Egypt signing a separate peace treaty with Israel and to substantial American economic and military assistance.

Meanwhile, during the same period, India moved closer to the USSR and hence there was a hint of political divergence between the two countries, though there was no bilateral dispute as such. Besides, India could not endorse the Egyptian strategy of separate peace with Israel without alienating the rest of the Arab world which had ostracized Egypt from the Arab fold, and with whom India was trying to cultivate a more meaningful and profitable relationship, hence India's cautious and qualified welcome to the Camp David Accord. Nevertheless, India firmly resisted pressure from various Arab countries to expel Egypt from the Nonaligned Movement (NAM) at Havana in September 1979.

The 1970s and 80s underlined the fact that, apart from some political understanding, there was little else to Indo-Egyptian relations. Indo-Egyptian economic relations failed to take off despite repeated attempts by the two governments. Nasser, Tito and Mrs. Gandhi tried to provide a new direction for the developing countries by setting an example of promoting economic cooperation through mutual granting of tariff preferences and other concessions and incentives in selected areas. However, this laudable experiment proved to be only a modest success.[66]

Indo-Egyptian economic relations were also plagued by a trade imbalance between the two countries. Initially, the imbalance was the result of Egypt buying more of Indian goods but failing to sell to India to the extent specified in the agreement. India's major import from Egypt was long-staple cotton. However, Egypt was not always able to fulfil its export commitment to India because of Egypt's preference for selling the same in hard currency areas.[67] Later, the problem was compounded when India became a net exporter of cotton.

In 1975, India and Egypt agreed to terminate the rupee trade and switch over to trading in convertible currency. By and large, Indo-Egyptian economic relations remained modest and low-key with little likelihood of any significant breakthrough in future either.

Indo-Egyptian attempts at technological collaboration also ended in total failure. The two countries sought to produce a supersonic military aircraft, with India building the HF 24 airframes while Egypt manu-factured the E 300 engines. The project fell through because of technical problems.[68] In the words of one commentator, "The whole project was a brain-child of Mr. Krishna Menon, who conjured up the idea of mating an Indian-built airframe with an Egyptian-designed jet engine, as a piece of political fantasy during the heyday of nonalignment."[69]

There were a number of other irritants in Indo-Egyptian relations in the late 1970s and 80s. In 1976, Egypt approached India for spare parts for its MIG 21s, which were more or less grounded because the Soviet Union had suspended all military supplies to Egypt. India could not possibly have obliged Egypt because of its contractual commitments to the USSR. India sent a negative reply almost six months after the initial Egyptian request.[70]

Egypt was also upset that India voted in favour of a resolution condemning Egypt for signing a separate peace treaty with Israel at the Havana Nonaligned Summit in 1979, contrary to the assurance that it received from the then Indian Foreign Minister. The two countries also failed to renew the agreement to train Egyptian nuclear scientists at Trombay, and the acrimonious negotiations between Air India and Egypt Air over the flights from one country to the other further vitiated the atmosphere between the two countries.[71]

To sum up, India's relations with Egypt acquired a larger-than-life image initially because of euphoria over nonalignment, India's exaggerated fears over a hostile Islamic bloc and the colourful and charismatic personalities of Nehru and Nasser. However, the passage of time exposed the limitations of Indo-Egyptian relations in both the political and economic spheres. While India did gain something from this relationship, it must be emphasized that India's close identification with Nasser was a principal cause for the alienation of many Arab states which resented Nasser's leadership and policies but had no quarrel with India, thereby seriously circumscribing India's already limited options in the region.

India and Iraq

India's relations with Iraq, potentially one of the more significant and powerful countries in the Middle East, have been rather chequered and took an unusually long time to mature and consolidate. In the following pages, an attempt will be made to analyse the initial impediments to the development of Indo-Iraqi relations, the Ba'athist coup in 1958 and its impact on subsequent Indo-Iraqi interaction and the factors that contributed to a breakthrough in their bilateral relations in the early 1970s, along with a brief discussion of future prospects.

Indo-Iraqi ties can be conveniently considered in two phases: the first phase lasting till 1958 when Iraq was under monarchy, and the second phase beginning with the coup in Iraq in 1958 which overthrew the monarchy and established a radical Ba'athist regime in Baghdad.

Indo-Iraqi relations till 1958

Indo-Iraqi relations started on a fairly positive note soon after India's independence, when the two countries entered into a treaty of friendship in November 1952.[72] However, as in the case of Iran, Nehru's penchant for nonalignment and Nasser again came in the way of India seriously cultivating Iraq on a bilateral basis.

The monarchical regime in Iraq was, like other monarchies in the region, politically conservative. But its championing of Islam was again politically motivated and meant to ward off the threat posed to the regime by radical Arab nationalism. "The rivalry between Egyptian and Iraqi leaders was not new: but 'Nasserism' heightened and gave a new edge to old rivalries."[73]

Hence, Iraq's affinity with Pakistan even before the Ba'athist coup was primarily political rather than religious. More importantly, the Pakistan factor was of much less importance in the Indo–Iraqi equation than it was in the Indo–Iranian equation simply because, unlike Iran, Iraq saw no direct stake, political or security, in the stability and viability of Pakistan.

Nevertheless, India failed to take a fairly detached view of Pakistani-Iraqi ties and develop its relations with Iraq independently of the Pakistan factor. This only goes to underline India's rather unwarranted obsession with Pakistan and pan-Islamism, which led to unnecessary distortions in India's Middle Eastern policy in general.

It was the fear of radical Arab nationalism as represented by Nasser that prompted the regime of Nuri Pasha to gravitate, as a counter, towards Islam, Pakistan and eventually the Baghdad Pact.[74]

The Baghdad Pact, 1955

The Iraqi decision to join the Western military alliance in 1955, which came to be known as the Baghdad Pact, was a blow to the development of Indo-Iraqi relations for various reasons. Firstly, India, in general, was opposed to military alliances. Secondly, India was particularly worried about the Baghdad Pact because of Pakistan's membership of it. India feared that Pakistan could exploit its membership of the alliance to put pressure on India in relation to bilateral disputes between the two countries.

As Nehru pointed out, "But, surely, nobody here imagines that the Pakistan Government entered into this Pact because it expected some imminent or distant invasion or aggression from the Soviet Union. The Pakistan newspapers and the statements of responsible people in Pakistan make it perfectly clear that they have joined this Pact because of India."[75] Thirdly, Iraq started extending overt political and diplomatic support to Pakistan over Kashmir only after the latter had joined the Baghdad Pact.

Looking back, one cannot help wondering whether India should have allowed Iraq's membership of the Baghdad Pact to cloud Indo-Iraqi relations to the extent it did. Iraq was not unfriendly towards India, nor was there any major bilateral dispute between the two countries. Iraq's motives for joining the Baghdad Pact had nothing to do with India. As Nehru himself pointed out, "other members of the Baghdad Pact have no hostility to India".[76] As we have already seen, the Baghdad Pact failed to evolve along the lines of NATO, regarding common defence against third parties, which greatly reduced its efficacy and solidarity.

However, Iraq did support Pakistan on the Kashmir issue much more vocally after both of them joined the Baghdad Pact. Iraq's basic stand had been that the Kashmir issue must be solved on the basis of a plebiscite and that the passage of time made no difference to this commitment which both sides had accepted earlier.

Iraq sent an *aide-mémoire* to the government of India in June 1956, presumably at the behest of Pakistan, to "point out that the Kashmir question is a factor of restlessness and tension and it has its effect on the security of this area and, Iraq being a member of the United Nations and the Baghdad Pact, feels that it cannot but be interested in anything that upsets the security of this area, which is on the whole linked with the security of the world".[77]

At a Security Council meeting in January 1957, the Iraqi representative argued that "The passage of time has neither changed the principles upon which the future of Kashmir was to be decided nor has made the method of a plebiscite less applicable now than it was eight years ago."[78]

In October 1957, the Iraqi representative, Mr. Khalaf, asserted in a Security Council debate that in relation to Kashmir "a solution is already prescribed by the Council ... and all that is to done is to implement the resolutions".[79]

As can be seen from the above, Iraqi support for Pakistan on the Kashmir issue was largely political and diplomatic and primarily meant to express its solidarity with a fellow member of the Baghdad Pact. To India's dismay and disappointment, this support continued even after the coup in Iraq in 1958 which installed a radical Ba'athist regime in Baghdad.

The 1958 Ba'athist coup and after
The Ba'athist coup in Baghdad in 1958 was a significant and welcome development from the Indian point of view for a variety of reasons. First and foremost, the coup in Baghdad sounded the death-knell of the Baghdad Pact which India greatly feared and firmly opposed. As Nehru told the Rajya Sabha:

> The whole conception and inception of the Baghdad Pact was based on unreality. It ignored the great forces and ferments in Asia today and merely thought in terms of coming to agreements with a certain stratum of rulers and a small group at the top. And suddenly we find that the very basis of the Baghdad Pact is gone. Baghdad and

Iraq have dropped out of it.[80]

Secondly, India expected that the advent of a Ba'athist regime in Baghdad would give "a boost to the forces of nonalignment and secularism in the Middle East".[81] The Ba'athist regime did adopt a nonaligned stance in foreign affairs, and followed a genuinely secular policy in both the international and domestic spheres. This, in turn, no doubt strengthened the forces of nonalignment and secularism in the region, a development which India could not but have welcomed with a sense of satisfaction and perhaps vindication.

Thirdly and lastly, India must also have hoped that the nonaligned and secular regime in Baghdad would, at least, dilute the strong political support that Iraq had been extending to Pakistan over the Kashmir issue. The fact that this did not happen for quite some time must have both disappointed and probably surprised New Delhi. This is primarily because India's earlier reservations about the monarchical regime and expectations in relation to the post-1958 Ba'athist regime were both based on misperceptions.

As has already been pointed out, even before the 1958 coup, Islam was hardly a consideration in Iraq's foreign policy pursuits, nor was it a factor in Iraq's close ties with Pakistan. More importantly, India was never a factor in Iraq's aligned posture between 1955 and 1958. Hence, it was rather naive on the part of Indian policy makers to have expected a dramatic change in Indo-Iraqi relations in strictly bilateral terms, even after 1958. Iraq's support for Pakistan's position on Kashmir continued beyond 1958 primarily because Iraq considered Pakistan's friendship as a useful factor in its rivalry with Egypt for Arab leadership.

The change of regime in Baghdad did little to scuttle the traditional rivalry between the Egyptians and Iraqis, and the Ba'athist regime in Baghdad, despite its ideological affinity with Nasser, was not inclined to play second fiddle to him. As one scholar pointed out,

> The most striking, and to many the most surprising, development was the extraordinary rapidity with which antagonism between Iraq and Egypt reopened after a brief lull following the fall of the royal regime ... . Qassim perceived that Nasser aimed at a "leadership" of the Arab world which prejudiced independent action by Iraq in external affairs ... . Without explicitly stating it, Qassim unmistakably implied the equality of Iraq with Egypt within the framework of Arab nationalism.[82]

Thus, in the post-1958 period, "India's relations with Iraq took a turn for the better, although the major development in relations came between 1966 and 1976".[83]

When the Sino-Indian border dispute erupted into a full-scale war in October 1962, Iraq extended strong support to India and criticized the Chinese actions quite explicitly. *Almowatin*, a widely circulated Iraqi daily, editorially condemned the unprecedented and unreasonable Chinese aggression over a large territory of India and demanded that they withdraw to positions they held prior to 8 September 1962. The Chinese action, the paper went on, compelled India to request arms from the West which she was never inclined to do earlier.[84] There was also a message of support for Nehru from Iraqi thinkers, academicians and lawyers.[85] The Iraqi Prime Minister, Abdul Karim Dassim, implicitly criticized China when he said: "The cause behind the fighting was high-handedness in view and the insistence on imposing this high-handedness."[86]

Incidentally, India and Iraq signed an agreement in December 1962 which accorded most favoured nation treatment to each other, and as a result Iraq became an important market for Indian tea, jute, textiles and spices.[87]

The Iraqi President, Mr. Mohammad Arif, paid an official visit to India in March-April 1964 and had extensive talks with Nehru. The first ever India-Iraq joint communiqué[88] "acknowledged the identity of views between India and Iraq on world issues such as nuclear disarmament, colonialism, racial discrimination".

In an implicit reference to the Sino-Indian border dispute, they asserted that "all disputes between states ... should be settled by peaceful means and not by resort to force, and that if aggression is committed in pursuit of territorial aims, its fruits must be denied to the aggressor".

The Iraqi President also "expressed gratification at the fact that India was the homeland of 50 million Muslims ... who enjoyed the fullest freedom of religious faith and worship".

The Indo-Pakistani war over Kashmir in September 1965 saw Iraq take a position which was consistent with her earlier stand in relation to the dispute. The Iraqi representative at the UN argued that "a lasting solution of the Kashmir problem must be based upon the principles of the Charter and the decisions of the competent organs of this Organisation".[89] Iraq did not accept the Indian contention that the plebiscite issue had become irrelevant in view of the free elections held in Indian-occupied Kashmir which was tantamount to the Kashmiris exercising their right to self-determination.

The then Foreign Minister of India, making a statement in the Rajya Sabha in November 1965, mentioned Iraq among other Middle Eastern countries and said: "The representatives of these countries made statements which cannot be construed as against our interests."[90] So, the Iraqi position during the 1965 Indo-Pakistani war was not construed as unfriendly even by the Indian government.

The year 1966 was a turning point in Indo-Iraqi relations. In February 1966, it was announced in Cairo that Iraq had given up its pro-Pakistan stand on the Kashmir issue. It was believed that it was Nasser who had weaned the then Iraqi President Arif away from the earlier pro-Pakistan posture.[91] This development went a long way to simplifying and expanding Indo-Iraqi relations.

The Iraqi Foreign Minister's visit to India, 1967

Dr. Adman Al-Pachachi, the first Foreign Minister of Iraq ever to visit India, said that Iraq supported India's stand on nuclear nonproliferation and stood by the resolution moved on the issue by the eight nonaligned powers. He asserted that Iraq adhered strictly to nonalignment and rejected any other form of grouping of states like that envisaged at the Islamic Conference.[92]

The Indo-Iraqi joint communiqué[93] also reflected the warming up of Indo-Iraqi relations. It said that a treaty of nonproliferation of nuclear weapons was essential to meet the "serious danger inherent in the spread of nuclear weapons". Such a treaty should be based on "the principle of an acceptable balance of obligations and responsibilities between the nuclear weapon states and the non-nuclear states".

The year 1968 saw Indo-Iraqi cooperation extending to the field of defence as well. India's then Defence Minister disclosed that India would provide more military instructors to train the Iraqis and would increase the training facilities, particularly for Iraq's Air Force.[94] In February 1970, India and Iraq signed an agreement on Technical and Scientific Cooperation.[95]

From the Indian point of view, during the Bangladesh crisis "Iraq was not hostile although it did not adopt a vocally sympathetic standpoint".[96] After the crisis was over, Iraq became the first Arab country to recognize Bangladesh in August 1972.

In June 1972, India threw its weight behind Iraq's decision to nationalize the Iraqi Petroleum Company.[97] This was significant, because the nationalization decision had led to a bitter war of words between Iraq on the one hand and the USA and the UK on the other, and to threats of economic sanctions against Iraq.

The importance of growing Indo-Iraqi ties

The upswing in Indo-Iraqi relations in the early 1970s was significant not only in itself but also for the openings it provided for Indian diplomacy in the region. As one newspaper put it, "Gone are the days when New Delhi's approach to the Arabs revolved round one or two countries in the region. India has acquired new friends in countries like Iraq and Yemen."[98] Consequently, India's approach to the region became more balanced and broad-based.

The opening up of Indo-Iraqi relations was a major contributory factor to the subsequent breakthrough that was achieved in Indo-Iranian relations. The Shah of Iran would in no way allow his principal Arab rival in the Gulf to cultivate India, an emerging regional power, on exclusive terms.

More importantly, it was also a lesson for Indian policy makers that it was not necessary to make an "either/or" choice between two contending countries, and that it was quite feasible to have good relations with both on the basis of mutuality of interests. India's success in cultivating Iraq without alienating Iran was ample proof of this. India's deepening relations with Iraq also facilitated the subsequent process of political understanding and fruitful economic cooperation between India and various Gulf states.

In October 1972, Iraq agreed in principle to give India a loan to cover the bulk of the foreign exchange requirements of the giant Mathura refinery, estimated at $75 million.[99] In April 1973, Iraq agreed to supply India with 30 million tons of crude over a ten-year period for the refinery to be set up at Mathura during 1977-78. Iraq also agreed to extend a credit of $50 million in the shape of supplies of crude oil.[100]

The Iraqi Vice-President, Mr. Saddam Hussein, visited India in March 1974 and had extensive discussions with Mrs. Gandhi, and the joint communiqué[101] issued on the occasion reflected the further strengthening of political and economic ties between the two countries. The establishment of a permanent Joint Commission and the agreements for securing a loan on soft terms to import 2.8 million tons of crude oil during 1974 and the supply of 112 million tons of crude over ten years after the Mathura refinery became operational were the major outcome of the visit.[102]

The visit reflected the close political affinity that existed between the two countries which, in turn, led to extensive economic cooperation. As one newspaper put it, "Iraq, committed to socialism and total independence in the field of foreign policy, is closest to India. Vice-President Saddam Hussein ... represents these attitudes more emphatically than any Arab leader today."[103]

Mrs. Gandhi's three-day visit to Baghdad in January 1975 was a definite success in both political and economic terms. The joint communiqué[104] issued on the occasion reflected the close coordination that the two countries managed to establish in their general views on international affairs and specific issues of mutual interest and benefit. Mrs. Gandhi "appreciated the successes achieved in consolidating the country's economic independence and gaining control over its national resources for the well-being of the people of Iraq". Regarding Iraq's border dispute with Iran, Mrs. Gandhi "expressed the Government of India's full awareness of the dimensions of these problems".

Indo-Iraqi political honeymoon
The latter part of the 1970s saw the establishment of the closest political and economic links between India and Iraq. This was largely due to the similarities in the problems that the two countries encountered during this period and their respective national ambitions and aspirations.

Both India and Iraq faced grave challenges to their national security and sovereignty in the early 1970s, India in relation to the Bangladesh crisis in view of the unsympathetic attitude of the West, and Iraq in relation to gaining control over its oil resources from foreign companies in the face of threats of economic sanctions, again from the West.

Consequently, both India and Iraq were left with little choice but not only to move closer to the USSR but also to formalize their close ties with it in the form of friendship treaties in 1971 and 1972 respectively. As the challenges which precipitated the friendship treaties were overcome, both India and Iraq "reverted to their normal foreign policy stance".[105]

Nevertheless, this period was also characterized by an orchestrated campaign, mainly Western inspired, that the USSR was trying to create a hostile ring round Iran and Pakistan by building an axis running from New Delhi through Kabul to Baghdad. It was also alleged that India and Iraq were secretly providing base facilities to the Soviet Indian Ocean fleet at Visakapatnam in the Bay of Bengal, and at Umm Qasr in the Shatt-al-Arab estuary in the Persian Gulf, respectively, which had no basis in fact whatsoever.[106]

This is the reason behind both countries reaffirming, time and again, their commitment to nonalignment, their opposition to major power meddling in the Indian Ocean, their determination to pursue independent foreign policies and their emphasis on national self-reliance, which they sought to attain by mutual cooperation in economic as well as technological spheres during this period.

Iraq and the Janata interregnum, 1977-79
The change of government in India made little difference to the buoyancy in Indo-Iraqi relations, despite the fact that Iraq extended its full support to and solidarity with the domestic policies of Mrs. Gandhi during the emergency period in India.[107] A high-level Iraqi delegation led by its Vice-President, Mr. Taha M. Marouf, visited India in July 1978 and had extensive talks with Desai and his senior colleagues. They covered a wide range of subjects and a "broad measure" of agreement on the issues discussed emerged.[108]

Indo-Iraqi relations in the 1980s
The Soviet intervention in Afghanistan in December 1979 brought India and Iraq much closer to each other politically. Both were opposed to the Soviet intervention in Afghanistan, and there was considerable similarity of views between the two on the developments in Afghanistan and the situation created by them in the region. Both agreed on the need to defuse the tension in the area and prevent the escalation of superpower rivalry in the region, including the Indian Ocean. Both were of the opinion that an injection of arms into the region would create further instability and heighten tension in the region.[109]

Commenting on the importance of the Indo-Iraqi ties, one newspaper said:

> ... the regime there [in Baghdad] is genuinely secular and non-aligned. Both these points are important for New Delhi: the first because the tide of Islamic fundamentalism is sweeping West Asia and a number of governments are finding it expedient to speak in the name of religion, and second, because the Soviet take-over in Afghanistan and the US response to it have exposed the whole region to superpower rivalry on a much bigger scale than it has been exposed ever before ... . For years, both India and Iraq have been trying to pursue policies which could strengthen their political and economic independence and keep the region free from the control of the superpowers.[110]

However, the fact remained that neither India nor Iraq was in a position to displease the Soviet Union over Afghanistan. Though it was primarily the Soviet action which escalated tensions in the region, both countries reserved their strongest criticism for the Western response to it. It was also ironical that, despite being two of the largest importers of arms in the region (mostly Soviet), India and Iraq chose to be critical of Western countries for large-scale transfer of arms to the region as a response to the Soviet presence in Afghanistan.

However, the Iran-Iraq war which started in September 1980 caused considerable strain in Indo-Iraqi relations. When the war broke out, the Indian Foreign Ministry described it as an "unfortunate development" because both countries were nonaligned and had friendly relations with India.[111]

However, there were reports in the foreign press that India had agreed to supply planes' and tanks' parts to Iran in its war with Iraq. The Indian Foreign Ministry described these reports as "mischievous and motivated".[112]

When the Israeli Air Force bombed and destroyed Iraq's Osirak nuclear reactor near Baghdad on 7 June 1981, India reacted sharply and condemned Israeli action as "stark adventurism and a blatant act of intervention and aggression".[113]

As the Iran-Iraq conflict continued unabated, for the first time since the Iraqi revolution in 1958 Indo-Iraqi relations started showing strains. Iraq did not like the shifting of the venue of the 7th Nonaligned Summit from Baghdad to New Delhi in 1983. According to the Gulf News Agency (GNA), Iraq had informed India many times of its "dissatisfaction" with the Nonaligned Movement's (NAM) role in ending the Iran-Iraq war. Iraq reportedly sent a low-level representation to Mrs. Gandhi's funeral to register its unhappiness.[114]

To sum up, Indo-Iraqi relations, like Indo-Iranian relations, took a much longer time to develop and consolidate than they should have done, primarily because of Nehru's passion for nonalignment and Nasser. This was so despite the fact that the Pakistan factor was of much less significance in relation to Indo-Iraqi ties than it was in the case of Indo-Iranian ties. India's initial reservations and misgivings about Iraq just because it was aligned and was under a monarchy were unwarranted and uncalled for. The fact that there was no dramatic upswing in Indo-Iraqi ties even after the coup in Baghdad in 1958 and Iraq's subsequent withdrawal from CENTO and its nonaligned orientation only served to expose the basic untenability and far-fetchedness of some of these assumptions that underlay India's policy towards the region. It is of significance to note that Indo-Iraqi ties really flourished only after India had started cultivating Iraq in bilateral terms on the basis of mutuality of interests in the political

sphere and complementarity of interests in the economic sphere subsequently.

Iraq will always be an important country for India in the Middle East
because Iraq will continue to be a major factor in Middle Eastern regional
politics and there has been no bilateral dispute whatsoever between the
two countries over the years. Given the complementarity of political
outlook and economic interests between the two countries, Indo-Iraqi ties
will continue to grow, occasional irritants notwithstanding.

2. India's Politico-diplomatic Interests in the Middle East: Iran and Saudi Arabia

India and Iran

Iran, apart from being a major and potentially one of the most powerful countries in the Middle East, is, perhaps, the most important country India has had to deal with in the region. This is primarily because Iran, from the beginning, considered that it had a direct and vital stake in the Indian subcontinent from both political and security points of view.

Consequently, Pakistan became an important factor in the Indo-Iranian equation for almost two decades, and placed artificial restrictions on the development and maturity of Indo-Iranian relations which remained in a state of somnambulance. While Iran was partly responsible for this, it appears, at least in retrospect, that India must accept the larger part of the blame for this sorry state of affairs.

India signed a treaty of friendship with Iran as early as March 1950.[1] However, the following two decades of Indo-Iranian relations hardly bore any resemblance to the sentiments expressed in the friendship treaty and remained cool and low-key, punctuated by moments of mutual suspicion and even hostility. The following pages will be devoted to a critical discussion of the reasons that prevented Indo-Iranian relations developing to their full potential in the two decades or so following India's independence, the factors that contributed to a breakthrough in their relations in the mid-70s and a brief look at the future prospects.

When India and Pakistan became independent in 1947, in spite of Pakistan's anti-Indian propaganda and the considerable sympathy that existed in the Iranian press and the people in general for Pakistan, the government of Iran remained unaffected, and was basically well disposed towards India, a fact acknowledged by Nehru himself.[2] Even before India's independence, Iran participated in the first Asian Relations Conference, held in New Delhi in March 1947, and extended its friendship and goodwill to India.

Nehru too extended sympathy and support to Iran in 1946 in its dispute with the USSR in regard to Azerbaijan and the withdrawal of Russian forces from Iranian soil, though he avoided any direct criticism of the Soviet Union. He made it clear that Indian opinion would strongly resent any aggression towards Iran or Turkey by any power.[3] Again, when Iran nationalized the Anglo-Iranian Oil Company in 1951, India extended her support to Iran to help her get rid of the remnants of Western imperialism in that country, though India appealed to both Iran and Britain to settle the issue through negotiations.

More importantly, during this period, Iran also tried to steer clear of great power influence and pursue an independent foreign policy akin to India's nonalignment, under the premiership of Mossadegh. As one observer put it, "Under Mossadegh, Iran refused like India to be drawn into one or other of the two great power blocs and clung tenaciously, if a little hopelessly, to her neutrality".[4]

However, unlike in India where there was a broad national consensus on India's nonaligned posture, Mossadegh's National Front had to contend with two other contestants for power in Iran who were opposed to Iran's policy of neutrality, namely the Shah, who favoured an alliance with the West in order to contain the Soviet threat, and the Tudeh (Communist Party of Iran) which desired an alliance with the USSR on ideological grounds.[5]

Alignment and alienation

However, the ousting of Mossadegh and the reinstatement of the Shah in August 1953 (with the help of the Central Intelligence Agency) put an end to Iran's experiment with neutrality and put her firmly in the Western alliance. The Shah never believed that neutrality would be in the interests of Iran. During World War II, in spite of Iran's declared neutrality, Iran was occupied by the allied powers and the Shah's father, Reza Shah, was deposed and exiled.[6]

However, Iran joining the Western alliance proved to be a turning point in Indo-Iranian relations in the sense that it created a political rift between the two major Asian nations which they failed to mend, despite a few feeble attempts, in the next two decades or so. The reasons for this are not far to seek.

The Nehru factor

Firstly, India displayed little understanding of the circumstances which almost compelled the Shah to align himself with the West. He had genuine fears of a Russian threat to Iran, particularly after Stalin delayed the withdrawal of Russian troops from Iran beyond the stipulated date of 2 March 1946 at the end of World War II. The Shah was also fearful that the Russians could destabilize his regime through the Tudeh Party, which had close links with the USSR. The Shah's domestic position too was anything but secure, having been installed in power by the CIA. Moreover, he considered alignment with the West as the only way of obtaining the economic assistance and arms to which he attached the highest priority.[7]

Nehru, on the other hand, had little time for aligned nations in those early days of pristine nonalignment. His attitude to aligned nations, as has already been pointed out, was "self-righteous". Hence, Nehru showed little appreciation of the genuine fears and misgivings that haunted the Shah in relation to his country's security and integrity. Consequently, for years, a barrier was created between Iran and India by Nehru's antipathy towards those in military alliance with the West.[8]

The Shah of Iran made his first visit to India in February 1956 on India's invitation, just four months after Iran had joined the Baghdad Pact. The visit was anything but a success in political terms. The Shah tried to impress upon the Indian leaders that his country's close ties with Pakistan were not directed against India and would not be at the cost of India's friendship.[9] That no communiqué was issued at the conclusion of talks between Nehru and the Shah was an ample indication of the fact that the two leaders were on different political wavelengths and merely agreed to disagree.

Nehru made a return visit to Tehran in September 1959. The visit only served to underline the political gulf that separated the two countries. According to Girilal Jain, Nehru's meeting with the Shah was a "near disaster" because the two leaders thought in "very different terms".[10] The joint statement issued on the occasion was deliberately confined to vague generalities and pious sentiments in order to conceal or at least gloss over disagreements on specific issues.[11]

The Nasser factor

The second factor that adversely affected Indo-Iranian relations was Nehru's close personal friendship with Nasser. Nehru's endorsement of Nasser as the leader of the Arab world and of his policies as progressive and dynamic naturally did not go down well with the Shah, who felt threatened by such policies.[12]

The Shah was already apprehensive about the Soviet threat and the vulnerability of his own domestic position, which was far from stable. Under the circumstances, Nasser's crusade against monarchies only tended to increase the Shah's sense of insecurity. The traditional Persian-Arab rivalries and suspicions and the sectarian divide between the Shi'ite Iran and the predominantly Sunni Arabs only accentuated the Shah's fears of isolation and encirclement.

Nasser's attempts at the unification of the Arab states, like the formation of the United Arab Republic (UAR) by the merger of Egypt and Syria, made the Shah conjure up visions of a coalition of radical Arab states leaning heavily upon Persian Iran.

The coup in Iraq in 1958 and the coming to power of a radical Ba'athist regime in Baghdad only confirmed the Shah's worst fears. After the coup, the new regime not only started moving closer to the USSR but also reopened the Kurdish question.[13] The Iraqi claims to Kuwait in the early 1960s and the civil war in Yemen and Egypt's active participation in it were perceived by the Shah as a direct threat to Iran's interests, particularly in the Persian Gulf.

Under the circumstances, it is hardly surprising that the Shah of Iran did not take kindly to India's "special relationship" with Egypt and Nehru's political preference in favour of Nasser and nonalignment.[14]

Islam and Pakistan as factors

The Shah tried to counter this threat from Arab radicalism as espoused by Nasser in two ways. First, he sought to make use of Islam as a counter-ideology to Nasser's radical Arab nationalism. It is in this context that one should understand the Shah's attempts to organize Islamic conferences, particularly in the 1960s.

Secondly, he tried to counter Iran's sense of isolation by cultivating non-Arab Muslim countries like Pakistan, with whom Iran had close ethnic and cultural ties. Ironically, Nehru's penchant for Nasser and nonalignment prompted the Shah to move closer politically to Islam and Pakistan, a development which the Indian policy towards the Middle East was purported to counter and neutralize.

Though Shi'ite Islam was declared the state religion in Iran, the Shah of Iran was not a religious man in any sense of the term. Despite his political conservatism, the Shah was a modern and forward-looking monarch. In fact, under the Shah, the emphasis in Iran was on pre-Islamic Aryan civilization. His title "Aryamehr" meant the "Light of the Aryans". In 1971, the Shah celebrated in a grand and pompous fashion the 25th centenary of the founding of the Persian empire by Cyrus the Great, emphasizing Iran's Aryan ethos and heritage.

Hence, Islam was hardly a factor in the Shah's support for an Islamic alliance in the 1960s or for his intimate relationship with Pakistan over the years. The Shah cultivated both Islam and Pakistan as a counterpoise to Nasserism and a possible Arab domination of the region.

Iran also firmly opposed Pakistani attempts to give a religious colour to "Regional Cooperation for Development" (RCD) which came into existence in 1964 to promote economic cooperation between Iran, Pakistan and Turkey. The Iranian Foreign Minister told the Majlis (the Iranian Parliament) that "... incidentally, Turkey, Pakistan and Iran are all Muslim countries but ... this unity, alliance and concord has no direct connection with Islam, nor does it have any specific religious aspects. Other nations of Asia ... may share in this regional alliance."[15] In fact, Iran even sounded India on joining the RCD as early as 1964, despite Pakistan's total opposition to such a move.[16]

It goes without saying that joining the Baghdad Pact had brought Iran and Pakistan closer both politically and militarily, a development which India could not but look upon with considerable disquiet and trepidation. As Nehru told the Lok Sabha, "... Baghdad Pact and SEATO ... have a direct effect upon us and naturally we have viewed them with suspicion and dislike".[17]

It must be stated that it was only after Pakistan joined the Baghdad Pact that it could count on the support of Iran and other Pact members on the Kashmir issue both at the UN and outside.[18] This support, in essence, was based on the UN resolutions which sought to settle the issue on the basis of a plebiscite in Kashmir. Both Iran and Turkey supported Pakistan on Kashmir because they considered Pakistan's membership of the Pact as essential for its viability and success. Besides, Iran solicited Pakistan's support in its dispute with Iraq over the Shatt-al-Arab waterway, as did Turkey in its dispute with Greece over Cyprus.

Nevertheless, Iran joined the Baghdad Pact for motives other than those that prompted Pakistan to join, and India-baiting was certainly not one of them. Nehru himself acknowledged this when he told the Lok Sabha in 1956 that "Other members of the Baghdad Pact have no hostility to India and they have not entered into the pact because of their anti-Indian feelings."[19] Consequently, the partial cooling of Indo-Iranian relations following Iran's adherence to the Baghdad Pact was anything but irretrievable.

Moreover, the Baghdad Pact, in its actual terms, failed to acquire the sort of teeth and efficacy that NATO managed to muster. The Pakistani attempt to convince Pact members that the threat to them could come from "any source other than the Communist nations" came to nought because of the opposition from the USA and Britain.[20]

Nor could Baghdad Pact countries agree on aggression against one being aggression against all on the lines of NATO. It also failed to raise a force of its own with a unified command. As a result, Pakistani-Iranian cooperation was confined to joint military exercises and political support to each other. And the Pact more or less collapsed when the coup in Iraq in 1958 installed a radical Ba'athist regime in Baghdad.

Though the Baghdad Pact was renamed CENTO, and its headquarters transferred to Tehran following Iraq's formal withdrawal from the Pact in 1959, the fast-changing regional and international scenario in the 1960s gradually made the Pact redundant.

The changing scenario of the 1960s

The onset of the 1960s saw the evolution of the new weapons systems based on ICBMs and IRBMs which brought about a definite reorientation in American security perceptions towards the region. "By 1964–65 the US strategic interests in the area had shifted from the land-mass of the northern tier to the Indian Ocean."[21] Consequently, US policy towards Iran tended to be a little more relaxed in this period than it was earlier.

These changing American perceptions had serious implications for Iran, which left her with no choice but to adjust her foreign policy posture to the emerging new realities[22] like: American reluctance to aid Iran in case of threat from sources other than the USSR; the gradual decline in economic and military aid from the USA; and the resentment over being discriminated against by the USA in comparison to Pakistan and Turkey in the supply of sophisticated arms.

Iran responded to the changing strategic scenario by trying to open up to the USSR, a process facilitated by the Iranian refusal to permit the USA to install anti-Soviet missile bases in Iran.[23] This was the beginning of the independent foreign policy that the Shah was to pursue with increasing vigour towards the end of the 1960s.

The Sino-Indian war over their disputed border in October 1962 saw Iran come out openly and strongly on the Indian side. The Prime Minister of Iran stated on 3 November 1962 that Iran "supports India at a time when she has fallen victim to an aggression".[24] In fact, it was reported that the Shah had advised Ayub Khan to send his troops in support of India following the Indian military debacle in the North East Frontier Agency (NEFA). Obviously, the Shah was not aware of the close links that

Pakistan had already established with China.[25]

However, the Indo-Pakistani war of 1965 over Kashmir saw Iran extend moral as well as material support to Pakistan. Reacting to the crossing of an international boundary into Pakistan by Indian forces near Lahore on 6 September, the Iranian Foreign Ministry declared that it was "an act of aggression committed by Indian forces against Pakistan".[26] At the UN, the Iranian representative argued in favour of a settlement "in accordance with the Security Council Resolutions" and "on the basis of the principle of self-determination, to which both parties had previously subscribed".[27] On the material side, the Iranian help to Pakistan was rather modest. However, it was reported that Iran did supply jet fuel, gasoline and some small arms and ammunition to Pakistan.[28] Iran also sent medical supplies and medical teams to Pakistan.

On the face of it, these Iranian actions could be construed as unfriendly to India. However, the Shah, in private, strongly urged Ayub Khan to bring the hostilities to an end. Nor did Iran interrupt its oil supplies to India. Generally speaking, Iran acted as a restraining influence on Pakistan in the latter's disputes with India.[29]

More importantly, from the Indian point of view, the Indo-Pakistani conflict gave a further fillip to Iran's quest for an independent foreign policy. The Shah was badly shaken by the American attitude to the Indo-Pakistani war. Despite its commitment to Pakistan under CENTO, SEATO and the bilateral defence agreement of 1959, the USA remained neutral in relation to the conflict. Moreover, the US arms embargo to both India and Pakistan worked out to India's advantage, because India was almost self-sufficient in small arms and ammunition production, whereas Pakistan was excessively dependent on the West for the same.

The Shah realized the limitations and the conditional nature of external assistance in safeguarding Iran's security and integrity and its basic unreliability. As a result, he "launched an accelerated weapons acquisition programme in 1966-67 which was independent of the CENTO".[30]

Besides, the Shah also tried to reduce his exclusive dependence on the West by striking an arms deal with the USSR in 1967 which included APCs and anti-aircraft guns. The deal was also meant to be a "lever" to persuade the West to sell sophisticated arms to Iran which worked "rather well".[31]

The changing Pakistan-Iran equation

The 1960s also saw a gradual change in the Pakistan-Iran equation, particularly after the Sino-Indian border war of 1962. First, the Shah did not approve of Pakistan getting too close to China. There were people in Tehran who believed that Chinese Communist influence had percolated into the officer cadre of the Pakistani army. The Shah reportedly once remarked that his friendship with Pakistan was intended to prevent it from getting itself more deeply involved with China.[32] Nor did Iran approve of China's ultimatum to India during the Indo–Pakistani war of 1965, and made it clear that China should not interfere in Indo-Pakistani issues.[33]

Iran also supported the Indian position at the preparatory meeting of the proposed Afro-Asian summit at Jakarta in April 1964: that the Nonaligned Summit should precede the Afro-Asian Conference and that the USSR should be invited to the latter. The Indian move was primarily meant to sabotage China's attempt to project itself as the leader of the Afro-Asian world following the Chinese military defeat of India in 1962.[34]

Secondly, the 1960s also exposed the limits of Iran's economic relationship with Pakistan, RCD notwithstanding. Economically, India was a bigger market. With a population of 25 million, Iran's development strategy had to be export oriented.[35] In 1958, India's trade with Iran was five times more than Pakistan-Iran trade. One reason for this was that India's oil needs and its oil imports from Iran were greater than those of Pakistan. But it must be noted that Iran's non-oil trade with India was also far more significant than that of Pakistan.[36]

Thirdly, following the Sino–Indian war in 1962 and the subsequent supply of American arms to India, Pakistan sought to upgrade its relations with China and normalize its ties with the USSR. "In 1963, bilateralism became the key concept in the new foreign policy of Pakistan, a policy in which links between two countries would exist quite apart from either's relations with any third country."[37] In other words, Pakistan's ties with China or the USSR had little to do with US-Pakistani relations. By the same token, "This policy could also mean that Iran's relationship with Pakistan had little bearing on Iranian relations with India."[38]

Fourthly, the 1960s saw the development of certain discordant notes in the Pakistani-Iranian relations. Pakistan, in this period, tried to patch up with the Arab countries, especially Egypt. Hence, Pakistan could not share Iran's hostility to Nasser and consequently Pakistan's support to Iran on regional issues slackened considerably. When a shooting incident took place on the Iran-Iraq border in December 1965, the Iranians were disappointed by the lack of response from Pakistan.[39] Iran was also upset when Pakistan voted in favour of Bahrain's membership of UNESCO in September 1966, implicitly acknowledging Bahrain's sovereign status which was not acceptable to Iran then.

Lastly and more importantly, the late 1960s saw the emergence of a strategic environment which enabled the Shah to redefine and enlarge Iran's role as a regional power. As a consequence, it became imperative for the Shah to look beyond the Persian Gulf and Pakistan for understanding and support in favour of Iran's new regional policy.

There were a number of factors which facilitated Iran's quest for a more assertive role in the Persian Gulf region. The limited superpower détente and Iran's own improved relations with the USSR enabled the Shah to shift his focus from his northern borders and concentrate on the Persian Gulf. The British decision in 1968 to withdraw its forces from the east of Suez by the end of 1971 dovetailed with Iran's new regional ambitions. The debacle that the Arabs suffered in 1967 at Israeli hands more or less destroyed the mythical appeal of Nasserism and left Nasser a weak and shattered man. This freed the Shah from his preoccupation with the radical Arabism which he had considered a serious threat to his regime, and allowed him to devote his attention to Iran's expanding role as a regional power.

Most importantly, by the mid-60s, the Shah had consolidated his domestic position considerably. The success of his domestic reforms known as the "White Revolution", the suppression of domestic opposition, Iran's rapid economic growth and the acquisition of sophisticated arms increased the Shah's self-confidence and enabled him to give real substance to what he termed "independent foreign policy".[40]

The changing tenor of Indo-Arab relations

The 1960s also saw the emergence of stresses and strains in Indo-Arab relations which necessitated the Indians taking a critical look at India's policy towards the Middle East. The disappointing response of the Arab countries to the Sino-Indian war of 1962 and the Indo-Pakistani war of 1965 brought about a widespread disillusionment in India, and questions were raised about India's unqualified support of the Arabs. The humiliation that Egypt and Nasser suffered after the 1967 military debacle awakened Indian policy-makers to the risk of too much dependence on Nasser. The 1967 war also led to the emergence of Iran and Saudi Arabia as important actors in the region, which India could not possibly ignore for long.

All these factors converged towards the end of the 1960s to create an environment which made it necessary for both Iran and India to set aside their old inhibitions and misgivings about each other, and embark on a new course of mutual understanding and accommodation on the basis of a growing consensus on a number of regional issues which were of concern and importance to both countries.

It was in such a positive and relaxed atmosphere that the Shah's visit to India took place in January 1969. During the visit, the Shah asserted that Iran wanted to pursue an independent policy and stand on her own feet.[41] He did not mince words regarding Iran's role as a regional power. "We owe a responsibility not only to ourselves but also to the region," he said.[42] He also made it clear that CENTO had long ceased to have any military significance and would remain so despite the Soviet action in Czechoslovakia.[43] He pointed out that India was a big country in the region and "a historical responsibility towards smaller nations of the region rests on her".[44]

The joint communiqué[45] which was issued at the end of the Shah's visit reflected, for the first time, something approaching political understanding between the Shah and an Indian Prime Minister. Thus, when India and Iran looked poised for a breakthrough in their relations, the developing crisis in East Pakistan vitiated the atmosphere between the two so badly that Indo-Iranian relations went into cold storage for the next three years.

The Bangladesh crisis, 1971

Iran's attitude to the Bangladesh crisis was fairly consistent with its earlier policy towards the Indian subcontinent. Unfortunately, the crisis revived many of the old fears and suspicions that Iran and India traditionally entertained about each other over the decades, and proved to be a stumbling block when Indo-Iranian relations seemed to be poised for a breakthrough.

From the very beginning of the crisis, following the brutal Pakistani crackdown in East Pakistan and the exodus of millions of refugees to India, Iran maintained that it was an internal matter for Pakistan and strongly advised all powers against interfering in Pakistan's internal affairs.[46] Iran was quite perturbed over the situation in the subcontinent, primarily because it could have had an unsettling and spill-over effect on Iran.[47]

When war broke out between India and Pakistan on 3 December 1971, Iran's response at the UN was much more muted than it had been in 1965 when Iran condemned India as the aggressor. The Iranian representative at the UN[48] criticized India's interference in "affairs which were essentially within the national jurisdiction of Pakistan".

However, what really caused resentment and disquiet in India was Iran's assistance to Pakistan in the military sphere. The Shah himself made no bones about the increased flow of military supplies to Pakistan through Iran. From the Indian point of view, the Indo-Soviet treaty was expected to serve as a deterrent as much against the overt dangers of Chinese intervention as against the covert threat of a large-scale flow of arms to Pakistan from Iran by the overland routes.[49] In fact, it was reported that the USSR deployed troops along the Iranian border to deter the Shah from aiding Pakistan in its war with India over Bangladesh in late 1971.[50] Pakistan itself acknowledged the help rendered by Iran during the Indo-Pakistani war of 1971 in a communiqué issued by Islamabad on 8 May 1973.[51]

Given Iran's close relations with the USA and President Nixon's strong opposition to the emergence of Bangladesh, one cannot help wondering to what extent the Iranian assistance to Pakistan was at the American behest. Nevertheless, while what Iran did to help Pakistan was significant, what it chose not to do was equally significant, if not more.

Despite the threats that Iran would stop supplying oil to India in case of war with Pakistan,[52] Iran never carried out the threat. During the war, the palace sent word to the small Indian business community in Tehran to assure it that it had nothing to fear from Tehran's support for Pakistan.[53] Iran also resisted the Pakistani pressure to activate CENTO and provide a legal basis for its clandestine assistance, nor did it indulge in any direct provocation.[54]

Iran also extended total political and diplomatic support to Pakistan after the Indo-Pakistani war of 1971 in order to bolster Pakistan's weak bargaining position vis-à-vis India, which held all the aces after its military victory. Iran openly committed itself to the integrity of what remained of Pakistan and firmly supported the Pakistani position on the issues of 93,000 Pakistani POWs detained in India, withdrawal of forces from occupied territories, the proposed trial of 195 POWs by Dacca on charges of genocide and the recognition of the state of Bangladesh.

The dismemberment of Pakistan in 1971 was seen by the Shah as part of a larger plan to encircle Iran. "At the core of the Shah's interpretation of the security threat ... was the perception of a pincer movement from Iraq to the west, India and Afghanistan to the east and the Soviet Union behind both."[55] The Indo-Soviet Treaty of August 1971, the Iraq-Soviet Treaty of April 1972, the July 1973 coup in Afghanistan and the secessionist movements in Baluchistan, Pakhtoonistan and Sind gave credence to such fears. The increasing Soviet naval presence in the Arabian Sea and the Indian Ocean made Iran wonder if it had to counter the Russian threat not only from the north but from the south as well.

Under the circumstances, the Shah considered that Iran had a vital stake in the survival of the remainder of Pakistan for two reasons. First,

Iran wanted both a stable eastern flank and Pakistani support in its rivalry with the Arab states. Secondly, any separatist movement in Baluchistan would give ideas to the large number of Baluchis living in Iran. The Shah told the *New York Times*: "We must see to it that Pakistan doesn't fall into pieces. This would produce a terrible mess." He went on to add ominously "But if Pakistan fell apart, the least we could do in our interest would be some kind of protective reaction in Baluchistan."[56] The interviewer interpreted this to mean that Iran would annex Baluchistan before anyone else did.

Thus, "During 1971-73, an attempt was also made to project the possibility of an Indo-Iranian confrontation as a source of threat perception for India as well Iran."[57] Hence, the relations between India and Iran in this period "could be distinctly characterized as chilly".[58] Nevertheless, the post-Bangladesh phase saw the transformation of the regional environment both in South Asia as well as in the Middle East in such a decisive way that it made it imperative for India and Iran to come to terms with each other in the light of new regional realities in both regions.

The post-1971 period saw a decisive change in the power balance in the subcontinent in India's favour and it emerged as the pre-eminent power in South Asia. As a result, "New Delhi could afford to see and formulate its policy towards other countries, relatively independently of the Pakistan factor."[59] Consequently, India, more sure of herself than before, was in a position to take the close Pakistani-Iranian relations in her stride and strive for better relations with Iran for their own worth. More importantly, as a result of the events of 1971, "India's security environment has greatly improved and the self-confidence of its foreign policy making elite has vastly increased".[60] Hence, India, for the first time since independence, was able to "rid itself of its rather unhealthy preoccupation with Pakistan and the Indo-Pakistani power balance"[61] and concentrate on playing a wider role in the international arena in consonance with her size, location and resources.

It was also at about this time that certain changes were occurring in the Middle Eastern region which prompted Iran to don formally the role of a regional power. The British withdrawal from the Persian Gulf was completed on 30 November 1971 as part of its east-of-Suez policy. On the very same day, Iran occupied the three disputed Gulf islands of the Greater and Lesser Tumbs and Abu Musa, near the Straits of Hormuz. This act symbolically and dramatically heralded the emergence of Iran as a regional power, a role which had the tacit support of the USA.[62] However,

The core relationships in their foreign policy arenas that New Delhi and Tehran had now evolved, linked one with the Soviet Union, and the other with the United States. This was bound to create complications in their bilateral relationship, since such a relationship could not be divorced from the total environment in which Indian and Iranian foreign policies were shaped.[63]

Nevertheless, the Arab-Israeli war of 1973 introduced certain new elements into the regional politics of the Middle East as well as South Asia, which further pushed India and Iran to explore the possibility of a rapprochement between the two countries in a much more persistent and determined way.

The Arab-Israeli War, 1973

The Arab-Israeli war of 1973, and the subsequent oil embargo which led to a steep increase in the price of oil, resulted in Iran's income from oil jumping from $4.9 billion in 1973 to $25 billion in 1975.[64] The Shah sought to use his increased oil revenues to: build up a powerful military machine in line with his regional ambitions; use Iran's phenomenal oil wealth "in influencing policies and winning friends"; and ensure the rapid industrialization of Iran before its oil reserves ran out.[65] The Shah realized that a friendly India could play a complementary role in the realization of Iran's major political and economic goals in the changed regional context in South Asia as well as in the Middle East.

The good showing of the Arab forces in the 1973 war and the remarkable unity displayed by them during the war must have caused some concern to the Shah, whose earlier security strategy for Iran was based on Arab disunity.[66] Hence, opening up to India was an opportune move on the part of the Shah.

The Shah was also upset by Pakistan's attempt to forge close links with Arab states like Saudi Arabia, the UAE and Libya, which could have security implications for Iran in the long run. He was particularly annoyed with Bhutto for hob-nobbing with Gaddafi, and refused to attend the Islamic Summit in Lahore in February 1974 because of his presence.

The Shah was also aware of India's growing relationship with Iraq in the early 1970s, his principal rival in the Gulf, and of the need to balance it by cultivating a fruitful relationship with India in the economic as well as political spheres. He further realized that only by providing alternative sources of economic assistance and political support could he wean India away from the USSR.

The tripartite agreement among India, Bangladesh and Pakistan in April

1974 further paved the way for Indo–Iranian détente. India was able to convince the Shah that she too had a stake in Pakistan's integrity and survival.[67] As a result, the Shah gave up his earlier policy of shoring up Pakistan militarily *vis-à-vis* India and instead accepted "an Indo-Pakistani rapprochement as the surest way of stabilising Iran's eastern flank".[68]

India too, for her part, had her reasons for making up with Iran. India did entertain serious misgivings about Pakistani-Iranian military links over the years.[69] Indian policy-makers realised rather belatedly that the only way India could dilute the close Pakistani-Iranian relations was by cultivating Iran on a bilateral basis relatively independent of the Pakistan factor, and by creating a stake for Iran in the improvement and consolidation of Indo-Iranian relations. More importantly, and in a much broader context, Indian policy-makers were also able to shed some of their past inhibitions and diffidence in their attitude to the Middle East as a whole, which had earlier hampered India's manoeuvrability in the region. As one Indian scholar put it,

> The long period of Indo-Arab relations has created a certain thinking in a section of the Indian elite that an improvement in India's relations with any other regional power, whether that power be Israel or even Iran, can be only at the cost of India's close ties with the Arab world … . India has already lost some initiative in West Asia by taking a negative stand *vis-à-vis* the Palestine question. That should serve as a warning and should prevent India from taking a similar negative stand on the Arab-Iranian relations also.[70]

It was against this backdrop that Mrs. Gandhi made her momentous trip to Tehran in April 1974. This was "the first time that there has taken place what can be called a meeting of minds between the Shah and the Indian Prime Minister".[71] The joint communiqué[72] issued at the end of Mrs. Gandhi's visit reflected the understanding and accommodation that the two sides were able to achieve on most major political issues and saw a substantial increase in the economic cooperation between the two countries.

Both sides "emphasised the vital importance of safeguarding stability and peace in the Persian Gulf and settlement of issues by the littoral states themselves … without outside interference". Both sides called "for complete withdrawal of Israeli forces from occupied Arab territories, and a just solution of the Palestinian problem". The Iranian side explained the situation "on their western borders" and the Indian side expressed "full understanding of the dimensions of the problem". As one newspaper put it: "The economic gains to India and Iran from the latest accords are obvious, but it is the political assumptions behind them which are far more significant."[73]

The Shah of Iran paid a return visit to India in October 1974; its real significance lay in the fact that India was the last lap of his tour of a number of littoral states of the Indian Ocean, namely Singapore, Australia, New Zealand and Indonesia. His tour was primarily meant to gain support for his proposal to establish an "Indian Ocean Economic Community".[74]

Even before he arrived in India, the Shah made certain statements which reflected the growing understanding between the two countries. In an interview, he envisaged the possibility of collaboration of the Indian and Iranian navies in keeping the Indian Ocean free of big power rivalries.[75] In Canberra, he accepted India's stand on its Peaceful Nuclear Explosion (PNE) at Pokhran in May 1974 on two counts. "Firstly, I must accept the word of a friend and secondly, a policy of peaceful uses of nuclear technology was in the Indian interest."[76]

The political understanding and economic cooperation that India and Iran achieved in 1974 was sustained and consolidated till the Shah of Iran visited India again in February 1978, when the Janata Party was in power.[77] The fact that the change of government made little difference to the deepening of Indo-Iranian relations was amply demonstrated by the joint communiqué[78] issued at the end of the Shah's visit. In an interview, the Shah described India's positive response to his proposal to forge an Indian Ocean Community as the "most encouraging development".[79]

As one newspaper pointed out, "Although the impression left by the Shah of Iran's four-day visit to India is mainly of a marked advance in economic cooperation between the two countries, the political under-standing behind this important development should not be ignored". It went on to add "That the Shah spent four days in India and only four hours in Pakistan also indicates a certain change in his assessment of priorities".[80]

The Shah's change of priorities was due to a number of factors. Throughout the 1950s and 60s, Pakistan was the stronger of the two countries. However, "An increase in Iranian power and prestige coincided with Pakistan's decline, which resulted from the 1971 defeat at Indian hands and the dismemberment of the country into Pakistan and Bangladesh."[81] Hence, there was a definite change in the Pakistani-Iranian equation in favour of the latter in the 1970s, a fact acknowledged by Bhutto himself when he bemoaned: "Before, when I talked with him [the Shah], I used to talk to him as a brother. Now, I have an audience."[82]

The growing disparity between Iran and Pakistan in the 1970s also caused disquiet and suspicion in some quarters in Pakistan regarding the Shah's intentions in relation to Pakistan. His comments about "protective reaction" in Baluchistan caused a flutter in Pakistan and fears were expressed that Iran was trying to interfere in the internal affairs of Pakistan.[83] Growing Indo-Iranian amity only added to the Pakistani fears. The Chief of the Pakistani Air Force, Nur Khan, quite bluntly remarked that "Iran and India could come closer to each other. India could claim half of Pakistan up to the river Indus, leaving the rest of Pakistan to Iran. A weak Pakistan could also go under the hegemony of Iran as well."[84] The Shah was also piqued by Pakistan's firm and open opposition to his grandiose scheme in relation to the Indian Ocean Community. Pakistan quite deliberately chose the eve of the Shah's visit to India to let its opposition to the idea be more widely known to the world.[85]

The Marxist coup in Afghanistan in April 1978 which brought the pro-Moscow government of Taraki to power revived the Shah's old fears of encirclement, as the new government lost no time in supporting the Baluchistan and Pakhtoonistan demands. The Shah was also reported to have said that Iran would intervene if Pakistan showed signs of cracking up.[86] Further, the Shah seemed to be in broad agreement with the Indian view that, despite the Marxist leanings of its leadership, the Afghans' fierce sense of freedom would make them rather unlikely stooges. He was not too impressed by the Pakistani attempt to project the happenings in Afghanistan as posing an immediate Soviet threat to the region which could be countered only by making Pakistan strong through arms aid.[87]

Khomeini's Iran and India

The fall of the Shah in February 1979 and the appearance of Ayatollah Khomeini on the scene "did affect the momentum" of Indo-Iranian relations.[88] The Indian Foreign Minister, Mr. Vajpayee, told the Lok Sabha that the developments in Iran were "positive" and described Khomeini as the "father figure of the Iranian revolution". "We are waiting for the day when we can welcome Iran in the nonaligned movement," he added.[89] In fact, "India viewed the revolution in Iran as a reflection of Iran's quest for identity and national self-assertion and a desire to charter an independent course without outside Big Power influence".[90]

However, Khomeini's regime soon became totally preoccupied with domestic problems like the American hostages issue and a breakdown in law and order following the purges of the Shah's suspected supporters. The Iraqi invasion of Iran in September 1980 left little time for the new regime to follow a vigorous foreign policy.

India reacted very cautiously to the abortive US attempt to rescue its diplomats, held hostage by Iran. The official statement said that whatever the extenuating circumstances, India could not condone such "military adventurism". While India was opposed to the violation of diplomatic immunities and sympathized with the fate of the American hostages, it felt that the US action "tended to complicate the situation further and to heighten the tension".[91]

Later, at a press conference, Mrs. Gandhi said that the US attempt to free its hostages in Iran could not be described as an attempt to invade that country nor could it be called an interference in the affairs of another country.[92] While India heartily welcomed Iran to the nonaligned fold,[93] it also had its misgivings about the new regime in relation to its Islamic fervour and its attempts to export it.

Generally speaking, while the two countries have a great potential to coordinate their foreign policies in relation to major regional issues and exploit the complementarity of their economies to the full, there could develop, in future, certain areas of friction and competition in their relations.[94] How effectively and how smoothly potentially contentious areas (such as the roles of their respective navies in the Indian Ocean, their attitudes to the Gulf states and their security concerns) are going to be tackled by the policy-makers on both sides will determine the nature of future Indo-Iranian interaction.

To sum up, Indo-Iranian relations failed to take off despite the absence of bilateral disputes between the two countries and even a certain harmony in their politico-economic interests. Nehru's preference for nonalignment and particularly for Nasser put off the Shah of Iran considerably. India's exaggerated fears about Pakistan's ability to forge Islamic solidarity in the region against India led its policy-makers to give more importance to the Pakistani factor in the Indo-Iranian equation than they should have done. As a consequence, India failed to pursue with the required vigour and persistence the policy of bilaterally cultivating Iran on the basis of mutuality of interests, despite the existence of a number of factors which would have facilitated such a course. That, perhaps, would also have been the surest way of weaning Iran away from Pakistan, a major objective of India's policy towards the Middle East.

India and Saudi Arabia

One of the more amazing and puzzling aspects of India's policy towards the Middle East has been India's relationship, or lack of it, with Saudi

Arabia over the decades. As one newspaper put it, "Relations between India and Saudi Arabia in the 26 years since the first Indian Prime Minister visited that country were hardly the kind that should have governed two major Asian nations".[95]

The Indian political leadership from the beginning entertained misgivings about Saudi Arabia, considering it a feudal and theocratic state, and was wary of cultivating it even on bilateral terms. Saudi Arabia was one of the major countries in the region in terms of its geographical and demographic size and economic potential, even in the 1950s. The fact that it was the guardian of the Holy shrines of Islam gave it an added aura in the Islamic world.

Given India's fears about the possible creation of an Islamic bloc under the inspiration and the goading of Pakistan, it was all the more important and necessary for India to have established an amicable and balanced relationship with Saudi Arabia; this would have pulled the diplomatic rug from under the feet of Pakistan and would have been a more effective impediment to the rise of any Islamic grouping than any other strategy that India could possibly have adopted. The reason why it was not done would remain one of many mysteries that characterized India's rather unimaginative and timid policy towards the Middle East.

The initial harmony
It was not as if there were irreconcilable differences in the political outlook of the two countries, in spite of the admittedly conservative and traditional nature of the political leadership in Saudi Arabia. There were many incipient tendencies in the policies of the Saudis, even in the early years, which could have been encouraged and promoted by India to its political advantage. The fact that India failed to do so was essentially because of India's own rather rigid and self-righteous posture in the 1950s and 60s which prevented India from broadening and diversifying its political base in the region, as we shall see in the following pages.

It should be noted here that Saudi Arabia was one of the participants in the first Afro-Asian Conference ever held in Bandung in Indonesia in April 1955, and was a signatory to the final communiqué issued after the conference.

When Pakistan joined the Baghdad Pact, the Saudi Embassy in Pakistan took the unusual step of issuing a press handout containing the text of the Radio Mecca broadcast which exhorted Pakistan to withdraw from the Pact and "return to the right path". It referred to Pakistan's action as "a stab in the heart of the Arab and Muslim states".[96] The strong Saudi reaction to the Baghdad Pact could not but have pleased India who herself vehemently opposed it for her own reasons.

The first top-level political contact between the two countries took place in December 1955 when King Saud came to New Delhi for a brief visit. The joint statement issued at the end of the visit reflected a certain harmony in the political outlook of King Saud and Prime Minister Nehru. Both the leaders emphasized that "a peaceful and non-militant approach to the issues which divide the world is an urgent necessity".[97]

More importantly, King Saud, speaking as the guardian of the Muslim Holy Places, publicly thanked Nehru and his government for their policy towards the Muslim minority in India. He declared: "I desire to say to my Muslim brethren all over the world with satisfaction that the fate of Indian Muslims is in safe hands."[98] This was a very significant statement, from the Indian point of view, in view of the persistent Pakistani criticism of the alleged discriminatory policy of the Indian government towards its Muslim minority.

Nehru paid a return visit to Riyadh in September 1956. In the joint statement that was issued on the occasion, both sides, referring to the Suez Crisis, emphasized that

in spite of the difficulties and tensions that have arisen over this question, it is possible to reach a settlement negotiated between the parties concerned without any derogation from Egyptian sovereignty and authority and maintaining the interests of other countries in the unrestricted use of the Canal as an open waterway.[99]

When Nehru arrived in Riyadh, he was greeted with the slogan "marhaba rasool al salam", which led to a lot of controversy and resentment in Pakistan. The Saudi Embassy in Pakistan issued a statement explaining that the phrase meant "Welcome Messenger of Peace" and not "Welcome Prophet of Peace" as interpreted by the Pakistanis.

But Pakistani feelings were not mollified. The Pakistani newspaper *Dawn*, in view of King Saud's and President Nasser's less than friendly attitude towards Pakistan, advised Pakistanis to "calmly and dispassionately take all these bitter truths into consideration and restrain to some extent their vain expectations from the so-called Muslim world".[100]

In view of all this, it is nothing less than astonishing that for the next 26 years, no Indian Prime Minister visited Saudi Arabia till Mrs. Gandhi made a trip to Riyadh in 1982. Neither the religious orthodoxy of Saudi Arabia nor Pakistan's perceived closeness to the Saudis over the years would fully explain the lack of verve in Indo–Saudi relations. Nor was there any serious bilateral issue that vitiated the political atmosphere between the two countries.

The Nasser factor

Looking back, the most plausible reason for this Indo–Saudi estrangement seemed to be political and ideological rather than religious. There is no gainsaying the fact that it was Nehru's endorsement of Nasser as the sole and undisputed leader of resurgent Arab nationalism that complicated India's relations with Saudi Arabia. Saudi Arabia, probably more than any other country in the region, felt threatened by the radical Arabism espoused by Nasser.

Nor did the threat from Egypt remain purely ideological. In the 1960s, Egypt became actively involved in the civil war in Yemen. Egyptian troops trained the Republican forces and also actively fought the Royalist tribesmen in North Yemen in support of the Republic of South Yemen, which was governed by a radical leftist regime. At the height of the civil war in North Yemen, as many as 70,000 Egyptian troops were involved in it.[101] This was often cited as one of the reasons for the defeat of the Arabs in the 1967 war. Moreover, during the Yemen civil war, Egyptian planes often bombed Saudi border towns like Najran with impunity.[102] Saudi Arabia, being a large country with a long coastline but with a relatively small population and a poorly trained and equipped army, felt quite vulnerable and almost defenceless. Under the circumstances, it is hardly surprising that the Saudis were annoyed with India for backing Nasser so consistently and so unequivocally, even when he had acted rashly and overambitiously on occasions.

Ironically, it was King Feisal's fears of Arab radicalism as represented by Nasser that prompted him to resort to pan-Islamism as a counter-strategy, a development India sought to resist and undermine by supporting Nasser.

Islam and Pakistan as a counter

In fact, "King Faisal's dedication to pan-Islamism had its genesis in the struggle for Arab unity and the Saudi-Egyptian rivalry for the leadership of the Arab world."[103] The Saudi attempts to organize various Islamic conferences in the 1960s should be seen in this context. Moreover, the opponents of Nasser were branded by Cairo as "reactionaries" and "agents of imperialism", and a number of unsuccessful plots were organized by the UAR to overthrow various monarchies and conservative regimes in the region.[104]

Against this background, it is anything but surprising that the Saudis looked upon Nehru's endorsement of Nasser's leadership of the Arab world with suspicion and resentment. Thus, it was India's own ideological reservations and misgivings about the so-called conservative Arab states and a lack of balance and sensitivity in its policy towards them that was primarily responsible for India's lack-lustre relationship with Saudi Arabia in the 1960s and even 70s. Hence, no consistent and determined effort was made to cultivate Saudi Arabia, which left India with no leverage worth the name with one of the most important states in the region and, at least since the mid-70s, one of the richest in the world.

It was in this context that the Saudis sought the assistance of Pakistan in bolstering their defence capability in the late 1960s. In August 1967, the Saudi Minister of Defence and Civil Aviation visited Pakistan, which resulted in a defence agreement between the two countries. As a result, Pakistani advisors were sent to Saudi Arabia to "help expand and modernize the Saudi Armed Force". The number of Saudi personnel in Pakistani military training institutions also went up "considerably".[105]

India was quite quick to react to this development. The Indian Foreign Minister, Chagla, reportedly conveyed India's concern to the Saudi Ambassador regarding the "disquieting" newspaper reports about the transfer of Saudi arms to Pakistan.[106] Indian policy seemed to have attributed the close Saudi-Pakistani ties more to Islamic solidarity than to mutuality of interests between the two countries. The only way India could have diluted Saudi-Pakistani amity was to try and cultivate the Saudis on the basis of mutuality of interests. However, Nehru's close identification with Nasser and his political distaste for the so-called conservative Arab states got in the way of such a possibility.

If India supported Egypt because it promoted India's security by its progressive policies in the region, the Saudis felt threatened by such policies and sought to enhance their own security by opposing Nasser. In the process, the Saudis cultivated Pakistan in order to counter the forces Nasser represented, and the lack of amity between Egypt and Pakistan facilitated this process. This also acted as a snub to India, intended or not, for throwing in its lot with Nasser. Nevertheless, the Saudi support to Pakistan *vis-à-vis* India, even against this background, was cautious and calculated and was never so substantial as to alienate India totally.

Kashmir
Regarding Kashmir, the Saudi position in general was that the issue should

be solved in accordance with the right of self-determination of the people of Kashmir. It was at variance with the Indian position in so far as it refused to subscribe to the subsequent Indian position that the issue of plebiscite had become irrelevant in the changed circumstances of Kashmiris having elected their own government in free and fair elections.

At this juncture, it must be noted that even Nasser, the reason for Saudi distancing from India, never supported India's position on Kashmir. His consistent stand on the issue was that India and Pakistan should settle their dispute through negotiations without outside interference. In view of India's own unwavering support of Nasser in relation to most Arab issues, which was, no doubt, irksome to the Saudis, it would be difficult to describe the Saudi position on Kashmir as anti-Indian.

Likewise, during the 1965 Indo-Pakistani war over Kashmir, the Saudi representative at the UN recalled that the Security Council had "passed resolutions reaffirming the right of the Kashmiri people to self-determination"[107] which, of course, was a fact. In view of India's almost non-existent relationship with Saudi Arabia in those years, it would be rather rash to characterize the Saudi attitude to India as unfriendly and hostile.

Again, during the 1971 Bangladesh crisis, the Saudi position was similar to that of many other countries which generally held the view that what was going on in East Pakistan was Pakistan's internal affair and that no other country had any right to interfere in the same. The Saudi representatives argued along the same lines at the UN throughout the crisis. Mr. Baroody, speaking at the Security Council on 16 December 1971, admitted that the conflict between East and West Pakistan was "most probably for economic as well as for political reasons ...". He also asserted that "only India and Pakistan can solve the problem, without interference from outside".[108]

By and large, the Saudi attitude to the Bangladesh issue at the UN was fairly balanced and conciliatory. Its position was akin to that of many other states, Muslim and non-Muslim, and it would be rather petulant to suggest that it adopted a hostile or unfriendly attitude towards India.

However, the Bangladesh episode did have a serious bearing on Indo-Saudi relations in the sense that it proved to be an obstacle to improving the political understanding between the two countries at a time when the situation in both regions was conducive to such an exercise. Even in the 1960s, despite Saudi Arabia's image as a politically conservative and socially backward country, there were a number of elements in Saudi's regional policy which would have been consonant with India's own thinking and preferences in the region.

The most striking thing about the Saudis' regional policy was its moderation. The financial support to Egypt and Jordan in their confrontation with Israel, the occasional appeal for Islamic solidarity and the calls for an Islamic summit and a Jihad against Israel after the burning of the Al Aqsa mosque might give an impression of religious orthodoxy and hawkishness.[109] However, King Feisal always favoured a peaceful solution to the Arab-Israeli dispute, and merely insisted on the implementation of the November 1967 Security Council resolution which only called for the withdrawal of Israeli forces to the pre-war positions.[110]

King Feisal was also more fearful of Communism than Zionism and was opposed to the increasing influence of the USSR in the region under the pretext of helping the Arabs against Israel. For him, the existence of the Jewish state would be more palatable than allowing the USSR to entrench itself in the region, provided Israel could be persuaded to withdraw from occupied Arab territories.[111]

King Feisal was also firmly opposed to any foreign power filling in the so-called vacuum created by the withdrawal of the British from the Persian Gulf in 1970. He was in favour of security being maintained by the states of the region themselves.[112]

The Saudis also realized the limitations of their relationship with Pakistan at about this time. Despite the mutual desire to increase "Islamic cooperation in industrial fields", there was very little progress in that direction because Pakistan's petroleum needs were quite low.[113] This, in turn, made the Saudis realize the importance and usefulness of cultivating India for both economic and political reasons.

After the burning of the Al Aqsa mosque in 1969, King Feisal called for an Islamic summit to discuss the issue. However, King Hassan of Morocco thwarted Feisal's efforts to have the summit at Mecca and managed to stage it in his own capital, Rabat. Feisal was not satisfied with his status as the "Joint Convenor" of the summit. Since the agenda at Rabat was confined to the burning of the Al Aqsa mosque and any new proposal on Palestine would not find favour with Iran and Turkey, Feisal came up with the idea of inviting India as a means of asserting his own authority and pre-eminence at the summit. India's anxiety to attend the summit in order to thwart any Pakistani attempts to rake up its bilateral issues with India suited Feisal admirably. However, Pakistan's President Yahya Khan's threat to boycott the summit in the event of India's participation carried the day and King Feisal's ploy backfired badly.[114]

Most importantly, the Arab debacle in the 1967 war reduced the prestige of Egypt in Arab eyes and more or less destroyed the mythical appeal of Nasser. Nasser himself realized the need to adopt a new strategy in the changed circumstances. His crusade against monarchies and feudal elements only drove the conservative Arab states more and more into Western arms. Nasser now decided to build a broad Arab national front by involving even these states which were earlier detested on ideological grounds. Egypt's withdrawal of troops from North Yemen removed the most important irritant between Egypt and Saudi Arabia and symbolized Nasser's new strategy of broad Arab unity. Nasser's death in 1970 marked the end of an era in Arab politics and the beginning of the end of India's "special relationship" with Egypt, which certainly removed a cloud hanging over Indo–Saudi relations.

When everything pointed towards a new beginning in Indo–Saudi relations by 1970, the crisis in East Pakistan in 1971 and the subsequent dismemberment of Pakistan put an end to any such hopes. After the fall of Dacca, Saudi Arabia extended total and continuous support to Pakistan in its dealings with India. It also withheld its recognition to Bangladesh until it got the green light from Pakistan in order to strengthen Pakistan's bargaining position *vis-à-vis* India and Bangladesh.[115] The Saudi Minister of State for Foreign Affairs, Mr. Omar Saqqaf, asserted that India's refusal to hand over the POWs to Pakistan, and its decision to refer some of them to Dacca for trial as war criminals, constituted "a flagrant violation of the Geneva Convention". India's attitude could result in "further deterioration in the situation", he warned.[116]

The post-1973 period

However, in May 1973, India struck an oil deal with Saudi Arabia, "hitherto considered most unlikely of Arab countries".[117] The Saudis agreed to supply 3.3 million tons of crude in three years from June 1973, at the rate of 1.1 million tons per year.

But during the oil embargo that followed the Yom Kippur war of 1973, Saudi Arabia exempted nine countries including Pakistan, Malaysia and Britain from the cut in oil supplies. India's name, however, did not figure on the list.[118] Nevertheless, a few days later, the Saudi Chargé d'Affaires, Suleman-el-Nasser assured New Delhi that there would be no cut in oil supplies to India.[119]

The Simla agreement of April 1974 signed by India, Pakistan and Bangladesh, the subsequent return of all POWs to Pakistan and the normalization of relations in the subcontinent paved the way for an Indian initiative to open a meaningful dialogue with the Saudis. The visit of D.P.

Dhar, the then Minister of Planning, to Jeddah in May 1974 was designed to facilitate such a process.

Consequently, the Saudi Oil Minister, Mr. Ahmed Zaki Yamani, paid a three-day visit to India in February 1975. Significantly enough, Mr. Yamani was the first Saudi dignitary to visit India since King Feisal's visit to India in 1955. At a press conference,[120] he expressed confidence that a "new era" in Indo-Saudi relations could begin. He revealed that an agreement to set up an India-Saudi Arabia joint commission for economic, scientific and technical cooperation would be signed soon. Mr. Yamani ruled out Saudi oil at concessionary rates for India and also any Saudi credit for supply of crude to India. He said Saudi policy was to have one price for everybody and to sell oil only on a cash basis. However, Saudi Arabia was prepared to extend long-term credit to India on soft terms for starting joint industrial ventures in either country. Regarding Pakistan, he said: "we are concerned with the integrity of Pakistani territory. We are a Muslim country and in Saudi Arabia we are concerned with our brothers all over the world, in Pakistan and in India."[121]

The real significance of Mr. Yamani's visit lay in the fact that "... the Saudi Oil Minister's visit revives a long neglected relationship".[122] The new political climate in the subcontinent following the Simla agreement facilitated a new understanding between Saudi Arabia and India and led to a remarkable leap in Indo-Saudi economic relations in the next few years.

However, in the political sphere, the understanding between the two countries did not reach the sort of level it should have, given the extent of commonality of interests and perceptions on the major issues confronting both South Asia and the Middle Eastern regions. India's suspicions about Saudi's close military links with Pakistan and Saudi Arabia's misgivings about the Indo-Soviet connection persisted despite the limited political understanding that the two countries managed to reach in the post-Simla phase.

Indo-Saudi ties in the 1980s

The fall of the Shah of Iran in early 1979, the Soviet invasion of Afghanistan in December 1979 and the outbreak of a full-scale war between Iran and Iraq in September 1980 only served to reinforce and exacerbate the old suspicions and fears between India and Saudi Arabia. Saudi Arabia's domestic vulnerability, its fears over Khomeini's brand of Islamic fundamentalism engulfing the whole region and the substantial Soviet military presence in Afghanistan only helped to increase Saudi's acute sense of insecurity, which drove her headlong into a closer and more extensive military relationship with the USA and Pakistan, a development India looked upon with considerable fear and suspicion. On the other hand, the Saudis did not take kindly to India's rather muted and low-key response to the Soviet invasion of Afghanistan.[123]

Ironically, it was these very fears and suspicions that India and Saudi Arabia entertained about each other that made them renew their efforts for better understanding and appreciation of each other's point of view and strive for some common political ground.

The Saudis were worried because the Soviet occupation of Afghanistan and the massive American build-up in the Indian Ocean had had an unsettling effect in the volatile Gulf region, which was vital for Saudi's own security. They were also nervous about relying almost exclusively on American military protection which would be of little use if an Iran-type situation were to arise in Saudi Arabia. A section in the Saudi hierarchy was also of the opinion that there was no harm in cultivating a country like India which could exert some influence on the USSR, instead of courting only Pakistan in an extremely uncertain situation.[124]

India, for its part, wanted to impress upon Saudi Arabia the need to use Saudi influence to find local solutions to regional problems without outside interference. India also hoped that improved relations with Saudi Arabia would act as some constraint on the Saudi inclination partly to underwrite Pakistan's arms purchases.[125]

It was against this background that the Saudi Foreign Minister, Prince Faisal, visited New Delhi in April 1981. Both the countries agreed that the Afghan issue should be resolved, leading to the elimination of "foreign military presence".[126] The Prince told the Indian Foreign Minister, Mr. Narasimha Rao, that Saudi Arabia was opposed to the establishment of foreign military bases in the Gulf and in Saudi Arabia. Both agreed that the Afghan problem should be solved through political negotiations.[127]

Later, at a press conference,[128] Prince Faisal said that his country did not view her bilateral relations with any country in the light of her ties with a third country. Admitting Saudi Arabia's close relationship with Pakistan in a number of fields, including the military, he asserted that his country would like to have close ties with India on their "own value". He denied reports that two Pakistani divisions were stationed in Saudi Arabia.

It was quite obvious that India failed to get the sort of assurance that it was looking for from Prince Faisal in relation to Pakistani-Saudi relations, particularly in the military sphere. Nor did Saudi Arabia share India's concern in relation to Pakistan's nuclear ambitions. Answering a specific question regarding Pakistan's nuclear bomb, he said Pakistan had denied such reports and "We have no reasons not to accept Pakistan's denial."

Though India and Saudi Arabia agreed on a number of issues in general terms, the divergence in their approach became apparent when it came to specifics. For instance, both agreed on a political solution regarding Afghanistan. But Saudi Arabia would do nothing either to stop or curtail Western assistance to the Afghan resistance as a first step in that direction. Nor was Saudi Arabia particularly receptive to Indian misgivings regarding Saudi financing of Pakistan's military acquisitions from the USA in response to Soviet intervention in Afghanistan. The Indian argument that it would create tensions in the region cut no ice with the Saudis.

A year later, Mrs. Gandhi visited Riyadh in April 1982, the first by an Indian Prime Minister since Nehru's visit to the kingdom way back in 1956. As one Saudi paper put it, the end of a long "communication gap" was a welcome gain in itself.[129] The joint communiqué issued at the end of Mrs. Gandhi's visit to Saudi Arabia reflected a general agreement on a variety of issues, but little else. On the contentious issue of Afghanistan, "the two sides called for a just and comprehensive settlement of the question on the basis of the withdrawal of all foreign troops, strict observance of the principles of non-intervention and non-interference, and full respect for the independence, sovereignty, territorial integrity, non-aligned status of Afghanistan and its membership of the Organization of Islamic Conference".[130] However, the fact that precious little was said about how it could be achieved was indicative of the fact that the two sides merely agreed to disagree on the specifics.

Though it was agreed that "the security and stability of the Gulf area is the responsibility of the Gulf states only, without any foreign interference or intervention", the unstated fact was that few Gulf states were in a position to defend themselves without outside help. More remarkably, both sides "recognised that the stability and security of the Gulf region and that of the Indian subcontinent were closely interlinked". This was an implicit acknowledgement that, just as India had a legitimate concern in the Gulf, Saudi Arabia too had a stake in the Indian subcontinent. But in real terms, neither had the capability to pursue their interests much beyond their borders, legitimate or otherwise. Later, at a press conference in Riyadh,[131] Mrs. Gandhi defended India's approach to the Afghan issue. She said:

Our view is that there should be no foreign intervention, military or subversive or of any other kind. We have expressed our views very clearly, both privately and publicly, to the Soviet leaders about the presence of their troops in Afghanistan, but have refrained from condemning them. If one condemned them, one would have to condemn all those who were interfering in other parts of the world in various ways.

It needs to be emphasized that the visit failed to elevate to a new level the limited political understanding that had already been established between the two countries. This was so because the general agreement on issues could not be extended to specific measures required to deal with any given issue. However, both countries displayed a certain maturity and sagacity in their approach to each other which enabled them to set aside minor irritants in their relations and emphasize and concentrate on those areas where their broad interests coincided in the long run. As one newspaper commented, Mrs. Gandhi's visit appeared "to have given the two countries an opportunity to break out of the restrictive relationship they had got locked into as a result of those old attitudes and suspicions".[132] The visit, also, did not result in any substantial economic agreements, which was a shade disappointing. Nevertheless, "It was perhaps appropriate in the context of the larger purpose behind Mrs. Gandhi's visit that bilateral economic cooperation should have been accorded somewhat secondary importance."[133]

To sum up, India failed to take advantage of certain early trends in Saudi policies which were complementary to those of India in relation to the Middle East, and thereby lost an early opportunity to develop a positive relationship with the Saudi kingdom. India's own reservations about Saudi religious orthodoxy and political conservatism made it throw most of its support behind Nasser, which only further alienated Saudi Arabia.

India also failed to realize that Saudi Arabia's intimate links with Pakistan in the 1970s and 80s were based on concrete national interests of both the countries and had little to do with religious affinity between them. India's undue emphasis on the religious factor made it treat Saudi Arabia almost as a lost cause for a considerable period of time; this betrayed a lack of deep and intelligent understanding of the politics of the Arab world on the part of Indian policy-makers, and placed artificial limitations on the growth of Indo-Saudi relations for decades.

It goes without saying that India's fixation with Pakistan and exaggerated fears about the emergence of an Islamic bloc cramped her diplomatic style in the Middle East. Besides, Nehru's strong preference for nonalignment and Nasser needlessly alienated the so-called conservative states in the region with whom India had no bilateral disputes whatsoever. Consequently, India's policy towards the region became ideologically rigid and politically diffident and resulted in avoidable distortions.

It is time India took a fresh look at its policy towards the Middle East in view of the momentous changes that occurred in the South Asian and the Middle Eastern regions in the post-1971 period, and adjusted its policies accordingly. India's claims to a regional role will gain credibility and substance only if India sheds some of her self-imposed inhibitions, and begins to play a much more confident and positive role in a region which has been of utmost importance to her in the past and will continue to be so in future.

3. India's Security and Strategic Interests in the Middle East

The fact that the Indian subcontinent has always had a vital link with the Middle East in security and strategic terms is borne out by both geography and history. This chapter seeks to evaluate the threat perceptions of the Indian policy-makers in relation to the Middle East after independence, the assumptions which underlay such perceptions and the strategies and policies they adopted to counter the same. This will be done in two parts, the first dealing with India's security concerns and responses in the region till the Bangladesh war in 1971, and the second thereafter.

The eastern Arab land-mass constitutes a link between three continents, namely Asia, Africa and Europe. This region has variously been described as "the gateway of Asia and Africa" and the "backdoor of Europe" by geostrategists. Consequently, this region has been a hotbed of international rivalry throughout recorded history. When the Suez Canal which linked the Red Sea with the Mediterranean was opened in 1869, "the Arab world became the nerve-center of international communications, both over land and sea".[1]

The British policy of preserving the Ottoman empire in the 19th century was primarily meant to safeguard its lines of communications to India from her European rivals. In fact, throughout the 19th and early 20th centuries, the region became a bone of contention among all major powers who had their covetous eyes on India.

Whether it was the British anxiety over the security of the imperial communication lines, Napoleon's expedition to Egypt, Czarist Russia's drive towards the Persian Gulf or the German *Drang nach Osten*, the ultimate object had invariably been India.[2]

Valentine Chirol, an Englishman, underscored the importance of the

Middle East in India's defence calculations when he defined the region as consisting of "those regions of Asia which extend to the borders of India, and which are consequently bound up with the problems of Indian political as well as military defences".[3]

India's security concerns and policies in the Middle East till 1971

It goes without saying that one of the fundamental concerns that governed India's policy towards the region was security. While the Middle East would have been an important region for India's security concerns under any circumstances, the partition of India and the creation of an exclusively Islamic state, Pakistan, in the subcontinent and the bad blood that accompanied it made the Indian political leadership particularly sensitive to a region which was not only predominantly Muslim but also had geographical contiguity and close cultural ties with Pakistan.

While Pakistan has always been and will always be a very important factor in India's security calculations in relation to the Middle East, it must be mentioned that India's security concerns in the region were by no means confined to it.

In fact, it will be argued that India's exaggerated attention to the Pakistan factor over the years rather cramped its approach to the security issues in the region which impinged on India's own safety and security.[4] As a result, India's security policy towards the region became rather self-conscious and overcautious, which, in turn, made it rather weak, un-imaginative and largely ineffectual.

Fears of an Islamic bloc

There were two major security concerns for India in the Middle East in the 1950s and 60s which were primarily Pakistan-related. The first was the possible emergence of a Pakistan-inspired Islamic bloc to the detriment and discomfiture of India's security.[5] Predictably, Pakistan did make an assiduous effort to forge an Islamic alliance among the Muslim states of the Middle East in the late 1940s and early 50s. However, Pakistani efforts came to nothing for a variety of reasons.[6] It was Pakistan's disappointment and disillusionment with pan-Islamism as a means of achieving its political objectives that primarily prompted it to opt for the Western alliance in the mid-50s.

The Baghdad Pact, 1955

The second major security concern that haunted the Indian policy-makers during this period was Pakistan's joining of the Baghdad Pact in 1955.

The Baghdad Pact, undoubtedly, constituted the most important challenge to India's security concerns in the Middle East in the 50s. The Pact was the outcome of (a) an Anglo-American drive to forge a military alliance among the Muslim countries of the Middle East to contain the Soviet influence in the region and to protect their oil interests and (b) the Pakistani drive to bring about an Islamic grouping in the region as a counterpoise to India.

> While the former threatened to bring the Cold War between the East and the West to India's doorstep, the latter sought to isolate India from a region so vital to its security and economic well-being. By 1955, the two forces converged, and the Baghdad Pact was born.[7]

Apart from his general opposition to military pacts, Nehru reacted very sharply to the Baghdad Pact, primarily because he saw a potential but real threat to India's security from it. Nehru told the Lok Sabha[8] in March 1956: "... SEATO and the Baghdad Pact, apart from being basically in the wrong direction, affect us intimately. In a sense, they tend to encircle us." He was certain that Pakistan joined the pact because of its antipathy to India. He was, however, "quite sure that the other members of the Baghdad Pact have no hostility to India ...". He was also "prepared to accept completely the assurance given to me by the leaders of the United States of America. I am quite sure they did not mean ill to us."

Nevertheless, Nehru was quite disturbed by the possible security implications that these pacts could have for India. His first fear was that "Countries get interlocked with one another, each pulls in a different direction and in a crisis they are pulled away in a direction they never thought of going". Secondly, he was also worried about Pakistan's ability to cause mischief by taking advantage of its membership of these pacts. "The danger is that any odd member of one of these pacts can set in motion something which would gradually pull in not only the members of the pact, but some other interrelated pact of which they are common members."

"That is why, both for larger reasons and for the narrow reason of self-interest, we have taken exception to SEATO and the Baghdad Pact," he explained.

But in purely military terms, the Baghdad Pact failed to pose the sort of threat to India that Nehru imagined or feared it could, for a variety of reasons. First, the Pakistani attempt to broaden the definition of aggression by insisting that the threat to the Pact members could emanate from "any source other than the Communist nations" did not cut much ice with the USA and Britain.[9]

Secondly, the Baghdad Pact failed to develop along the lines of NATO for various reasons which have already been referred to. When the coup in Baghdad in 1958 installed a radical Ba'athist regime in power, the Pact more or less ceased to exist. Nehru, explaining the larger reason behind the collapse of the Baghdad Pact, said:

> The major fact in West Asia is the growth of Arab nationalism in a very powerful, resurgent way ... . This fact, which was patent, was neither liked nor appreciated by many powers, and an attempt was made to split the Arab countries, in fact, Arab nationalism .... While the Governments carried on a cold war against each other, the people in almost every Arab country were powerfully affected by this tide of Arab nationalism. Thus, in the countries associated with the Baghdad Pact, there was a hiatus between the Governments looking in another direction and those rather ranged against this spirit of Arab nationalism. How big this hiatus was can be seen from the *coup d'état* in Baghdad ... . [10]

Non-Pakistani security concerns

Though Indian policy-makers exaggerated the role of Pakistan and Islam in relation to India's security concerns in the Middle East, there were other important security considerations for India in the region which had little to do with either Pakistan or Islam. "Closely connected with India's security interests was the question of the international communication lines which lie across the Arab world."[11]

Even in ancient and medieval times, trade between the Indian subcontinent and Europe was carried through the Arab lands both on land and by sea. It was the unreliability of these routes because of the unsettled conditions in the region during the 15th century that prompted Vasco da Gama to discover a sea route to India. However, when the Suez Canal was thrown open to international traffic in 1869, the Middle Eastern route regained its significance.

The strategic significance of the Suez Canal for India's physical and economic well-being need not be overemphasized. "The Suez Canal indeed cut down the maritime distance between Bombay and London by 4500 miles and in course of time became the veritable life-line of world trade. About three-fourths of India's import and export trade passed through the Suez Canal."[12] Besides, the Middle Eastern region became an important staging post for India's air services to the West.

The vital importance of this waterway for India's economic plans in general and trade and commerce in particular was driven home in a telling fashion during both the Suez Crisis in 1956 and the six-day Arab-Israeli war in 1967 when the Suez Canal was closed temporarily.

During the Suez crisis in 1956, Nehru was quite open about India's vital interest in the normal operation of the Suez Canal. He told the Lok Sabha in August 1956: "India is not a disinterested party. She is a principal user of this waterway, and her economic life and development is not unaffected by the dispute, not to speak of worse developments, in regard to it."[13]

The then Minister of External Affairs, Mr. Krishna Menon, explained to the Lok Sabha in much more detail in March 1957 India's vital stake in the Suez Canal. He emphasized that "the Suez Canal to a certain extent is much more our life-line than it may be the life-line of the Western countries. In the autumn of last year, 70 per cent of our exports and 69 per cent of our imports passed through the Canal. This country carried somewhere about 650,000 tonnage through the Canal in that twelve-month period. Therefore, the re-opening which is vital to the progress of our Five-Year Plans, to our economic life and to our food prices, is a matter of great concern to us."[14]

The story was not much different when the Suez Canal was closed to all traffic following the Arab-Israeli war in June 1967. The then Commerce Minister, Mr. Dinesh Singh, told the Rajya Sabha in July 1967 that judging from the previous year's exports, the freight charges for 1967 might go up by roughly Rs1.8 crores per month as a result of surcharge levied by shipping companies following the closure of the Suez Canal. He further said that if the closure of the Canal was for a short period, no assistance might be necessary to the exporting industries. If the closure was for a long period, assistance might be necessary and the government would consider it then.[15] The closure of the canal also seriously affected India's food supplies from the USA. The week-long detour round the Cape of Good Hope by ships carrying foodgrains to India disrupted their even supply at a critical juncture.[16]

Despite the fact that the normal operation of the Suez Canal was in the vital interest of India, she failed to contribute much towards that end primarily for two reasons. Firstly, India refused to take any initiative to solve the Arab-Israeli dispute in view of the Arab refusal to recognize and negotiate with Israel, which made repeated conflicts and repeated closure of the Suez Canal almost inevitable. Secondly, obtaining the cooperation and goodwill of Israel was also necessary for the normal functioning of the Suez Canal. India's decision more or less to ignore Israel diplomatically made any such possibility rather remote. Nor should it be forgotten that Israel could have been used as an alternative transit point for Indian economic dealings with the West in case of extreme emergencies. In fact, Israel offered transit facilities to India through Israel for India's trade with the West which, it was said, could have saved India Rs 38 crores a year in freight charges.[17]

But India remained more or less a passive spectator, except during the earlier Suez Crisis in 1956, in relation to an issue which was of great and direct importance to her.

The Indo-Pakistani wars and the Middle East

The first real test of India's fears and suspicions in relation to Pakistan's ability to garner support in the Middle East, particularly in the military sphere, in any possible conflict with India came in September 1965 when war broke out between the two countries over Kashmir. Kashmir is the only Muslim majority state in India and Pakistan did try her best to give the conflict a communal colour in order to gain the support and sympathy of the Muslim Middle East.

While the diplomatic support to Pakistan from the Middle Eastern countries during the war was substantial, the same could not be said of military assistance. Among the Middle Eastern countries which provided material assistance to Pakistan during the conflict, Iran, perhaps, was the most important. Even Iran's material assistance to Pakistan was rather modest and limited.[18] On the other hand, as we have already noted, the Shah, in private, urged Ayub Khan to bring the hostilities to an end. More significantly, the Shah made no attempt to interrupt Iran's oil supplies to India. Thus, the military assistance that the Middle Eastern states provided to Pakistan during the Indo–Pakistani conflict of 1965 was almost negligible.

The Indo-Pakistani war in December 1971 over the Bangladesh issue again saw the Middle Eastern states throw their diplomatic weight behind Pakistan, but little else. Iran once again turned out to be the Middle Eastern country most concerned about the developments in the subcontinent and provided considerable material assistance to Pakistan. The extent of Iranian help to Pakistan during the Indo-Pakistani conflict became clear when Pakistan issued a communiqué on 8 May 1973 on the subject. During the conflict, the entire fleet of Pakistan's civilian aircraft took shelter in Iran and they were allowed to fly essential supplies to Pakistan from there.

Iran also sent fire-fighting equipment and experts when oil tanks in Karachi were set ablaze. Iran allowed the passage of strategic materials to Pakistan through its territory. It also supplied certain items in critical shortage, including ammunition and aircraft, and helped in maritime reconnaissance.[19]

Nevertheless, Iran, despite the threats to interrupt oil supplies to India,[20] chose not to carry out the threat. More significantly, Iran resisted Pakistani pressures to activate CENTO to provide a legal basis for Iran's assistance to Pakistan. Iran also did not indulge in any direct provocation nor interfere with the overflights of Indian aircraft.[21]

In addition to Iran, a few Middle Eastern countries provided token assistance to Pakistan during the conflict. However, suffice it to say that the material assistance that Pakistan received from the Muslim countries of the Middle East during the Bangladesh war was neither substantial nor decisive and proved to be of little more than symbolic value.

The Indo-Pakistani wars of 1965 and 1971 exposed certain fallacies that seemed to have governed India's security policy towards the Middle East till then. Firstly, India's misgivings that Pakistan would be able to gain the support of the Middle Eastern countries on the basis of Islamic solidarity in any conflict with India proved to be rather unwarranted and grossly exaggerated. The professions of Islamic solidarity on these occasions proved to be little more than rhetoric. Secondly, it also became very clear during these two wars that each Middle Eastern country weighed these conflicts in terms of its national interests and acted on that basis alone. For instance, Iran was the country which provided most assistance to Pakistan during these wars, primarily because it considered Pakistan's continued existence as a viable state to be in Iran's national interest, not as an expression of Islamic solidarity. Thirdly and lastly, there seemed to be very few countries in the Middle East which were capable of and willing to provide the sort of help to Pakistan which could have tilted the scales in its favour in its conflict with India.

India's security concerns in the Middle East since 1971

The Indo-Pakistani war in December 1971 over the Bangladesh issue and the subsequent dismemberment of Pakistan constitutes a watershed in India's strategic perspective in relation to the Middle Eastern region.

At one level, India's strategic gains were substantial. India won a moral victory over the USA, a political victory over China and a decisive military victory over Pakistan. With the separation of Bangladesh, Pakistan was reduced to one-tenth of India's size. With the loss of its Eastern wing,

Pakistan lost its strategic relevance for SEATO. From being the largest Muslim country in the world in terms of population, the population of what remained of Pakistan roughly equalled that of Muslims in India. Moreover, as a direct consequence of the Bangladesh crisis, "even Pakistan's tomorrow seemed uncertain as regional and separatist elements in the new Pakistan became bolder".[22]

On the other hand, India's victory over Pakistan was as much military as it was psychological. For the first time since independence, India was able to rid herself of her unhealthy preoccupation with Pakistan and look beyond the subcontinent for a role commensurate with her size and resources. In fact, "India emerged as a dominant power in South Asia, with no formidable competition in sight".[23]

Moreover, India's "north eastern flank no longer raised a serious security problem for its military strategists".[24] India, in the event of another war with Pakistan, need no longer worry about fighting a two-front war. Besides, with the collapse of East Pakistan, the secessionist movements in north-east India also received a serious jolt. It was also widely believed that it was the Bangladesh crisis that prompted Sheik Abdullah to come to some sort of political understanding with Mrs. Gandhi over Kashmir in 1975.[25]

However, at another level, Pakistan's strategic position was considerably strengthened. The separation of East Pakistan "has resulted in a more concentrated Pakistani defence system ...".[26] Moreover, Pakistan's policy towards the Middle East, since the secession of East Pakistan, became "more concerted and coordinated within the framework of a calculated strategy than it has ever been before".[27] Bhutto toured eight Middle Eastern countries in January 1972 and followed it up with another 14 in May and June of the same year. Countries like Iran, Saudi Arabia, Turkey and the UAE did not recognize Bangladesh till Pakistan recognized it in February 1974 as a token of support to Pakistan.

Given the close cultural and ethnic links between Pakistan and the Middle East, it is but natural that Pakistan tends to look towards the latter for support and sustenance. Moreover, "Pakistan enjoys a special position *vis-à-vis* this region by virtue of the fact that she occupies the sensitive transitional zone which links the Middle East with South Asia."[28]

At this critical juncture, the relationship between South Asia and the Middle East underwent a fundamental transformation as a result of the Arab-Israeli war of 1973, the oil embargo that followed it and the subsequent steep rise in oil prices.

By 1968, ... it was hard to assess which region – the Middle East or South Asia – was more influential in relation to the other or within the wider international system. By the end of 1973, however, there was no longer ambiguity. In five years, the historic balance of relationships had decisively turned, and seems likely to hold for the foreseeable future. The Middle Eastern-Iranian area had become the source of substantial influences playing on South Asia; there were virtually no influences at work in the opposite direction. The 1973 Arab-Israeli war and the Arab oil embargo had changed the situation in a flash.[29]

The two superpowers also became much more closely involved in the region, the USA primarily because of oil and the USSR because of the proximity of the region, a development which could not but have caused disquiet in India.

The accumulation of petro-dollars in the Middle East in the mid-70s following the oil bonanza resulted in the large-scale purchase of sophisticated and advanced arms by a number of states in the region, particularly Iran, Iraq, Saudi Arabia, Libya and some of the Gulf sheikhdoms. The Western countries, hard hit by the steep rise in oil prices, were only too keen to supply these countries with extremely advanced weapons systems for economic gain regardless of the political consequences of such arms transfers to a region as volatile as the Middle East.

The security implications [for India] of these trends are more long-term and arise from Pakistan's military ties and involvements in the region, from the strategic interests and arms transfer policies of the great powers in both the Middle East and South Asia, and from various economic dependencies and linkages that have developed between the states of the subcontinent and the oil-exporting Islamic states.[30]

Hence, Pakistan started looming large in India's defence calculations in relation to the Middle East much more in the 1970s than at any time before. The most important reason for this was the fact that quite a few Middle Eastern countries envisaged their own national interests coinciding with those of Pakistan much more during this period than ever before. "Whatever the causes, Pakistan and the Middle East have converged economically, politically and psychologically. While the relationship is still evolving, it rests on a mutuality of interests that promises to be enduring."[31]

As a result, most of the security issues that confronted India in the 1970s and 80s in relation to the Middle East were in some way or another Pakistan-related, as we shall see in the course of this account.

Pakistan and Iran

The dismemberment of Pakistan in 1971 despite its membership of CENTO and SEATO had an unsettling effect on the Shah of Iran. He considered the survival of the remainder of Pakistan as vital to Iran's own security and stability primarily for two reasons. Firstly, Iran wanted a stable eastern flank and Pakistani support in its rivalry with the Arab states. Secondly, any secessionist tendencies in Baluchistan could cause disquiet in his own considerable Baluchi minority. In a broader context, he suspected and feared the development of a Moscow-New Delhi-Kabul-Baghdad axis to the detriment of Iran's security and regional ambitions.

Consequently, the Shah made a public and unequivocal commitment to the territorial integrity of Pakistan in 1972 by stating that any attack on Pakistan would be considered an attack on Iran itself.[32] Besides, the accumulation of petro-dollars following the hike in oil prices in the aftermath of the 1973 Arab-Israeli war sent Iran on a massive arms purchasing spree. In four years between 1974 and 1978, Iran spent $36 billion on arms purchases compared to about $12 billion spent by India during the same period.[33] There was a genuine concern in India that Iran might transfer some of these advanced weapons systems to Pakistan in any future conflict between India and Pakistan.[34]

However, the rapidly changing geopolitical situation in the world in general and in the regions of South Asia and the Middle East in particular in the 1970s saw the convergence of the economic and strategic interests of India and Iran which were emerging as preponderant powers in their respective regions.

Indeed certain common features are discernible in Iran's and India's security scenarios and their behaviour as dominant regional powers. Both attach the greatest possible value to the attainment of security autonomy, and both have to live with dependence on external security for a fairly long time. Both are therefore anxious to maintain and assert as much independence and initiative as possible within the framework of their relationship with their respective patron power.[35]

So both India and Iran saw the need to coordinate their foreign policies, both to exploit the complementarity of their economic and security interests at the regional level, and also to avoid any possible friction, if not conflict, between them. India convinced the Shah of Iran that it had a vested interest in the integrity of what remained of Pakistan, and the Shah, in turn, categorically stated that unless India attacked Pakistan, it would not face, either directly or indirectly, the arms Iran was acquiring.[36] Isolating the Pakistan factor from Indo-Iranian relations enabled Mrs. Gandhi and the Shah to strive "to unite Iran and India in strategic cooperation for shared objectives in Southwest and South Asia".[37]

The Indo-Iranian strategic understanding was so sound that India chose to look rather indulgently at the acquisition of fancy weapons systems by the Shah and the latter readily accepted India's rationale behind its Peaceful Nuclear Explosion (PNE) in May 1974. The Shah's grandiose scheme for the eventual emergence of an Indian Ocean Economic Community[38] and his desire for close collaboration between the navies of India and Iran[39] to keep the Indian Ocean free from outside encroachment underscored this understanding.

However, the strategic understanding and cooperation between India and Iran more or less collapsed with the fall of the Shah and the triumph of the Islamic revolution under the spiritual leadership of Ayatollah Khomeini.[40] At one level, the Islamic revolution in Iran improved India's security environment. Khomeini's Iran embraced nonalignment which asserted Iran's independent foreign policy posture. This resulted in the drying up of supplies of sophisticated weapons from the West, particularly the USA. It also meant the end of military collaboration between Iran and Pakistan under CENTO as Iran withdrew from CENTO following the Islamic revolution. Khomeini's Iran was also less ambitious in its foreign policy endeavours compared to that of the Shah, both by design and by necessity. The Islamic regime was completely preoccupied with its domestic problems and as such had little time for external affairs, nor did it have the same sort of ambition that the Shah had for Iran. Khomeini's Iran seemed to be more inclined towards spreading its ideological rather than politico-military influence in the region. Moreover, the tacit strategic support that Iran had from the USA for its regional role under the Shah was neither sought by Iran nor extended by the USA in the changed circumstances.

However, the security scenario for India was exacerbated at another level, following the Islamic revolution in Iran. The panicky reaction of the USA to the fall of the Shah (one of the "twin pillars" of US policy in the Middle East) and to the subsequent Soviet invasion of Afghanistan increased and upgraded US military presence in the Indian Ocean, which was of great concern to India. Iran's alleged proclivities for exporting Islamic revolution also caused considerable disquiet in India, given its large but poorly integrated Muslim minority. Lastly, the Iran-Iraq war also put India in a diplomatic tightspot. It had developed considerable political understanding and a fruitful economic relationship with both, which now seemed to be in some danger. Besides, "The lessons of the Iran-Iraq war suggested the possibility of Arab financing of Pakistani wars against India in the future."[41] Furthermore, the eclipse of the Shah made it imperative for the USA to shift its focus to its other "pillar" in the region, Saudi Arabia, which again had serious security implications for India.

Pakistan and Saudi Arabia

With the fall of the Shah, Iran ceased to be the American-sponsored policeman of the Middle Eastern region. The Soviet invasion of Afghanistan in December 1979 which closely followed on the heels of the Islamic revolution in Iran and the ousting of the Shah sent panic waves through the entire Middle East, and revived the historical fears of the West in relation to the Soviet drive towards the warm waters of the Indian Ocean. As a result, Saudi Arabia became a willing strategic partner and the linchpin of US policy in the region in the 1980s in order to contain the possible Soviet penetration of the region. The Reagan administration's adoption of Pakistan as a frontline state so that it could act as a conduit to American arms to Afghan resistance brought the USA, Saudi Arabia and Pakistan together in a strategic drive to insulate the region from further Soviet encroachments.

The Saudi-Pakistani cooperation in the military sphere did not begin with the Soviet invasion of Afghanistan but did elevate it to a new level. The initial contacts for cooperation were made in 1963, though the first formal agreement was reached in 1967 wherein Pakistan agreed to send a small number of its officers to oversee the development of the Saudi Army and the Air Force.[42] The Saudis were reportedly impressed by the performance of the Pakistani armed forces against a much bigger Indian army during the Indo-Pakistani war of 1965. Generally speaking, the Saudi-Pakistani military links remained rather modest and sporadic in the 1970s. However, the beginning of the 1980s saw the close convergence of Saudi-Pakistani security interests for a variety of reasons.

The Islamic revolution in Iran posed an ideological threat to the Saudi royal family as well as to Zia ul Haq's military regime in Pakistan. Khomeini's branding of these two regimes as un-Islamic and his repeated calls for their overthrow caused great concern in both the countries. Saudi Arabia was particularly concerned about the disquiet in the Shia population in its eastern province following Khomeini's triumph in Iran. Pakistan too had a substantial Shia population and was concerned about the impact of Khomeini's exhortations on them. More importantly, even when the Shah was at the helm in Iran, Pakistan took with a pinch of salt Iranian assurances in relation to Pakistan's security and integrity. With the advent of Khomeini, Pakistan lost even that psychological assurance. In fact, "Pakistani-Iran relations since 1978 have had a deep-seated but unarticulated element of fear and unpredictability."[43]

The Marxist coup in Afghanistan in 1978 which was closely followed by the Soviet invasion of Afghanistan in December 1979 caused considerable panic in both Riyadh and Islamabad. The Saudis construed the Soviet action as a possible first step in the USSR's inexorable march towards the Indian Ocean. The Soviet presence in Afghanistan, Saudis feared, could embolden the Marxist regime in South Yemen, whose hand was suspected in the attack of Muslim zealots on the Grand Mosque in Mecca, to indulge in further mischief.

The outbreak of hostilities between Iran and Iraq in September 1980 further underlined Saudi Arabia's military vulnerability despite her large arsenal. As far as Pakistan was concerned, the Soviet presence on its western borders was genuinely unsettling in view of the Indo-Soviet treaty and its own less than satisfactory relations with Afghanistan.

Saudi Arabia and Pakistan also shared a deep sense of disappointment and disenchantment with the US policy towards its allies and friends. The Saudis were particularly appalled by the American inability or unwillingness to stand by the Shah of Iran and help him in any tangible way in his hour of crisis, despite the fact that he was the pillar of US policy in the region. Pakistan's disappointment with the American response to its wars with India in 1965 and 1971 hardly needs any repetition. "Faced with mounting threats, Riyadh and Islamabad thus embarked on a two-track policy of calling on Washington's help while augmenting their security through joint moves."[44]

In addition to these general reasons, there were a number of other smaller but not insignificant factors that facilitated the expansion and consolidation of military links between Saudi Arabia and Pakistan. For the Saudis, given their own acute manpower shortage and the political liabilities that accompanied the direct American presence in the kingdom, the Pakistanis seemed to provide the best way out. Pakistan possessed a significant military establishment and a well-trained and professional army which was tested in the battlefield. While Pakistanis were Muslims, they were not Arabs. As such, it was easier to isolate them from local politics.

For the Pakistanis, the Saudi connection, in addition to the financial rewards that it provided, gave them access to highly advanced US weaponry which they could not lay their hands on either because of monetary considerations or for political reasons. Pakistanis also could have hoped that the increasing Pakistani-Saudi military cooperation "might expand the US Saudi commitment, either implicitly or explicitly, to the defense of Pakistan".[45]

However, information regarding the specifics of Saudi-Pakistani military collaboration is understandably sparse and nebulous. It was widely believed that Saudi Arabia, at least partly, financed Pakistan's purchase of 40 F-16 fighters from the USA.[46] It was also reported that in 1980 the two countries reached an agreement whereby Pakistan agreed to station two of its army divisions in Saudi Arabia which would be equipped and maintained by the latter. Besides, two compensating divisions were to be raised in Pakistan, which again would be financed by Saudi Arabia. Nevertheless, there was little evidence to suggest that the agreement was actually implemented. Pakistan had only two brigades in Saudi Arabia as of 1985.[47] It was also widely rumoured that Pakistan declined to accede to the Saudi request to withdraw Shias from its troops stationed in Saudi Arabia on the grounds that such action would divide her professional army along sectarian lines and was hence unacceptable.

It goes without saying that Pakistani-Saudi military links caused great consternation and concern in New Delhi. The Washington-Riyadh-Islamabad axis not only facilitated Pakistani access to sophisticated American weapons but also greatly reduced its financial burden by the Saudi underwriting of the costs of these weapons to a fairly substantial extent. It left India with no alternative but to match the Pakistani weapon acquisitions, which put the already overstretched Indian economy under great pressure. Besides, India also had to contend with the possibility that Saudi Arabia could transfer part of her newly acquired arms to Pakistan in any future confrontation between India and Pakistan.

The "Islamic Bomb"

Another major source of concern to India in the 1970s in relation to the Middle East was the potential threat posed by what was dubbed the "Islamic bomb" to India's strategic environment in general and national security in particular. The "Islamic bomb" was so called because it was alleged to be the product of Pakistan's technology and Middle Eastern finance in the 1970s. If true, this development could pose serious security concerns to Indian policy-makers and radically transform the strategic equation between South Asia and the Middle East, mostly to India's disadvantage. In analysing this issue, we will confine ourselves to the origins of the "Islamic bomb", how "Islamic" it is and what were the ways and means in which India could counter this potential threat in the context of her own nuclear ambitions and capabilities.

Pakistan's quest for nuclear technology began in 1953 with the establishment of the Pakistan Atomic Energy Committee, which was soon upgraded to an Atomic Energy Commission, primarily in response to India's expanding interest and activities in relation to nuclear technology. However, Pakistan's nuclear programme moved at a snail's pace until it came under the influence of Zulfikar Ali Bhutto.[48] Bhutto himself, from his death cell in 1979, referred to the crucial role that he had played in the development of Pakistan's nuclear programme:

> When I took charge of Pakistan's Atomic Energy Commission, it was no more than a signboard of an office. It was only a name. Assiduously and with great determination, I put my entire vitality behind the task of acquiring nuclear capability for my country ... . Due to my singular efforts, Pakistan acquired the infrastructure and the potential of nuclear capability.[49]

However, Bhutto's nuclear ambitions for Pakistan can be traced back to a much earlier period. Addressing the National Assembly of Pakistan in 1965, Bhutto asserted: "If India builds the bomb, we will eat grass and leaves, even go hungry. But we will get one of our own, we have no alternative."[50] Bhutto's zeal for nuclear capability for Pakistan, apart from rivalry with India and security considerations, seemed to have a technological dimension as well. He argued: "If Pakistan restricts or suspends her nuclear programme, it would not only enable India to blackmail Pakistan with her nuclear advantage, but would impose a crippling limitation on the development of Pakistan's science and technology".[51]

Bhutto took over a dismembered and distraught Pakistan in December 1971 following the crisis in East Pakistan and the subsequent Indian military intervention which gave birth to Bangladesh. It was probably this humiliating defeat that crystallized Bhutto's thinking on the nuclear issue and set him irreversibly on the course to nuclear capability. According to Bhutto's former press secretary, Khaled Hasan, Bhutto convened a meeting of Pakistan's top scientists in Multan in January 1972, one month after he took over as President. He reminded the gathering of Pakistan's humiliating defeat a month earlier at Indian hands and his determination to see Pakistan acquire nuclear capability.[52] Soon after, Bhutto took personal political charge of Pakistan's Atomic Energy Commission. In 1973, talks were initiated with France for setting up a reprocessing plant at Chasma, near Rawalpindi. Thus, Pakistan's quest for nuclear capability started in earnest well before India's nuclear test.

India's nuclear explosion on 18 May 1974 at Pokhran in Rajasthan, not far from the Pakistani border, however, proved to be a mixed blessing for Pakistan. It acted as a spur and a convenient excuse for Pakistan to accelerate its own nuclear programme and justify it to its own people. On the other hand, it made it much more difficult for Pakistan to obtain external assistance in relation to both nuclear technology and materials because Western countries, following India's nuclear test, tightened the laws concerning nuclear proliferation considerably and kept a close watch on nuclear threshold states.

Pakistan, which started negotiating with France in 1973 to buy a plutonium-reprocessing plant despite American pressures not to do so, signed a deal for the same in 1976. However, France backed out of the deal in 1978 under American pressure. While negotiations were going on with France, Pakistan thought it unwise to put all its nuclear eggs in one basket. Hence, as an alternative strategy, a determined bid was made to pursue the uranium-enrichment path to nuclear capability, which culminated in the establishment of the Kahuta plant in which Dr. Abdul Qadeer Khan, popularly known as the father of the "Islamic bomb", is said to have played a vital role.[53]

Bhutto's political reaction to India's nuclear explosion was also uncompromising and defiant. He told a press conference in Lahore on 19 May 1974: "Pakistan would never succumb to nuclear blackmail by India. The people of Pakistan would never accept Indian hegemony or domination in the subcontinent. Neither would it compromise its position on the right of the people of Kashmir to decide their own future."[54]

Pakistan also tried to use India's nuclear test to its advantage in other ways as well. Bhutto warned the USA that unless it lifted its embargo on arms sales to Pakistan, Islamabad would be forced to match India's nuclear capability. In the event, the USA did lift its arms embargo on Pakistan, if only partially. Pakistan also suggested an Indo-Israeli collaboration[55] in the nuclear test conducted by India in order to rouse the feelings of the Middle Eastern states (to whom Pakistan was moving closer politically) against India's nuclear test, and probably also as a ploy to attract Middle Eastern petro-dollars to assist Pakistan's own nuclear effort.

It was Bhutto's own reference to the "Islamic" nature of the Pakistani bomb in his testimony from his death-cell that added a new and ominous dimension to the Pakistani nuclear programme. "The Christian, Jewish and Hindu civilizations have this capability. Only the Islamic civilization was without it, but that position was about to change."[56] While there is no conclusive evidence to establish a definite link between Pakistan's nuclear programme and Middle Eastern petro-dollars, there is sufficient circumstantial evidence not to brush aside such reports lightly. For instance, there were persistent reports that Libya was underwriting Pakistan's purchase of uranium from Niger.[57] There were also reports of Saudi Arabia, the UAE and Turkey assisting Pakistan's nuclear activities.[58]

Be that as it may, the Pakistani professions of commitment to peaceful uses of nuclear technology started sounding rather hollow following a series of incidents in the 1980s. In 1984, Nazir Vaid, a Pakistani national, was caught trying to smuggle 50 electronic switches out of the USA which could be used for detonating nuclear bombs and was deported.[59] At about the same time, Pakistan tried to purchase high-speed industrial cameras from the West which could be used for designing the conventional explosive trigger of a nuclear bomb.[60] Again in July 1987, one Arshad Pervez was arrested in Philadelphia on charges of trying to smuggle "maraging" steel to Pakistan which could be used in the rotors of centrifuges.[61]

In an interview with an Indian journalist, Kuldip Nayar, in early 1987, Dr. Khan confirmed that Pakistan did possess nuclear capability.[62] "What the CIA has been saying about our possessing the bomb is correct and so is the speculation of some foreign newspapers."[63] More importantly, Dr. Khan was quite outspoken about the implications of a Pakistani bomb for India. "Nobody can undo Pakistan or take us for granted. We are here to stay and let it be clear that we shall use the bomb if our existence is threatened." He went on to add, "I personally think that the only way to stop nuclear warfare between us [India and Pakistan] is to come to an agreement."[64] Hinting at the futility of any Indian attack on Kahuta, Dr. Khan asserted, "India knows what price it would have to pay for attacking Kahuta. In any case, the plant is well protected and we have not put our eggs in one basket."[65]

Though Dr. Khan vehemently denied giving the interview later, the timing of the interview was of utmost significance. The Pakistanis knew that the real worth of nuclear weapons was their "deterrence value" not their "use value". The interview came at a time when the Indian Army was conducting a massive military exercise called "Operation Brasstacks" close to Pakistan's border, and there was persistent speculation of a pre-emptive strike on Kahuta either by India alone or in collaboration with Israel. It was also probably a hint to the Americans not to link the nuclear issue with the American aid package to Pakistan by presenting the Americans with a nuclear *fait accompli*.

Now let us examine India's possible response to the Pakistani bomb in the context of India's own nuclear policies and ambitions. It is obvious that India sees in technology the means to achieve economic progress and military might which would revive its political fortune and enable it to deal with the developed countries on equal terms and possibly from a position of strength.

Nehru was acutely conscious of this when he observed in 1948:

Consider the past four hundred years of history, the world developed a new source of power, that is steam - the steam engine and the like - and the Industrial age came in. India with all her many virtues did not develop that source of power. It became a backward country in that sense; it became a slave country because of that ... now we are facing the atomic age; we are on the verge of it ... if we are to remain abreast in the world as a nation which keeps ahead of things, we must develop this atomic energy .... [66]

It goes without saying that India's nuclear and space programmes are amongst the most sophisticated, advanced and comprehensive in the world. They have been designed to meet India's civilian and military needs simultaneously.[67]

In view of India's nuclear capabilities as demonstrated by the Peaceful Nuclear Explosion (PNE) at Pokhran in May 1974 and the simultaneous development of rocket technology which would provide India, if it so desired, with the required delivery systems, the inevitable question that arises is whether India would exercise its nuclear option and cross the nuclear threshold or persist with its current policy of voluntary nuclear abstention.

In trying to answer this question, first we must examine the basic attitude of India's political leadership to the issue of the application and adaptation of science for military purposes. From the very beginning, the Indian leaders have been neither unaware of nor averse to the idea of military applications of science. Nehru made this quite clear as far back as 1946. "I hope Indian scientists will use the atomic force for constructive purposes. But if India is threatened she will inevitably try to defend herself by all means at her disposal."[68]

He more or less reiterated this position while participating in the Constituent Assembly debates in 1948: "Indeed, I think we must develop it [nuclear technology] for peaceful purposes ... of course, if we are compelled as a nation to use it for other purposes, possibly no pious sentiments of any of us will stop the nation from using it that way."[69] Thus the Indian leaders, since independence, despite their pacifist and peaceful professions, have been aware of the military potential of scientific knowledge and had no qualms about making use of it if the situation demanded it.[70]

It must also be borne in mind that India's nuclear development, in general terms, has been independent of China's or, much later, of Pakistan's nuclear threat. India's quest for nuclear technology began, in earnest, in 1948 when neither China nor Pakistan were factors in India's nuclear calculations. Moreover, India has had serious disagreements with the superpowers on the question of instituting international controls on the nuclear programmes of developing countries. "India ... viewed international controls in atomic energy as downright dangerous and discriminatory, and as a form of economic and technological colonialism."[71]

Thus, India's nuclear outlook has been that of a potential great power which is determined to follow an independent path in terms of its own national interests and perceptions in defiance of objections from other great powers. While China and Pakistan continue to influence India's nuclear policy, they have never been fundamental to it, though they could serve as convenient excuses when India decides to go nuclear.

The probable answer to this question must also be discussed in the context of the two major objectives that underlie and govern all of India's foreign policy endeavours, namely the attainment of great power status and the security of the nation. As we have already seen, it has been India's endeavour since independence to emerge as an independent and autonomous centre of power, an objective which it pursued with tenacity and relentlessness despite occasional setbacks and pitfalls.

The fact is that there has been a consistency in India's policies of national centralization and unification since independence, as well as a foreign policy that has been global in its objectives. Criticism from outsiders has not deflected India from its recognition of itself as a major nation that has achieved great power status.[72]

This leads us to the crucial and related question of security, which has been a dominant theme of India's external posture ever since independence. Simply put, the question is: can India remain nonaligned and non-nuclear and still cope with the security threat? The answer, at least in the long run, seems to be an emphatic no.

Let us now consider the options that are open to India if it chooses to remain non-nuclear. First, India can abandon its nonalignment and seek nuclear guarantees from the superpower of its choice. Given India's experience in the matter in the 1960s, this is easier said than done. Moreover, nuclear guarantees obtained even after a formal alignment have not been considered particularly effective or reliable by the Indians. To quote Mrs. Gandhi, "In the final analysis ... the effectiveness of a nuclear shield would depend not on the spirit in which protected powers accepted it, but on the vital and national interests of the giver."[73]

Abandonment of nonalignment may also prove to be too high a price for such unreliable nuclear guarantees. As we have already seen, non-alignment is fundamental to India's foreign policy. It is both a strategy and an outlook. It is the essence of India's existence and continuance as an independent and autonomous entity, and its abandonment would simply mean that India could not and would not go it alone.

Giving up nonalignment may also have serious internal repercussions for India. The internal stimulus for nonalignment is much more important than the external one. This explains the survival and strengthening of nonalignment despite an abatement in the Cold War. The delicate internal balance which has been so assiduously built over the years on foreign policy issues in India may disappear, giving room for significant internal bickering and strife which India can certainly do without.

If an aligned India is unlikely to get credible nuclear guarantees, there is little reason to believe that a nonaligned India would be able to do so. Hence, the logic of nonalignment inevitably leads India on the path of the development of nuclear weapons. If India were to achieve a credible nuclear deterrent, it would only strengthen and give substance and credence to its nonalignment. No credible nuclear umbrella would be provided to a nonaligned India. Nor could India's misgivings about being provided a credible nuclear shield even after alignment be brushed aside lightly. Thus, alignment and development of nuclear weapons appear, at least in the long run, to be mutually exclusive options for India. As Mrs. Gandhi made it clear in 1967, "We for our part may find ourselves having to take a nuclear decision at any moment and it is therefore not possible for us to tie our hands."[74]

While India has been justifiably concerned about Pakistan's nuclear programme, it is difficult for India to be self-righteous about it. India cannot deny to Pakistan what it claims to be within its own right to pursue. However, nuclear proliferation in South Asia might have serious implications for regional and even global security. It can undermine confidence in the nonproliferation regime and the will of the nuclear powers to maintain it. Given the strategic linkage between South Asia and the Middle East, it can suck into the equation certain Middle Eastern states, particularly Israel, with unpredictable consequences. Alternatively, "The competition between Pakistan and India for political and economic advantages in the Middle East ... creates powerful albeit shortsighted temptations to use nuclear leverage in more substantial ways."[75]

Nevertheless, at the subcontinental level, given the necessary political wisdom and will, India and Pakistan could come to some sort of *modus vivendi* which would spare the region many of the apocalyptic predictions that have been made in relation to possible nuclear holocaust.

Possession of nuclear capability by both India and Pakistan could eliminate both conventional and nuclear conflict between the two countries and initiate a process of negotiation as the only feasible way of settling bilateral disputes. The recent agreement between the two countries not to attack each other's nuclear installations is a step in that direction.

Nevertheless, the only practical way in which India can counter the threat of an "Islamic bomb", apart from keeping its own powder dry, is to cultivate the Israeli option. Indo-Israeli interests converge in this crucial aspect, and there is an urgent need for Indian policy-makers to make Israel an integral part of their security thinking in relation to the Middle East.

Islamic fundamentalism

Another major security concern of India in the 1970s in relation to the Middle East was the growing tide of Islamic fundamentalism[76] in the region. India was always wary of Islamic groupings in the region and opposed them consistently and firmly ever since independence. However, the rise of Saudi Arabia as an economic superpower in the region and the Islamic revolution in Iran towards the end of the 1970s posed more of an ideological than a political threat to many countries, including India.[77]

In the case of India, the threat is of considerable importance in the context of India's troubled secular polity, a large and vocal Muslim minority, the existence of an unfriendly and avowedly Islamic Pakistan and India's own delicate but substantial relations with the Muslim Middle East. In analysing this issue, we will confine ourselves strictly to the nature of the threat that Islamic fundamentalism poses to India and a critical appraisal of the ways and means that the Indian leadership adopted to deal with it.

> One of the cardinal tenets of Islamic Fundamentalism is to protect the purity of Islamic precepts from the adulteration of speculative exercises. Related to fundamentalism is Islamic revival or resurgence, a renewed interest in Islam.[78]

However, in a multi-religious country like India, which has been undergoing a sustained process of modernization since independence, any religious revivalism and orthodoxy could create serious problems and get in the way of political integration of various religious communities for national purposes.

Ever since independence, the policies and strategies adopted by the Indian political leadership to integrate the religious minorities, particularly Muslims, into the national mainstream have been rather half-hearted and diffident. The Pakistani factor and Hindu sensitivities to the Muslim Middle East in relation to the Indian Muslim minority put the Indian leadership on the defensive from the beginning.

The external props that the Indian National Congress resorted to in order to persuade the Muslims to join the national political mainstream before independence and which spilled over into the post-independence period were totally unnecessary and proved to be counterproductive in the long run. The INC's support of anachronistic issues like Khilafat, frequent appeals to anti-imperial solidarity and vociferous demands for justice to Palestinians did touch a responsive chord among Indian Muslims.

But these were grossly inadequate to induce Indian Muslims to join the national mainstream, because they did not address the most fundamental issue that was exercising the Muslim community in India, i.e. the political status of Indian Muslims in India after the British departure. It was the INC's failure, whatever the reasons, to solve this basic problem that eventually led to the partition of India.

There is some justification for the INC to resort to these external and artificial props in desperation in the face of an active "divide and rule" policy of the British and the veto they exercised over granting independence to India on the ground of keeping communal peace. However, the failure of such policies before independence and the departure of the British from India should have alerted the Indian political leadership to the irrelevance and untenability of such policies after India's independence. But that was not to be.

Nehru not only considered secularism as fundamental to India's survival as one nation but also described it as his greatest contribution to independent India. Nevertheless, Nehru failed to approach the issue head-on and left the job only half done. The most striking failure of Nehru, in this sphere, was his reluctance and eventual failure to enact a common civil code for the entire country, without which no country can realistically claim to have laid a sound basis for a secular society.

Admittedly, Nehru did have his reasons for not doing so. He was worried about the impact of such a measure on the Indian Muslim community, which was experiencing a sense of psychological insecurity following partition and the communal violence that accompanied it. Nehru was also concerned that any attempt at domestic reform in relation to the Muslims might give the conservative elements in the community an opportunity and a pretext to raise the slogan of Islam being in danger. Besides, he felt that

> The fate of India is largely tied up with the Hindu outlook. If the present Hindu outlook does not change radically, I am quite sure that India is doomed. The Muslim outlook may be and, I think, is often worse. But it does not make very much difference to the future of India.[79]

But in the event, Nehru was wrong and the Muslim outlook did make a difference. It gave the conservative elements among Hindus a potent and plausible argument to accuse Nehru of double standards and of pampering the Muslim minority. There were demands that Hindu personal law should also be left untouched by the government. The fact that no other religious minority except the Muslims were given such a privilege made matters worse and there were accusations of appeasement. It also created the impression that Muslims were opposing and avoiding the family planning programme so vital to the nation's progress on religious grounds, and hence their loyalty to the country was suspect. This, in turn, enabled the extremist elements among the Hindus to argue that Muslims would outnumber Hindus in due course in India, and hence the latter should also oppose family planning.

As Dr. S. Gopal points out,

> Paradoxically, in his efforts to make the Muslims feel at home in India, Nehru declined to enact a common civil code and insist on monogamy and rights of divorce, property and inheritance for all

Indians of whatever faith. Nehru prided himself on what he had done for the emancipation of women, which was to him the test of a civilization; but he had to reconcile himself to the denial of equality, proclaimed by the constitution, to Muslim women. In the interests of unity and integration, this aspect of the social revolution, on which Nehru laid great store, was deliberately held back from completion.[80]

It is difficult to agree with Dr. Gopal, at least in retrospect, that Nehru's lack of decisiveness in this regard was in the "interests of unity and integration". If anything, it had just the opposite effect. Nehru had the stature, appeal and the necessary trust among people, both Hindus and Muslims, to have pushed through such legislation. If he could not do it, it is unfair to expect any of his successors even to touch it. Hence, a reform which Nehru himself considered to be of the utmost importance was put more or less permanently in cold storage.

What was worse was the fact that the lesser and less scrupulous leaders who followed Nehru made the issue a political football to be kicked around for short-term electoral gains. Sending an official delegation to the Islamic Conference in Rabat in 1969 and parading India as the third or fourth largest Muslim country in the world were the results of such an attitude. As B.G. Verghese so aptly pointed out, "the tragedy is that while secularism means modernity, in regard to Indian Muslims the concept of secularism has been retrograde, tradition-bound, even superstitious".[81]

Moreover, in the 1970s serious compromises were made in relation to India's secular credentials for short-term electoral gains. The government's inability or unwillingness to deal with the real problems facing the Muslim community in India, such as economic and educational backwardness and unemployment, and the cosmetic and almost comical measures it resorted to (like more Urdu teachers, more newsprint for Urdu newspapers, more Qawalis on radio and TV) in order to curry their favour will be of no avail in the long run.[82]

On the eve of the general elections in December 1979, there was a series of dinners hosted by the ambassadors of Saudi Arabia, Libya and other Arab countries in honour of Mrs. Gandhi, which could not be dismissed as coincidental. It is possible that either Mrs. Gandhi was trying to project her image and that of her party in a favourable light to the Indian Muslims, or the Arab diplomats themselves were implicitly suggesting to the Muslim voters in India that they favoured Mrs. Gandhi for the leadership of the country.

The editorial in one of the leading newspapers accurately portrayed the implications of these "political dinners":

> The Muslim community, as one of our numerically and politically important minorities, deserves not only a fair but a generous deal, but any such arrangement arrived at with the patronage or support of a foreign government would be intolerable. It would be bad for the foreign government concerned and worse for the Muslim community in India and the local political leaders who promote or encourage such liaison in the name of building international bridges. The impact on members of the majority community of efforts to build an Islamic brotherhood across the oceans basically to gain a few million votes ... can prove to be disastrous.[83]

There was also the case of conversion of Harijans to Islam in the village of Meenakshipuram in Tamil Nadu in the early 1980s, reportedly with Middle Eastern money, which caused considerable communal tension in the country. The report of the Intelligence Bureau regarding the conversions was quite disturbing. It said:

> The proselytizing effort of the Muslim organizations and institutions has received a fillip because of the inflow of money from the Gulf region, Saudi Arabia and other Muslim countries and the Pan-Islamic Agencies. Promises of jobs and scholarships in the Muslim countries and deputations of some of the more promising of the converts to places like Madina University for higher religious learning are being made. As an atmosphere favourable for conversions is created ... it is likely to attract more and more attention of the Muslim countries and foreign Islamic organizations.[84]

However, even such a potentially explosive issue was used for narrow political gains without any regard for its long-term implications. The then Chief Minister of Kerala, Mr. K. Karunakaran, allowed two "black-listed" visitors from Kuwait, Hashim-al-Rifai and Yakub-al-Rifai, to visit Kerala in January 1986 to keep his Muslim League partners in good humour, despite the fact that their entry into India was banned by the Home Ministry. Hashim-al-Rifai was the Chairman of the World Muslim Minority Community, an international Muslim organization. It was this organization that was reported to have provided huge sums of money for the conversion of Harijans to Islam in Meenakshipuram.[85]

The only real threat that Islamic fundamentalism poses to India is that it could delay the integration of the Muslim community with the rest of the population for national purposes. It is a threat to the extent that it distorts and disorients the Indian Muslims. However, the Islamic fundamentalists in India work on the "periphery" of the Muslim community there, not from its "core".[86]

To sum up, while Islamic fundamentalism is not a major concern, it is "always at the back of our mind".[87] Nevertheless, the best way to counter it is to address the real and material problems of the Muslims in order that they would be, psychologically and materially, in a position to resist fundamentalist appeals. The propensity for soft options and short-term gains of successive governments made India "more Islamic, in a very narrow way, than most Muslim countries".[88]

The Shah Banu controversy is a case in point.[89] The case became a cause *célèbre* when the (Indian) Supreme Court upheld the ruling of a lower court granting a maintenance of Rs 500 to a Muslim woman, Shah Banu, who had earlier been divorced by her husband according to Muslim law (Shariat). The Orthodox Muslims considered this as an unwarranted infringement of their personal law and approached Rajiv Gandhi's government for its reversal. According to Vasant Sathe, an erstwhile Cabinet Minister in Rajiv Gandhi's government, the reversal of the Supreme Court judgement made Rajiv's government lose credibility with both Hindus and Muslims. As he frankly stated:

> We ourselves are responsible for giving credence to this communal feeling because, in the name of secularism, we ourselves were not secular. In the name of pragmatism, the government had succumbed to fundamentalists.[90]

What is needed is a bold and imaginative policy which emphasizes long-term national gains as opposed to short-term electoral benefits.

Soviet intervention in Afghanistan

The Soviet intervention in Afghanistan in December 1979 constitutes a watershed in India's security perceptions in relation to the Middle East. In fact, it crystallized and aggravated most of the security concerns that India had in relation to the region in the 1970s. As a consequence of the Soviet military occupation of Afghanistan, "the traditional strategic divide in South Asia - between Pakistan and India - was now meshed with the Soviet-US divide in the Persian Gulf, the Indian Ocean, and indeed in the global arena".[91] It heralded a "new Cold War" between the two superpowers with all the attendant implications for India's security. President Carter made it very clear that

> Any attempt by any outside force to gain control of the Persian Gulf region will be regarded as an assault on the vital interests of the United States of America, and such an assault will be repelled by any means necessary, including military force.[92]

And the Carter Doctrine was born. The Carter administration went on to develop the concept of a "regional security framework" for Southwest Asia which envisaged a massive US naval and military build-up in the Indian Ocean, including Diego Garcia and some of the littoral states like Egypt, Oman, Kenya and Somalia.[93] It was clear that

> the developments of 1980 marked a major threshold in the evolution of US strategy in the region. Not only was the US military presence at its highest level in history but there was also an underlying conviction that this region represented a major strategic zone of US vital interests, demanding both sustained attention at the highest levels of US policy making and direct US engagement in support of specifically US interests.[94]

More importantly for India, Pakistan became a "front line" state and once again a key member of the US military strategy in containing further Soviet inroads into the region. In fact, Pakistani-US relations were at a low ebb following the overthrow and hanging of Bhutto by his army Chief, Zia ul Haq, the seizure of the Grand Mosque in Mecca by Muslim fanatics which resulted in the burning down of the American Embassy in Islamabad and US concern about Pakistani efforts to acquire nuclear capability which led to the termination of all US military and economic aid to Pakistan in April 1979. The Soviet intervention in Afghanistan, however, changed all this. A two-year $400 million package of aid was proposed by the Carter administration to Pakistan which was turned down by Zia as "peanuts". Nevertheless, negotiations continued between the two countries, for Pakistan knew only too well that it was the only possible conduit of Western arms to the Afghan resistance after the fall of the Shah of Iran.

When Ronald Reagan took over as President in January 1981, he showed much less concern and sensitivity to Indian misgivings in relation to the proposed US military aid to Pakistan than Carter did. Pakistan became a part of American "strategic consensus" *vis-à-vis* the USSR, and in return the Reagan administration announced a package of $3.2 billion in economic and military aid to Pakistan over a six-year period, including the sale of 40 F-16 aircraft. Besides, the Reagan administration virtually turned a blind eye to Pakistani nuclear ambitions in order to forge a strategic alliance against the USSR when Congress waived the provisions of the Symington Amendment to the Foreign Assistance Act, which would have prohibited such aid in the absence of progress on nonproliferation.

Another disturbing development, as far as India was concerned, was the intimate links, particularly in the security sphere, that Pakistan managed to establish with the Gulf states after the Islamic revolution in Iran and the Soviet invasion of Afghanistan. Pakistan-Saudi military ties have already been discussed in some detail. Pakistan also managed to establish a military foothold in other Gulf states like Kuwait, the UAE and Oman. The Gulf states, including Saudi Arabia, given their meagre manpower resources, would be in no position to intervene directly in any Indo-Pakistani war. However, the substantial financial resources that these states command and the availability of compatible US-supplied war material in these countries as well as in Pakistan could make the costs prohibitively high for India in any future war with Pakistan.[95]

India was also extremely concerned about the spread of Islamic fundamentalism as a consequence of the Soviet occupation of Afghanistan. The Western trumpeting of the struggle between the Afghan resistance and the Soviet occupation forces as a "jihad" for short-term gains and the close involvement of avowedly Islamic regimes like Saudi Arabia, Iran and Pakistan in it, India feared, could boomerang badly with serious implications for the whole region. Hence "The possibility that an extremist Islamic government could take over in Kabul continues to excite very real Indian anxiety."[96]

There is very little doubt that India's rather subdued reaction to the Soviet occupation of Afghanistan caused considerable consternation and disquiet in the Islamic world and "isolated India from the conservative Islamic countries of Southwest Asia".[97] These countries were already suspicious of India's treaty with the USSR and of India's close political and economic ties with Iraq, which had a similar treaty relationship with the Soviet Union. India's apparent acquiescence to, if not approval of, the Soviet occupation of Afghanistan[98] gave further credence to the charge that India was acting as the USSR's cat's paw in the region. India's stand on Afghanistan also made its position in the nonaligned movement rather uncomfortable and awkward. While India's treaty with the USSR diluted her nonaligned credentials considerably, India's perceived acquiescence to the Soviet occupation of a nonaligned Afghanistan made matters worse. Most importantly, the Soviet occupation of Afghanistan struck a mortal blow to India's newly acquired and somewhat grudgingly acknowledged status as a regional power. The Soviet action posed

> an unprecedented threat to India's hard-earned status as South Asia's regional power, dismantling the favourable balance of regional power in South Asia that India had been able to bring about with its victory over Pakistan in the Bangladesh war in 1971, and the South Asian security regime erected on that balance.[99]

It provided Pakistan with an opportunity to taunt India's inability to do anything about regional security in relation to the Soviet presence in Afghanistan despite India's self-proclaimed role as a dominant power in South Asia. It appeared as though India was over-anxious about her regional status without any stomach for corresponding responsibilities.

To sum up, India's threat perceptions in relation to the Middle East seem to exaggerate the importance of Islam in forging military alliances. However, the reality has been otherwise. Pakistan's increasing military links with Middle Eastern states in the 1970s and 80s were, unlike before, based on mutuality of interests and as such tend to be more enduring. Consequently, India needs to evolve realistic and imaginative policies to counter these threats effectively.

India's traditional policy of supporting Arab causes in general and the Palestinian cause in particular is no longer adequate to counter the new and serious threats that could emanate from the region in the changed circumstances of the 1970s and 80s. For instance, neither India's pro-Arab stance nor consistent support of the Palestinian cause dissuaded Saudi Arabia from elevating its political and military relationship with Pakistan to new heights, in spite of Indian protests, in the late 1970s and 80s following the Islamic revolution in Iran and the Soviet occupation of Afghanistan. Nor does it appear that any of the Middle Eastern states share India's concern and anxiety about Pakistan's nuclear ambitions, and this stance is unlikely to change, no matter how strongly India supports the Arab causes.

Pakistani-Saudi security links and Pakistan's increasing role as a provider of security services, including direct presence in the Gulf sheikhdoms, have to be watched closely by India. The possible nuclearization of Pakistan could have serious implications for the Middle East and rule out any soft options for India in this regard. Should such development lead to a nuclear arms race between India and Pakistan, there is every possibility that Middle Eastern countries could get sucked into it in more than one way. Pakistan, given her limited resources, might be forced to depend more and more on the oil-rich countries of the Middle East to sustain such a costly arms race with India. This may result in Pakistan playing a more direct and decisive role as a security provider in the region, which could not but cause concern to India. Alternatively, it may place Pakistan under considerable obligation and even pressure to transfer nuclear technology to any of the Muslim countries of the Middle East. Any such eventuality would inevitably drag Israel into the picture. "The potential thus exists ... for some quite dramatic fusions of South Asian and Middle Eastern security interests as a result of developments in the nuclear arms race between India and Pakistan."[100]

Given the seriousness and probability of these developments, India needs to take a bold and pragmatic view of the changing security scenario in relation to the Middle East. There seem to be only two dependable and realistic ways of dealing with the situation. One is to develop bilateral relations with the Middle Eastern states on mutuality of interests in order to discourage them, to the greatest extent possible, from moving too close to Pakistan either politically or militarily. The second is to upgrade gradually India's relations with Israel, particularly in the security sphere where the interests of India and Israel seem to coincide, in order to demonstrate to the Middle Eastern states that India is not devoid of options in the region and would make use of them if forced to do so.

4. India's Economic Interests in the Middle East

India's economic interaction with the Middle East has always been a factor in the calculations of Indian policy-makers ever since independence. However, in this chapter, we will concentrate on India's economic relations with the region since the oil boom in the mid-70s. In doing so, an attempt will be made to evaluate the relative importance of economic factors *vis-à-vis* India's politico-strategic interests in the region. It will be argued that despite the substantial increase in India's economic stake in the region, India has more enduring political and security interests in the Middle East. While trying to put India's economic interests in the region in perspective, an attempt will be made to quantify India's economic dealings with the region and their importance to India's overall economic goals and strategies.

It is pertinent, at this stage, to make some general observations in relation to India's foreign economic policy before we proceed to deal with India's economic interaction with the Middle East in specific sectors. Firstly, India is a large country with a huge population and fairly well-endowed with a variety of natural resources. As such, one need not overemphasize the importance of the domestic market in India's plans for national development.

> While there can be variations of emphasis, the centrality of the domestic market in India's developmental strategy cannot be denied. A continental economy of India's size has no structural compulsions to pursue a path of export-dominated growth, let alone export-led growth. If it must still push its exports, it is because exports help pay for those critical inputs which are so necessary to build a national economy. In other words, exports are a means, not an end in themselves.[1]

Secondly, India (or anyone else for that matter) neither anticipated the oil bonanza nor was it ready to take full advantage of it. It was more or less an accident which caught India napping in an economic sense. In the short run, it only served to expose the limitations and obsolescence of India's industrial structure.

Thirdly and lastly, self-sufficiency has been a central and long-standing goal of India's economic planning and development. As such, we need to examine India's economic ties with the Middle East in the light of this important objective of India's national endeavour.

Trade

Although India's trade with the Middle Eastern countries since the oil boom has gone up considerably in absolute terms, its share in the total imports of these countries has been remarkably small. Since Indian businessmen enjoyed a large and well-protected domestic market, they hardly ever felt the urge or the need to export to the rest of the world on highly competitive terms. As one World Bank official put it, "From the very beginning, the attitude of accepting exports as an integral part of policy has been missing in India."[2] So when the oil boom came in the mid-70s, India neither anticipated it nor was it ready for it.

Consequently, India failed to take full advantage of the buying spree that the oil-rich Middle Eastern countries indulged in following the accumulation of petro-dollars. A glance at Table 1 makes this crystal clear. In 1955, when the combined imports of the Middle Eastern countries totalled about $1.4 billion, India's exports to these countries amounted to $45 million - a mere 3.3 per cent of the total. In 1975, when the imports of these countries were valued at $27 billion, India's share of it was $694 million and its share in the total imports fell to 2.6 per cent. In the decade after 1975, a period of phenomenal increase in Middle Eastern imports from the rest of the world, India's share in it further declined to just 1 per cent.

Despite India's geographical proximity and age-old cultural and commercial ties with the region, India failed to penetrate the Middle Eastern markets to the extent it could have. The reasons for India's rather lack-lustre performance are many. The major reasons, however, are the inability of Indian exporters to ensure quality and delivery schedules at competitive prices. Poor packaging is often mentioned as another factor. Besides, it has also been a matter of concern to the Indian government that most of India's exports to the region continue to be perishable goods and consumer items, rather than the engineering goods and durables that

Table 1 India's Share in Total Imports of Middle Eastern Countries 1955-85

	Total imports by country US $ millions			India's exports to each country US $ millions			India's % share of exports to each country		
	1955	1975	1985	1955	1975	1985	1955	1975	1985
Bahrain	174	1,198	3,159	4.8	21.0	32.5	2.76	1.75	1.03
Iran	337	10,343	11,635	11.0	325.0	77.5	3.26	3.14	0.67
Iraq	272	4,215	10,556	4.8	76.0	29.0	1.76	1.80	0.27
Kuwait	94	2,390	5,934	7.4	56.0	99.8	7.87	2.34	1.68
Oman	8	1,047	3,080	1.4	23.0	52.7	17.50	2.20	1.71
Qatar	17	410	1,162*	2.9	13.0	26.5*	17.06	3.17	2.28*
Saudi Arabia	245	4,214	33,696*	1.3	72.0	215.6*	0.53	1.71	0.64*
UAE	NA	2,669	7,043	NA	79.0	235.6	NA	2.96	3.35
Yemen, North	14	294	2,962	NA	19.0	21.8	NA	6.46	0.74
Yemen, South	210	313	1,600	11.2	9.0	19.7	5.33	2.88	1.23
Total	1,371	27,093	80,827	44.8	694.0	810.7	3.27	2.76	1.00

* 1984

Source: South, March, 1988, p.33.

it would like to sell in larger quantities.[3]

Labour

India's labour exports to the Middle East have been substantial ever since the mid-70s. Table 2 depicts the steady increase in the annual labour outflows to the region from India, which reached a peak in the mid-80s. Table 3, on the other hand, provides an estimate of the Indian migrant population in the Middle East between 1975 and 1987, when it reached its peak of about a million. However, two important characteristics distinguish the migration of Indians to the Middle East compared to the earlier migrants from India. Firstly, most of these migrants are at the "lower end of the spectrum of skills as also of incomes" whether in India before their departure or in their work place in the Middle East. Table 4 underlines this point in no uncertain terms. Secondly, an overwhelming majority of these migrants are "temporary migrants" who return to India after a definite period of work overseas, often not more than two years.[4]

Given the facts that the Indian economy has always had a large labour surplus and also the temporary nature of migration to the Middle East, the impact of the Middle Eastern migration on unemployment in India at a macro level is almost negligible. Moreover, it looks as though India's

Table 2 Annual Labour Outflows from India: 1976-86

Year	Number
1976	4,200
1977	22,900
1978	69,000
1979	171,000
1980	236,200
1981	276,000
1982	239,545
1983	224,995
1984	205,922
1985	163,035
1986	113,649

Source: Ministry of Labour, Government of India, New Delhi.

The above figures refer to the number of Indian workers who obtained emigration clearance from the Protector General of Emigrants.

Table 3   Estimates of the Indian Migrant Population in the Middle
East: 1975-87

Country	1975	1979	1983	1987
Bahrain	17,250	26,000	30,000	77,000
Iraq	7,500	20,000	50,000	35,000
Kuwait	32,105	65,000	115,000	100,000
Libya	1,100	10,000	40,000	25,000
Oman	38,500	60,000	100,000	184,000
Qatar	27,800	30,000	40,000	50,000
Saudi Arabia	34,500	100,000	270,000	240,000
UAE	107,500	152,000	250,000	225,000
Others	-	38,000	21,000	21,000
Total	266,255	501,000	916,000	957,000

Source: Deepak Nayyar, International Labour Migration from India: A Macro-
Economic Analysis, Working Paper No.3, Asian Regional Programme
on International Labour Migration, UN Development Programme, New
Delhi, 1988, p.14.

Table 4   The Skill Composition of Labour Outflows from India:
1984-86

	1984		1985		1986	
	Number	%	Number	%	Number	%
1. Unskilled workers	88,575	43.0	55,710	34.2	45,577	40.1
2. Skilled workers	86,041	41.8	86,037	52.8	53,432	47.0
3. White-collar workers	7,477	3.6	5,753	3.5	7,351	6.5
4. High-skill workers	6,495	3.2	7,378	4.5	5,958	5.2
5. Others	17,361	8.4	8,157	5.0	1,331	1.2
Total	205,922	100.0	163,035	100.0	113,649	100.0

Source: Ministry of Labour, Government of India, New Delhi.

manpower exports to the Middle East have already reached a plateau. India
has also been encountering stiff competition from other labour exporting
countries like South Korea, Thailand, Sri Lanka and the Philippines.

Remittances

Closely related to India's labour outflows to the Middle East are the remittances that the Indian migrant labour has been sending home ever since the oil boom in the Middle East. Table 5 details the estimated composition of remittances to India from various sources between 1974 and 1985. It is obvious from the above Table that from a modest figure of Rs 259 million and about 11 per cent of the total remittances in 1974-75, the Middle Eastern component of India's overseas remittances has increased dramatically thereafter and has constituted more than 50 per cent ever since 1977-78. It goes without saying that the Middle Eastern remittances constituted an important source of foreign exchange earnings for India in the late 1970s and 80s. They played a considerable role in easing India's balance of payments situation and enabled it to enjoy fairly large foreign exchange reserves for a considerable length of time.

However, it must be noted that the gross inflow of remittances constituted just 1.5 per cent of India's Gross Domestic Product (GDP) in the mid-80s when the remittances were at their peak.[5] In the words of an Indian scholar, the Middle Eastern remittances had little more than a "cushioning effect" on India's balance of payments situation.[6] Besides, the remittances from the Middle East constituted not only the money remitted to support families while abroad but also "once-and-for-all repatriation of savings on return home" in view of the temporary nature of emigration to that region. This is one of the principal reasons for the huge remittances from the region during the period under consideration. It must also be borne in mind that the greater part of India's Middle Eastern remittances were used up to pay for the oil imports from the Middle East.

There are also people who are worried about the impact of the Middle Eastern remittances on the Indian economy in the long run.

> Some disturbing trends are discernible which will have a more lasting impact on the [Indian] economy and on society than the crucial but temporary relief provided by this money in meeting the country's external payments obligations.[7]

Oil

India's dependency on oil imports from the Middle Eastern countries constitutes an important segment of India's relations with the region. Tables 6, 7 and 8 depict India's import of crude oil from 1971-72 to 1985-86, country by country. As Table 6 indicates, India imported its crude oil requirements from 1971-72 to 1976-77 from five Middle Eastern countries,

Table 5 Estimated Composition of Remittances to India by Origin: 1974-85. (Rs Million)

Year	North America	Western Europe	Britain and Australia	Middle East Oil-Exporting Countries	Other Developing Countries	Total Remittances	% of Middle Eastern Remittances
1973-74	432	189	442	74	287	1,424	5.20
1974-75	670	349	443	259	481	2,202	11.76
1975-76	1,105	502	620	1,316	694	4,237	31.06
1976-77	1,651	664	590	2,704	628	6,237	43.35
1977-78	1,382	786	1,026	4,868	1,111	9,173	53.07
1978-79	1,566	949	1,013	4,813	1,097	9,438	51.00
1979-80	2,210	1,192	1,631	7,904	1,784	14,721	53.69
1980-81	2,100	1,684	2,548	12,194	2,771	21,297	57.26
1981-82	3,355	1,866	2,195	10,975	2,438	20,829	52.69
1982-83	3,363	1,828	2,494	13,708	2,915	24,308	56.39
1983-84	3,871	2,119	2,460	15,000	3,033	26,483	56.64
1984-85	4,589	2,220	2,550	17,140	3,320	29,819	57.48

Source: Deepak Nayyar, op.cit., p.26.

Table 6 Country-wise Imports of Crude Oil 1971-72 to 1976-77
Qty: '000 Tonnes ; Value: Rs/Crores

Country	1971-72		1972-73		1973-74		1974-75		1975-76		1976-77	
	Qty.	Value	Qty.	Value	Qty.	Value	Qty.	Value	Qty.	Value	Qty.	Value
Iran	10,014	116.12	9,382	113.75	8,885	250.04	6,460	426.02	5,782	451.09	5,992	509.70
Iraq	40	0.51	213	3.71	1,168	49.87	3,099	217.22	2,779	219.65	2,984	247.01
Saudi Arabia	2,897	30.39	2,489	28.91	3,821	116.48	4,457	273.75	3,817	279.17	4,028	322.05
UAE	–	–	–	–	–	–	–	–	1,246	101.85	967	90.92
Egypt	–	–	–	–	–	–	–	–	–	–	77	6.23
Total	12,951	147.02	12,084	146.37	13,874	416.39	14,016	916.99	13,624	1051.76	14,048	1175.91

Source: Ministry of Petroleum and Chemicals, Government of India, New Delhi.

Table 7 Country-wise Imports of Crude Oil 1977-78 to 1982-83
Qty: '000 Tonnes ; Value: Rs/Crores

Country	1977-78 Qty.	1977-78 Value	1978-79 Qty.	1978-79 Value	1979-80 Qty.	1979-80 Value	1980-81 Qty.	1980-81 Value	1981-82 Qty.	1981-82 Value	1982-83 Qty.	1982-83 Value
Iran	6,191	537.99	3,601	299.37	3,714	574.34	5,901	1,281.91	5,035	1,246.09	3,456	797.78
Iraq	3,349	288.42	5,981	530.07	5,758	762.58	3,629	675.94	1,623	400.92	3,445	876.45
Saudi Arabia	2,941	242.34	2,410	193.22	3,017	352.25	2,520	503.44	3,680	815.68	6,189	1,431.81
UAE	872	79.68	1,117	99.88	1,417	198.42	1,553	326.39	1,605	410.84	1,196	307.42
USSR	962	82.90	1,548	128.63	1,998	275.61	1,782	362.97	2,000	493.30	2,588	610.80
Qatar	–	–	–	–	217	24.33	19	3.99	–	–	–	–
Kuwait	–	–	–	–	–	–	419	92.93	–	–	–	–
Egypt	192	14.87	–	–	–	–	50	8.30	–	–	–	–
Algeria	–	–	–	–	–	–	195	53.29	792	225.52	–	–
Malaysia	–	–	–	–	–	–	51	11.42	–	–	–	–
Mexico	–	–	–	–	–	–	129	28.39	–	–	–	–
Venezuela	–	–	–	–	–	–	–	–	563	144.03	75	19.48
Total	14,507	1246.20	14,657	1251.17	16,121	2187.53	16,248	3,348.97	15,298	3,736.38	16,949	4,043.74

Source: Ministry of Petroleum and Chemicals, Government of India, New Delhi.

Table 8 Country-wise Imports of Crude Oil 1983-84 to 1985-86
Qty.: '000 Tonnes ; Value: Rs/Crores

	1983-84		1984-85		1985-86	
	Qty.	Value	Qty.	Value	Qty.	Value
Iran	3,340	743.42	1,840	468.82	3,456	868.32
Iraq	3,500	778.36	2,650	668.02	2,147	541.05
Saudi Arabia	4,600	1,010.22	4,520	1,121.28	2,398	595.14
UAE	970	218.97	540	134.56	2,173	503.70
USSR	3,430	761.70	3,110	792.54	2,570	647.25
Egypt	-	-	-	-	514	114.95
Qatar	-	-	-	-	-	-
Kuwait	50	10.27	370	82.58	302	59.77
Oman	-	-	610	162.54	1,584	356.61
Algeria	-	-	-	-	-	-
Malaysia	-	-	-	-	-	-
Mexico	-	-	-	-	-	-
Venezuela	-	-	-	-	-	-
Neutral Zone	80	18.11	-	-	-	-
Total	15,970	3,541.05	13,640	3,430.34	15,144	3,686.79

Source: Ministry of Petroleum and Chemicals, Government of India, New Delhi.

namely Iran, Iraq, Saudi Arabia, the UAE and Egypt. But as Tables 7 and 8 demonstrate, India thought it wise to diversify its oil imports from 1977-78 onwards for economic as well as political reasons. India's oil imports thereafter were not only spread among more than a dozen countries, but also one-third of them were non-Middle Eastern countries.

India also, during the same period, made a vigorous and fairly successful effort to reduce its dependency on Middle Eastern oil for both economic and political reasons. Table 9 depicts India's crude oil production from 1979-80 to 1986-87. Crude oil production in the 1970s (1970-71 to 1980-81) had increased by 55 per cent, from 6.8 million tonnes to 10.51 million tonnes. In the next two years, output doubled to 21.1 million tonnes. A further 24 per cent increase was achieved in 1983-84 and production reached 26.0 million tonnes.[8]

During 1984-85, crude oil production increased by 11.4 per cent to 29.0 million tonnes. As a result of increased production of oil, the level of self-reliance in oil improved to about 70 per cent during 1980-85.[9]

Table 9   India's Crude Oil Production 1979-80 to 1986-87
         (Million Tonnes)

79-80	80-81	81-82	82-83	83-84	84-85	85-86	86-87
11.8	10.5	16.2	21.1	26.0	29.00	30.2	30.5

Source: Economic Survey 1984-85, p.17; Economic Survey 1987-88, p.25.

It should also be remembered that India has never had a problem in relation to oil supplies as such. Even during the two Indo–Pakistani wars in 1965 and 1971, when the political support of Middle Eastern countries to Pakistan was considerable, the oil supplies to India were never interrupted.

India's basic problem was the high price of oil and the fact that it had to pay for it in hard currency. However, the Middle Eastern countries made it very clear from the very beginning that there was no question of a dual price system for oil, one for the developing countries and one for the rest. Hence, the future price of oil will always be determined by market forces and India's political support for Arab causes will have no impact on it.

Loans and Aid

It is also instructive to see the extent to which India benefited from the Middle Eastern oil bonanza in terms of loans and aid. Table 10 makes it very clear that India's traditional good relations with the Middle East did not cut much ice with the oil-rich countries of the region so far as providing loans to India was concerned. As the Table below clearly illustrates, the Middle Eastern component of the total authorized loans that India has been able to obtain between 1974-79 and 1985-86 has never exceeded 5 per cent and as such is not very significant.

As far as aid is concerned, India has not been able to obtain a single dinar in the form of a grant as of 1986.[10]

Civil construction and industrial projects

As Table 11 makes clear, India was one of the principal beneficiaries in relation to civil engineering and construction projects in the Middle East. India enjoyed a natural advantage over her rivals in this area because of cheap labour and the proximity of the region. However, the same cannot be said of India's industrial projects in the region, as Table 12 indicates.

Table 10 Authorized Loans from the Middle Eastern Countries
(Rs. Lakhs)

	1974-79	1979-80	1980-81	1981-82	1982-83	1983-84	1984-85	1985-86
Iraq	60.41	1.33	78.77	–	–	–	–	–
Iran	932.21	11.65	16.56	–	–	–	–	–
UAE	52.50	–	–	–	–	–	–	–
Kuwait Fund	51.24	–	–	52.50	30.03	30.66	–	14.70
Saudi Arabia Fund	58.96	–	–	–	17.23	–	–	28.72
Abu Dhabi Fund	12.92	–	–	–	–	–	–	–
OPEC Special Fund	26.85	15.00	37.50	–	22.50	16.87	–	–
Total	1,195.09	27.98	132.83	52.50	52.53	64.76	–	43.42
Total authorized loans from all sources	6,592.80	779.94	2,896.80	2,160.06	1,878.28	1,473.58	2,594.95	3,301.50
% of Middle Eastern share	18.13	3.59	4.59	2.43	2.80	4.39	–	1.32

Source: Report on Currency and Finance 1985-86, pp.156-157, The Reserve Bank of India.

Table 11   Civil Engineering and Construction Projects
         (Rs Crores)

	1979 (Cumulative)	1980	1981	1982
Iraq	526.19	1,040.20	967.38	173.51
Libya	473.83	114.95	600.43	107.14
PDRY	25.69	1.40	0.77	-
YAR	61.60	72.30	-	-
Qatar	9.19	-	24.84	0.12
Kuwait	286.27	18.64	-	58.00
Saudi Arabia	43.15	-	-	5.71
UAE	185.76	64.29	0.27	0.21
Oman	32.00	5.38	2.09	-
Total	1,643.68	1,317.16	1,595.78	344.69
Total for all countries including Middle East	1,684.61	1,324.10	1,604.81	421.06
% of Middle Eastern share	97.57	99.48	99.44	81.86

Source: Handbook of Export Statistics, 1981-82, Project Export Supplement, p.14,
        Engineering Export Promotion Council, Calcutta.

India's participation in the industrial projects in the region has been rather uneven and demand also seems to be tapering off a bit.

India did make considerable gains from the tremendous upsurge in the purchasing power of oil exporting countries in the Middle East following the steep rise in the price of oil in the mid-70s; "it was more in the nature of a spill-over than anything else. It was not the outcome of any concerted effort. Looking at these gains, it is generally lamented that India missed an opportunity."[11]

Moreover, there is a need to appreciate the serious limitations, international as well as domestic, within which India had to respond to and take advantage of the Middle Eastern markets. In the international context,

it is not sufficiently recognised that the Arab Gulf market is, in its present orientation at any rate, closer to the Western market, whether in the matter of skills, technology, finance or commerce. The entire industrial edifice is built on Western technology; the outlet or market

Table 12 Industrial Projects
    (Rs Crores)

	1980 (Cumulative)	80-81	81-82	82-83
Iraq	182.47	–	–	–
Saudi Arabia	106.82	15.12	23.99	–
Libya	194.28	17.44	–	–
Iran	4.15	–	16.17	2.47
Kuwait	4.67	–	–	–
Qatar	2.48	–	–	–
Syria	–	–	10.18	11.20
Bahrain	–	–	–	1.80
Total	494.87	32.56	50.34	15.47
Total for all countries including Middle East	653.73	112.40	104.64	161.47
% of Middle Eastern share	75.70	28.97	48.11	9.58

Source: Handbook of Export Statistics, 1981-82, Project Export Supplement, p.3, Engineering Export Promotion Council, Calcutta.

for the hydro-carbon and petro-chemicals is in the West; and the investments too are from the West.[12]

Consequently, "All their economic policies and management are, therefore, geared to respond to the changing nature and sensitivities of the Western market."[13] It must be pointed out, therefore, that these structural limitations impose severe restrictions on India's efforts to increase its economic stake in the Middle East beyond a certain point.

There are also serious domestic constraints which would get in the way if India tried to expand its economic interaction with the Middle East in a big way. The Indian economy, which has so far largely developed around its large and protected domestic market, is facing serious constraints in penetrating highly competitive international markets. "The obsolescence of its technological base is becoming more obvious with India's increasing desire to participate in the external market."[14] It is difficult to envisage India overcoming this serious handicap, at least in the short run, given its institutional, financial and infrastructural constraints.

Above all, India's economic interaction with the Middle East should take into account its own developmental priorities and strategies, and should not be allowed to lead to distortions and scarcities in the domestic market.

All things considered, India's economic stake in the Middle East needs to be seen in its proper perspective. The Middle Eastern oil boom was an accident. While it was extremely useful to India in the short run, its long-term viability and utility for India are doubtful. It looks as though it is a passing phase, an extended one at best. It only served to rationalize and justify India's traditional policy of friendship with the Middle Eastern states rather than being its outcome. India, in this sense, has more enduring political and security interests in the region. It should be remembered that India's policy was not fundamentally different even in the 1950s and 60s, when India's economic stake in the Middle East was less than substantial. Besides, India's economic breakthrough with major Middle Eastern countries followed political understanding and accommodation, and not vice versa.

5. Indo-Israeli Relations

> If unrequited love exists in international relations, then this is the story of Israel as a suitor and India as an unresponsive partner.[1]

This comment from the *Israel Economist* sums up the nature of Indo-Israeli relations in the last four decades. Ironically, there has been no conflict of interests - at least in bilateral terms - between the two countries over the years. In fact, at times there has been the odd convergence of interests. Nevertheless, Indo-Israeli relations failed to take off; they remained cool but correct, friendly but low-key, intermittent but secretive.

It is no exaggeration to say that Israel has been one of the blind spots of India's foreign policy endeavours. In certain respects, it demonstrates the falsity and far-fetchedness of some of the assumptions that underlie it. What is more remarkable, and perhaps disturbing, is that no attempt seems to have been made to undertake a thorough reappraisal of India's policy to a region which has undergone momentous changes since the early 1970s.

In the following pages, an attempt will be made to trace the Indian attitude to the Palestinian issue at the UN and to the creation of the state of Israel. The factors and personalities that governed India's subsequent policy towards the Jewish state will also be examined in the light of India's own foreign policy objectives in the region. In addition, it will be argued that the changing politico-strategic scenario at the global, regional and subcontinental levels since the early 1970s has made it imperative for India to have a fresh look at the state and status of Indo-Israeli relations in the context of India's overall policy to the region.

India's policy towards Israel in the post-independence phase appears to be a hang-over from the attitude of the Indian National Congress (INC) towards the Palestinian question.[2] Its approach to the problem was influenced by moral, emotional as well as pragmatic considerations. While both Gandhi and Nehru had much sympathy for the long-suffering Jews, they considered it anything but moral to "impose" the Jews on the reluctant Palestinians through unlimited immigration, and thereby reduce the Arabs to the status of second-class citizens in their own land.

Nehru's response was emotional in the sense that he had participated in a prolonged and successful freedom struggle against British imperialism in India. He saw the Palestinian question as part of the larger issue of colonialism. He inferred that the British were pitting Jewish "religio-nationalism" against Arab nationalism, in order to retain their tenuous imperial possessions in the region.

At a more pragmatic level, the INC and its leaders could in no way support any nationalism which was exclusively based on religion. That would have been fundamentally at variance with their professed secular form of nationalism. In short, Nehru saw a parallel between the Muslim League's demand for Pakistan and the Zionist demand for a Jewish state on the one hand, and an opportunity for the British to resort to their age-old "divide and rule" policy on the other. It is against this background that we need to look at India's approach to the Palestinian issue, after the British (finding the problem intractable) washed their hands of it by referring the matter to the UN.

The INC, on the other hand, was no longer a national movement to adopt a highly moralistic attitude to issues. It had, under the stewardship of Nehru, transformed itself into a fully-fledged political party, committed to the preservation and promotion of India's national interests in a balanced and pragmatic manner. But as it turned out, India's policy towards Israel, once it came into existence, was neither balanced nor pragmatic and failed to subserve India's interests in the region, as we shall see in the course of this chapter.

At the UN

On 2 April 1947, the UK requested that Palestine be placed on the agenda of the next regular session of the General Assembly. On 21 and 22 April, five member countries (Egypt, Iraq, Syria, Lebanon and South Africa) requested the Secretary General to include an additional item on the agenda of the Special Session, viz. "The termination of the Mandate over Palestine and the declaration of its independence".

The General Assembly eventually adopted a resolution constituting a Special Committee comprising 11 members, including India.[3] The purpose was to "ascertain and record facts and to investigate all questions and views relevant to the problem of Palestine".

During these debates, the Indian representative, Mr. Asaf Ali[4], adopted a balanced and conciliatory approach to the Palestinian question. He recalled that in India "the Jews have never suffered throughout their history". Stating that the issue must be settled amicably by the Arabs and the Jews between themselves, he underlined the untenability of religion as the sole basis of statehood.

The Special Committee, known as the United Nations Special Committee on Palestine (UNSCOP), held its first meeting on 26 May 1947 and finalized its report[5] on 31 August 1947. The UNSCOP Report contained 12 general recommendations, of which 11 were unanimously approved. These 11 recommendations, *inter alia*, provided for the termination of the Mandate, independence for Palestine after a transition period under UN supervision, preservation of the Holy Places, minority rights, economic union and an appeal to both parties to eschew violence.

Furthermore, the committee came up with two alternative plans:

1. **Plan of Partition with Economic Union**: This was supported by seven members of the Committee (Canada, Czechoslovakia, Guatemala, The Netherlands, Peru, Sweden and Uruguay) and came to be known as the **Majority Plan**. It envisaged the partition of Palestine into two states, one Arab and the other Jewish, with the internationalization of Jerusalem under UN jurisdiction.

2. **Federal State Plan**: This was supported by three members (India, Iran and Yugoslavia) and came to be known as the **Minority Plan**. This plan called for an independent state of Palestine comprising an Arab state and a Jewish state, with Jerusalem as their capital. The federal state would have a federal government, and governments of Arab and Jewish states. There was to be a single Palestinian nationality and citizenship, with guaranteed equal rights for all minorities and free access to the Holy Places.

Mrs. Vijaya Lakshmi Pandit, who led the Indian delegation to the UN at the 1947 session, explained India's stand on the Palestinian issue to the Ad Hoc Committee on 11 October 1947. She asserted that peace in Palestine and the Middle East was of vital importance to India because of its geographical proximity to the region. The fundamental issue was the termination of the Mandate without delay and the recognition of Palestine as an independent state. Palestine was predominantly an Arab country, and this predominance should not be altered to the disadvantage of the

Arabs. Once Palestine became independent, the Jews could be given wide autonomy in areas where they were in the majority. India herself had suffered in the past because of the different interpretations of the promises of the governing power and hence she could not but sympathize with the Arab viewpoint.[6] Later, the Indian representative at the UN, Mr. Bajpai, argued that India had opposed partition earlier and did so now, because it was convinced by its own experience and by history that brute force never solved this kind of problem.[7]

However, as it turned out, the Zionists accepted the Majority Plan which partitioned Palestine into a Jewish and an Arab state. But the Arabs rejected both the Majority and Minority Plans because the former destroyed the territorial integrity of their homeland and placed a large Arab population in the proposed Jewish state as a permanent minority, and the latter because of its implicit partitionist content.

Three sub-committees were appointed and various modifications were suggested with a view to arriving at an agreed solution. Ultimately, however, the Majority Plan submitted by UNSCOP was adopted by the General Assembly with certain modifications.

The plan was adopted by vote - 33 in favour, 13 against, and ten abstentions. India voted against the plan along with the Arab countries, and Afghanistan, Cuba, Greece, Iran, Pakistan and Turkey. The UK, Ethiopia, Yugoslavia, and several Latin American countries abstained. The other permanent members of the Security Council favoured the plan. Interestingly, the Indian delegation and its leader Mrs. Pandit, it appears, were disgusted when they were asked to vote against the partition plan.[8]

After the partition plan was adopted, the Arab Higher Committee rejected it and refused to cooperate in its implementation. Instead, it requested the British government to hand over Palestine to "its Arab peoples". Thereafter, sporadic attacks against the Jews began on 30 November 1947 and gradually spread to the rest of Palestine. The Arabs, with the help of about six to seven thousand volunteers from neighbouring countries, seemed to have had the upper hand till the end of March 1948.

However, in early April 1948, the Israeli Haganah reversed this trend, scored a chain of victories, and consolidated the Jewish hold over the zones assigned to them by the General Assembly resolution. On 14 May 1948, the provisional government, with Ben Gurion as the Prime Minister and Defence Minister, issued its declaration of independence and announced the creation of the state of Israel. On 15 May 1948, the regular armed forces of Trans-Jordan, Syria, Lebanon, Iraq, Egypt, along with a small force from Saudi Arabia, were sent to Palestine to deal with the nascent state of Israel.

The Secretary General of the Arab League justified the Arab action on the ground that, with the end of the Mandate, there was no legally constituted body to administer law and order, and to protect life and property in Palestine. The Arab states would hand over the government to the Palestinian Arabs once law and order were restored.

However, the Arab forces failed to achieve their military objectives, while the Israelis, in the meantime, were able to acquire arms from Europe and elsewhere, and to recruit a number of Jewish veterans of World War II. After three broken truces, the General Armistice Agreements between Israel on the one hand and Egypt, Lebanon, Jordan and Syria on the other were negotiated on the Greek island of Rhodes in January 1949.

India's position: a reformulation

As can be seen from the foregoing analysis, India's attitude towards Palestine had gone through two distinct phases. First, it considered the Palestinian problem as a colonial question and regarded the elimination of colonialism (i.e. the ending of the British Mandate and the establishment of an independent Palestine) as the fundamental issue. India regarded the Jewish question as a minority problem, to be settled by extending to the Jews the rights and safeguards normally accorded to minority groups in other countries. In this phase, its criticism was primarily directed against the British exploitation of Arab-Jewish differences to perpetuate its rule over Palestine.

The second phase began with the large-scale migration of Jews from Central and Eastern Europe to Palestine between 1935 and 1947, primarily because of Nazi persecution. While India profoundly sympathized with the suffering of the Jews, it was opposed to a separate state for Jews in Palestine on two grounds. Firstly, it regarded any state exclusively based on religion as untenable. Secondly, it considered a remote historical connexion with the area as an insufficient ground for the creation of a separate Jewish state. Hence, it supported the Minority Plan, which envisaged a single Palestinian state based on federal principles.

The Indian approach to the Palestinian question contained two important elements. Firstly, it opposed the partition of Palestine as a solution, which was consistent with its own domestic stand *vis-à-vis* the Muslim League's demand for Pakistan. Hence, India advocated substantial autonomy for Jews in areas where they were in the majority.

Secondly, it de-emphasized the religious basis of the conflict between the Arabs and the Jews in Palestine. Rather, it sought to project it as a

political struggle, which again was calculated to dilute Pakistan's efforts
to flaunt its Islamic credentials to gain support and sympathy in the region.
Such a stand was also taken by India in order to subserve its domestic
political requirements as a multi-religious state.

Explaining India's stand, Nehru said:

We took up a certain attitude in regard to it which was roughly a
federal State with autonomous parts. It was opposed to both the
other attitudes which were before the United Nations. One was
partition which has now been adopted; the other was a unitary State.
We suggested a federal State with, naturally, an Arab majority in
charge of the federal State but with autonomy for the other regions
- Jewish regions.

After a great deal of thought we decided that this was not only a
fair and equitable solution of the problem, but the only real solution
of the problem. Any other solution would have meant fighting and
conflict. Nevertheless our solution ... did not find favour with most
people in the United Nations. Some of the major powers were out
for partition; they, therefore, pressed for it and ultimately got it.
Others were so keen on the unitary State idea and were so sure of
preventing partition at any rate or preventing a two-thirds majority
in favour of partition that they did not accept our suggestion.

When during the last few days somehow partition suddenly
became inevitable and votes veered round to it, owing to the pressure
of some of the powers, it was realised that the Indian solution was
probably the best and an attempt was made in the last 48 hours to
bring forward the Indian solution, not by us but by those who wanted
a unitary State. It was then too late.

I point this out to the House as an instance, that in spite of
considerable difficulty and being told by many of our friends on
either side that we must line up this way or that, we refused to do
so, and I have no doubt that the position we had taken was the right
one and I still have no doubt that it would have brought about the
best solution.[9]

It should be noted here that the creation of Israel had followed the partition
of the Indian subcontinent by just a few months, and this inevitably
influenced and shaped India's perceptions and policies towards the region
in general and towards Israel in particular.

When Israel applied to the UN for admission, the matter was put to the vote in the General Assembly on 11 May 1949. Israel was admitted to membership of the UN by 37 votes to 12 with nine abstentions. In addition to the six Arab states, India, Iran, Afghanistan, Pakistan, Ethiopia and Burma voted against the resolution. Explaining India's stand, the Indian delegate stated that "India could not recognise an Israel which had been achieved through the force of arms and not through negotiations."[10] India's reason for voting against Israel's admission to the UN is rather curious. It is an open secret that both the Arabs and Jews indulged in violence and terror. In fact, it was the Arabs who used armed force to overturn the UN's decision to partition Palestine, whereas Israel had accepted the decision.

Moreover, the state of Israel was a reality by then and could not be wished away. Hence, it would have been advisable for India to have either abstained or absented itself, rather than vote against Israel's admission. Such a decision would have been tactful, realistic and perhaps even fair. It is this ambivalence on the part of India which later led to diplomatic hair-splitting with regard to the recognition of Israel and the exchange of ambassadors, which should have followed each other logically.

Recognition issue

Once the state of Israel was proclaimed, its provisional government approached various countries, including India, for recognition in the middle of June 1948 and, according to Nehru, the government of India decided to "defer consideration of this question".[11] Explaining further, he said, "The obvious reasons were that a new State was formed and we had to wait. Normally we should have to be satisfied and know exactly what the international position is before taking any step."[12] It is obvious from the above that the Indian government delayed the recognition of Israel because the situation in the Middle East in relation to the Arab–Israeli dispute was still fluid and confusing. India thought it wise to delay the recognition rather than accord premature recognition to the Jewish state.

More importantly, India was aware of the hostile attitude of the Arab states to Israel and their refusal to recognize it. The Arab governments imposed economic sanctions against Israel, and Egypt maintained that it was in a state of war with Israel. Egypt also felt that "Recognition of Israel would encourage the Zionists to pursue their aggression and their incursions on Arab rights ...".[13] Moreover, India had hopes of co-ordinating her foreign policy pursuits with these countries in the interest of Afro-Asian solidarity.

India also had to contend with the emerging Pakistan factor, which, if not handled with care and delicacy, could complicate its relations with the Muslim Middle East. Pakistan refused to recognize Israel, and had declared that "recognition of Israel was constitutionally wrong and morally unjust".[14] Any hasty action on India's part could be used by Pakistan as a political stick with which to beat India.

Moreover, even after partition (and the communal holocaust that accompanied it), India was left with a large Muslim population which was still recovering from the physical and psychological wounds of partition and was going through an acute sense of insecurity. A Muslim member of the Indian Constituent Assembly pointedly asked Nehru whether he would keep the Muslim sentiments in view regarding the recognition of the state of Israel.[15] Nehru's reply was that the "Government have to keep in mind all the factors governing a particular situation".[16]

Answering another question in the Constituent Assembly in December 1949 on the same issue, Nehru explained the reasoning of his government: "The Government of India have had the question of the recognition of Israel under constant review. Israel is now a member of the United Nations and its recognition by other member States cannot obviously be indefinitely deferred."[17]

India's recognition of Israel eventually came on 17 September 1950, in the form of a terse one-liner from the government of India: "The Government of India has decided to accord recognition to the Government of Israel".[18] However, the government communiqué also contained a fairly detailed account of the factors and circumstances that prompted the Indian government to accord recognition to Israel. It was explained that "as in the case of Communist China, India's decision to recognize Israel is the recognition of an established fact".[19] For "the Government of Israel has been in existence for two years and there is no doubt that it is going to stay".[20]

Again, "India and Israel have been working together for the last two years in the United Nations and other international bodies, and Israel has been throughout this period collaborating with other members of the United Nations for furthering the cause of world peace and establishing better economic and social conditions in all parts of the world".[21] Hence, "continuing non-recognition is not only inconsistent with the overall relationship but even limits the effectiveness of the Government of India's role as a possible intermediary between Israel and the Arab states".[22]

Stating that "India will always value the friendship of Egypt and other Arab states" the government of India emphasized that "the recognition of

Israel does not mean that there is no difference between India's attitude and that of Israel over questions like the status of Jerusalem and Israel's frontiers. These questions would be judged by India on merit and due regard would be given to Arab claims."[23]

It is clear, therefore, that the delay in India's recognition of Israel had little to do with India's opposition to the partition of Palestine as imagined in some quarters. India had to take into consideration a number of factors, both internal and external, and weigh them in terms of its own national interests before it could cross the Rubicon. Hence, India's cautious and belated recognition of the Jewish state was both understandable and justified.[24]

Diplomatic relations

However, what cannot be easily understood or justified is, having recognized the state of Israel, that India refused to establish diplomatic relations with it, which was both illogical and ill-advised. Scholars like K.P. Mishra argued that India's recognition of Israel was a reflection of India's desire to "subscribe to the principle of defactoism even if it was at the risk of some misunderstanding or alienating the sympathies of some of her best friends in the world".[25] India, he further argued, made a distinction between "recognition as a legal act and the establishment of diplomatic relations as a purely political act ...",[26] presumably in deference to the sentiments of the Arab countries.

Nevertheless, it is not difficult to see that Mr. Mishra had adopted a purely legalistic approach to an essentially political question. This line of reasoning almost appears like a convenient after-thought. Moreover, it was neither consistent with the official communiqué issued by the government of India, nor with the subsequent behaviour of the Indian government which came very close to establishing diplomatic relations with Israel.

The communiqué itself referred to the Indo-Israeli co-operation in the UN and other international bodies to promote world peace, and to the possibility of India acting as a go-between between the two warring parties. The Indian government could not possibly have envisaged such a role for itself without the necessary diplomatic apparatus to facilitate such a process. In fact, India all but established full diplomatic relations with Israel in 1952. In early 1952, the Director-General of the Israeli Foreign Office, Mr. Walter Eytan, came to Delhi as a guest of the Indian government, and had negotiations with Indian officials about diplomatic relations between the two countries. Nehru agreed that it was time the issue was "reconsidered". In Mr. Eytan's own words ,

> Before Israel's representative left New Delhi, he was informed that
> the Prime Minister [Nehru] had approved the proposal.... . A draft
> budget for the Indian Legation was being prepared, though the
> formal decision to establish diplomatic relations still remained to
> be confirmed by the Cabinet. This was to be done as soon as the
> new Government was set up following the elections a few weeks
> later.[27]

However, nothing came of these talks and Eytan was left wondering as to
the reason for this "sudden change of mind" on the part of the Indian
government. Michael Brecher[28] unravelled this mystery almost a decade
later. According to him, it was Maulana Azad's "forceful intervention"
against normalizing relations with Israel that was responsible for India's
backtracking. Maulana was worried about the repercussions of such a move
in the Arab world, particularly at a time when the Kashmir dispute was
raging both in and outside the UN. Such a move could provide Pakistan
an opportunity to fish in troubled waters. He was also sensitive to the
unsettling effect it could have on the Indian Muslims. These were weighty
arguments and carried the day, probably against Nehru's own better
judgement and preference. However, an Israeli consul was permitted to
function in Bombay in 1953, but no counterpart was established in Israel.

Be that as it may, there is still no convincing explanation as to why
diplomatic relations were not established at the time of extending
recognition to Israel. Exchanging ambassadors two years after recognition
"would suggest a conscious act of friendship" and "this was precisely the
Indian error".[29] Both Nehru[30] and Krishna Menon[31] admitted as much,
but why it was not done is a question which probably will never be
answered, at least in a satisfactory manner.

This inexplicable slip looks all the more inexcusable, at least in
retrospect, for it pushed the Indian policy into a rut from which India
found it impossible to extricate itself over the years. In the process, India,
instead of playing a positive and purposeful role in the Middle East, seemed
to have settled down for something akin to diplomatic self-abnegation in
the region.

Nehru was half-apologetic when he tried to explain India's stand on
the issue again in 1958 at a press conference in New Delhi.

> This attitude was adopted after a careful consideration of the balance

of factors. It is not a matter of high principles, but it is based on how we could best serve and be helpful in the area ... . After careful thought, we felt that while recognising Israel as an entity, we need not at this stage exchange diplomatic personnel.[32]

While this attitude was certainly not a "matter of high principle", it is difficult to see how it was "based on how we could best serve and be helpful in that area". In fact, it made India forgo whatever leverage it had with Israel, foreclosed even the limited diplomatic options it had earlier, and reduced India to a passive spectator in the region.

While India has always had close bonds of friendship with the Muslim countries of the Middle East, it is not often emphasized that there was also much mutual admiration and goodwill between the Jewish and Indian leaders, in spite of India's opposition to the Zionist demand for a Jewish state and the subsequent partition of Palestine.

The Jewish leaders had great admiration and love for Indian leaders like Gandhi and Nehru. Gandhi was revered for his moral leadership and spiritual disposition. Gandhi had very close and trusted Jewish friends from his South African days, which prompted him to remark, "I am half a Jew myself." Some of them tried to win Gandhi's approval for the Zionist aspirations in Palestine, without much success.[33]

Nehru was admired because "his was the voice of rationalism, modernity, progress, and westernisation".[34] He had profound sympathy for the Jewish sufferings under Nazi tyranny. He also had entertained the "idea of starting a new university that would be staffed wholly or mainly by [Jewish] refugee intellectuals" in India. Unhappily enough, this idea proved to be a non-starter because of the lukewarm attitude of the British administration.[35]

There was also tremendous goodwill and affection for India among Jews in general because the Jewish communities which settled down in India over the centuries experienced no anti-Semitism whatsoever. This almost unique experience of Indian Jews endeared India to Jews the world over, and they looked up to India with gratitude and respect.[36]

There was also an ideological affinity between the ruling classes of the newly formed states of India and Israel. "Socialist Israeli leaders expected to find a common language with Asian socialist leaders such as Nehru and U Nu, and to open paths to them on the basis of their common socialist ideology."[37] In the early 50s, the socialist parties of Israel Mapai and Histadrut played a key role in forging ties between Asian leaders of similar ideological persuasions, which culminated in the first Asian Socialist

Conference in Rangoon in 1953 to which Israel was an invitee.

Moreover, there was some convergence of political outlook between Israel and the nonaligned stance that was being adopted by an increasing number of Afro-Asian countries, with India being one of its leading lights. By joining the Nonaligned Movement (NAM), "Israel hoped to rid itself of charges levelled against it by Nehru and other Asian leaders that Zionism came to Palestine under the protection of British bayonets", and "between 1948 and 1950 there was a marked preference among its leaders for pursuing a foreign policy independent of the two superpowers of the cold war".[38]

According to an Israeli scholar,[39] there were at least five general factors that moulded Israel's "attempt at maintaining an international orientation of nonalignment".

The first factor was "the recognition of the unity of the Jewish people, scattered throughout the world and in each of the two blocs, and the responsibility for its condition and fate".

The second was "the historic fact that the State of Israel had been established through the consent and support of both world blocs; Israel was to a certain extent grateful to both superpowers and anxious to sustain good relations with them in order to overcome the difficulties of realizing independence".

The third was "concern for world peace and the desire to abstain from encouraging great power rivalry by aligning itself with one of them".

The fourth was "the desire to maintain internal peace within the country's Labor movement". "Israel's extremely delicate situation during its formative years provoked fears within the leadership of a political conflict with the Israeli Left, which was viewed as an important political power... ." These fears necessitated attempts at "forming an undisputed basis for Israel's international policy".

The fifth and the last factor was "self-esteem". The "conception of ... a nation with its own morality and responsibility, seeking to be free of any external links so as to be able to choose its own path according to its own concepts, principles and aspirations".

The political line of nonalignment was thus motivated by a positive foreign policy consideration unlinked to international power combinations, as well as a pragmatic assessment of the current international constellation ... .

Israel hoped that nonalignment would open the door for her to the Afro-

Asian world. It would enable her to "combat growing political enmity and economic boycott practised against it by the Arab States", and "break through the wall of hostility which Arab States attempted to erect around its borders".[40]

Given all these factors, Israelis hoped that Nehru, a "non-Muslim but highly respected by the Arabs, would be willing and able to moderate Arab hostility and, perhaps, provide a bridge between Israelis and Arabs".[41]

However, that was not to be. India's decision not to establish diplomatic relations after recognizing Israel definitely impaired whatever chances there were for India's mediatory role in the region. This is in complete contrast to India's approach to China. In the case of China, India not only recognized China, to the obvious displeasure of the USA, but also went out of its way to facilitate its integration in the international community. The latter was done on the ground that isolating China would only drive it further into Russian hands.

The same logic was not applied in the case of Israel. It is difficult to envisage to what extent such a course would have helped the cause of peace in the region. However, the very fact that it was not given an honest chance is a misfortune in itself.

To be sure, at least a part of the responsibility for what happened lies on Israel's shoulders. At one stage India was prepared to accept Israel's representative in New Delhi, but Israel's insistence on reciprocity precluded any such possibility, which certainly was a mistake on Israel's part.[42]

There was another complication as well. Countries such as the USA and the USSR, which recognized Israel immediately after its creation, established their embassies in Tel Aviv. However, by the time India recognized Israel, Western Jerusalem had become its capital. Israel's insistence that all new embassies should be located in Jerusalem was not acceptable to India.[43]

It goes without saying that India could have established diplomatic relations with Israel. That it was not done proved to be a serious handicap in India's dealings with the region thereafter.[44] The passage of time only exacerbated the Arab-Israeli dispute. Gradually India ceased to be a factor in potentially the most destabilizing dispute in a region which was of utmost importance to India, as India found to its dismay at Bandung.

Bandung, 1955

The Bandung Conference of 1955 was a turning point in the history of Indo-Israeli relations, in the sense that it symbolized the culmination and crystallization of various undercurrents which affected them. The conference took place at Bandung in Indonesia from 18 to 24 April 1955. This Afro-Asian conference was sponsored by five countries, namely India, Indonesia, Pakistan, Ceylon (Sri Lanka) and Burma. They declared that all independent states would be invited.

However, it was decided to exclude Israel from the conference despite the fact that Israel was recognized by many states, including three of the sponsors, India, Burma and Ceylon.[45] The way this decision was arrived at was important because it set the pattern for almost all future Afro-Asian conferences in dealing with the Arab-Israeli dispute.

There were two informal meetings in Colombo (Ceylon) and Bogor (Indonesia),[46] which served as preparatory meetings for Bandung. At Colombo, the Pakistani Prime Minister, Mr. Muhammad Ali, introduced a draft resolution which described the creation of Israel as a violation of international law, condemned Israel's aggressive policy, and expressed concern over the plight of the Palestinian refugees.

Nehru, while sympathizing with the Arabs, pointed out that since India recognized Israel, he could not condemn it as a violation of international law. Moreover, the Pakistani resolution would adversely affect the UN's efforts to settle the dispute. After some debate, it was decided to delete two paragraphs from the Pakistani resolution and retain only the reference to the Palestinian refugees.

At Bogor, U Nu told Nehru that if Israel were not invited to Bandung, Burma might stay away. Nehru, while accepting that, on the basis of logical and geographic principle, Israel ought to be invited, pointed out that an Arab boycott of Bandung would mean that the whole of the Middle East would go unrepresented, in which case India should consider whether her own participation would be worthwhile.

Pakistan and Indonesia were strongly opposed to Israeli participation from the beginning. Burma was now rather subdued in her support for Israel. Ceylon was in favour of inviting Israel, and proposed that the Arabs should be "approached and reasoned with". Indonesia pointed out that the Arab League had already warned that an invitation to Israel would be considered an unfriendly act. Nehru summed up the discussion by saying that though such invitation might be justified, he did not think the matter should be pressed against the wishes of the Arab states. And so it was decided.

At the conference itself, Nehru maintained a very balanced approach to the Palestinian question, taking a principled stand and at the same time keeping India's interests in mind. First, he sought to relegate the religious factor to the background by emphasizing the political nature of the conflict. He also refrained from directly criticizing Israel. He told the delegates to understand "the forces behind the [Zionist] movement" and added, "Obviously it becomes a matter of power politics ...".[47] He also took exception to Mr. Ahmad Shukairy, a Palestinian (a member of the Syrian delegation), who, in the course of his speech, said that a negotiated settlement was not possible.[48]

The final communiqué issued after the conference had this to say on the Palestinian issue:

> In view of the existing tension in the Middle East, caused by the situation in Palestine, and of the danger of that tension to world peace, the Asian-African Conference declared its support of the rights of the Arab people of Palestine and called for the implementation of the United Nations resolutions on Palestine and the achievement of the peaceful settlement of the Palestine question.[49]

"Although the practical significance of this resolution was limited, the symbolic victory of the Arabs was not."[50] Nasser, who represented Egypt at Bandung, later remarked, "It is just a resolution. However, it has some moral value."[51]

Nevertheless, the Bandung Conference had some really important consequences for all the parties involved. Firstly, Israel was rejected as an Asian country by the majority of Afro-Asian countries. After Bandung, Israel had no chance whatsoever of participating in any of their official or unofficial gatherings.

> The Third World is regarded in Israel as a potentially powerful catalyst for effecting an Arab-Israel reconciliation. Friendly with both Israel and the Arab States, desirous of maintaining stable relations with both protagonists, basically unhampered by preconceptions or prejudices regarding either, and neutral in the dispute, Third World nations are seen in Jerusalem as a force which will provide moral backing for - indeed, will insist upon - the commencement of direct negotiations between the protagonists as a first stage toward conclusive peace agreements.[52]

The Bandung Conference put paid to any such hopes.

Secondly, as a logical consequence of this, Israel was also excluded from the NAM which was predominantly Afro-Asian and was formally launched in Belgrade in 1961. This in essence meant that the "no war-no peace" stance of the Arabs was acquiesced to (if not accepted) by the majority of Afro-Asian nations. This, in turn, sidelined both the nonaligned as a collectivity and India as a country (which was on good terms with both the Arabs and the Israelis) as possible mediators between the two antagonists. The result was a dangerous and potentially explosive deadlock.

Thirdly, it was also clear by then that the superpowers were trying to manipulate and exploit this dispute to further their own narrow interests in the region. A peaceful solution to the problem at this stage would not only have been easier, but it would also have minimized the chances of superpowers meddling in the affairs of the region (which again was the avowed objective of the NAM).

Nehru recognized this explosive situation, but expressed his helplessness to do anything to stop the rot in his talks with Brecher. It is worthwhile to quote at length Brecher's interview with Nehru.

NEHRU: It is not logical, my answer, but there it is. When the proposal was made for Israel to be invited … it transpired that if that were done the Arab countries would not attend … . We felt that logically Israel should be invited but when we saw that the consequences of that invitation would be that many others would not be able to come, then we agreed. Our approach … is that it is good for people who are opponents to meet.

BRECHER: Yes, but the Arabs have refused every invitation to sit and talk about the question of peace in West Asia.

NEHRU: It is obvious that there is the way of war to settle the question and, if you rule out war, then the only way is to meet - or allow things to drift.

BRECHER: But drift has the great risk surely that it may itself lead to war.

NEHRU: Yes, I know, but actually there is no other way.[53]

Therefore, the Bandung Conference only allowed "things to drift" with regard to the Middle East. Moreover, it had inadvertently contributed to the Palestine issue reaching a boiling point.

The impact of the Bandung Conference on Israel was "devastating". It felt both humiliated and isolated. As one high ranking Israeli official put it,

Bandung was our greatest diplomatic setback. It was the greatest trauma we ever suffered. That two and one-half billion people could be united in such a way against 1.8 million people in Israel was in itself soul-shattering to all of us in the Foreign Ministry.[54]

The general sense of insecurity and concern that enveloped Israel following the reverses it suffered in the international arena prompted Ben Gurion to return from his self-imposed seclusion and take over as Prime Minister from Sharett. Sharett was considered too "soft" in foreign affairs and was also thought to have placed too much faith in the UN and the major powers to ameliorate Israel's deteriorating security environment. "The change in leadership was interpreted at home and abroad as signifying a stiffening of foreign policy and a more aggressive Israeli stand on all fronts."[55] Consequently, the year 1956 saw an "agonizing reappraisal" of Israel's foreign policy so that the future policy would be "geared to facts, not hopes".

In the long run, the reappraisal brought about powerful diplomatic drives upon Afro-Asia. In the short run, it dictated a stiffening of Israel's policy *vis-à-vis* her neighbours, which led directly to the 1956 Sinai Campaign [the Suez crisis], designed to extricate her from the unendurable daily provocations and an adverse balance of power.[56]

The Suez Crisis, 1956

The Suez Crisis of 1956 constituted a watershed in India's relations with Israel. Here, we will confine our analysis to the impact this crisis had on Indo–Israeli relations.[57]

When the USA and the UK withdrew their offer of assistance to the construction of the Aswan Dam, Egypt reacted by nationalizing the Suez Canal. While efforts were still under way to settle the dispute, Israeli forces invaded Sinai on 29 October 1956. To make things worse, Israel was joined in this venture by the UK and France a few days later, in accordance with the prior understanding reached with Israel.

India's reaction to this development was sharp and forthright. An official statement issued on 31 October denounced Israeli aggression as a flagrant violation of the UN Charter, and in opposition to all the principles laid down in the Bandung Conference.[58] Nehru publicly branded Israeli action as "clear naked aggression", and was critical of the British and French backing it received.[59]

Whatever might have been the provocations, the open Israeli attack on

Egypt created much anger and resentment in India. The fact that Israel collaborated with ex-colonial powers like the UK and France in attacking a Third World country dissipated whatever sympathy and understanding the Indian leadership and the intelligentsia had had for Israel. The attack also gave credence to certain notions which existed in certain quarters in the Afro-Asian world about Israel. It reinforced the view that Israel was an outpost of Western imperial interests, and that it was essentially a European country in the wrong continent.

Nevertheless, the Suez Crisis did have a silver lining as far as India was concerned. India's posture towards Israel till then was rather inconsistent and awkward. "Indian attitudes subsequent to 1956 almost betrayed a sense of relief that what was an uncomfortable posture could now be continued with a feeling of moral righteousness."[60]

The Suez Crisis came at a particularly awkward moment for Israel. It took place on the very day the former Israeli Foreign Minister, Moshe Sharett, met[61] with Nehru in New Delhi. Sharett himself was strongly against the Sinai campaign but, having presented with a *fait accompli*, he had no choice but to defend Israel's action. Regardless of the merits or otherwise of the Israeli Sinai campaign, one unfortunate outcome of this action was that whatever possibility that might have existed for full diplomatic relations between India and Israel had now definitely receded.

The Israelis, for their part, were not exactly amused by the vacillation and ambivalence that characterized the Indian government's approach to the Jewish state. They found the Indian attitude to Israel to be at variance with what India had been preaching in international forums, like friendship with all, judging issues on their merits and accepting political facts of life. Their disappointment in Nehru was intense; it was as if their personal trust in him was shattered. Ben Gurion made a pointed reference to this when he said:

> I cannot understand how Mr. Nehru fits his behaviour to Israel with Gandhi's philosophy of universal friendship. Mr. Nehru gave definite promises to the Director-General of our Foreign Ministry eight years ago that he would soon establish normal diplomatic relations with Israel, but so far he has not kept his word.[62]

Later, in an article reviewing Israel's position in world politics, Ben Gurion was sharply critical of Nehru.

Nehru too claims allegiance to neutrality .... He is not even neutral in regard to Israel and the Arabs, for he has close ties and normal relations with the Arab countries but he has stubbornly refused to establish diplomatic relations with Israel, and in his frequent visits to the Middle East he has on every occasion - and not by accident - overlooked Israel.[63]

At this juncture, it must be emphasized that "difficulties of finance and personnel" were never the consideration in India not establishing diplomatic relations with Israel. Nor was it ever the thought that Israel was not important enough for India to have fully-fledged diplomatic ties, as alleged in some quarters.[64]

Covert contacts

It was India's inability or unwillingness to take initiative of any sort or adopt a more active diplomatic posture towards the Arab-Israeli dispute that more or less compelled it to keep its relationship with Israel under wraps. Whatever may have been India's official and public posture towards Israel over the decades, there is no gainsaying that India has always maintained a working but covert relationship with the Jewish state.

Surprisingly enough, there have been extensive contacts between the two countries - official and private - at various levels.[65] This in itself is ample proof of the fact that Israel is not as insignificant a factor in India's policy calculations as it appears. To dismiss Israel as expendable to India's policy concerns in the Middle East seems to be a mere rationalization at best.

After Israeli Foreign Minister Moshe Sharett's secret visit to India in 1956, another approach was made to Nehru in Washington by the then Israeli Foreign Minister, Abba Eban in, 1960. Nothing came of this meeting either.

It was about this time that the Israeli Foreign Office instructed its officials not to broach the subject of diplomatic relations with their Indian counterparts again. As Yaakov Shimoni, the Deputy Director-General of the Israeli Foreign Ministry, explained, "Until then our policy was to ask for an exchange of ambassadors on every possible occasion ... but we have some pride left ... . We were tired of being told, 'Please do not worry us' and being put off repeatedly."[66]

The next important contact between the two countries was at the time of the Sino–Indian war of 1962. The Indian military debacle shook Nehru, and in his hour of need he turned to Israel.[67] India mainly sought light mortars of 81 and 120 millimetres from Israel. Even in times of such grave national crisis, New Delhi could not get over her self-imposed inhibitions with regard to Arab sensitivities to such a deal.

Hence, Israel was asked if the weapons could be delivered in ships that did not fly the Israeli flag. Ben Gurion's blunt reply was, "No flag, no weapons." In the end, the Israeli cargo ship *Jarden* arrived in Bombay with "automatic rifles, mortars, grenades, etc.". The Israelis, for their part, imposed no preconditions such as exchange of ambassadors, and responded promptly to the Indian call for help.

In January 1963, the then Chief of the Indian Army, General J.N. Chaudhuri, invited his Israeli counterpart, General Shateel, and the Chief of Military Intelligence, who were on an official visit to Burma, to visit New Delhi on their way back for an exchange of views following India's military debacle against China. This could not possibly have been done without Nehru's knowledge and approval.[68]

Again, India received a modest amount of military hardware from Israel during the 1965 war over Kashmir with Pakistan. According to Israeli Consul-General Yaakov Morris, Israel supplied heavy mortars to India during the conflict. He also said that Israel supported India's case on Kashmir, and recalled the Israeli stand in the UN that Kashmir belonged to India. He offered transit facilities through Israel for Indian trade with the West which could save India Rs 38 crores a year in freight charges. He further said that Israel would appreciate any Indian efforts to bring Israel and the Arabs to the conference table for direct negotiations.[69]

Moments of pettiness

While India maintained covert contacts with Israel ever since her creation, its public stance *vis-à-vis* Israel often lacked diplomatic finesse, and at times almost bordered on pettiness and uncivility.

For instance, the Israeli Consul in Bombay wanted to hold the National Day reception of his country in New Delhi in April 1964. But the Indian government refused him permission on the ground that he would exceed his functions as Consul in Bombay.

The establishment of the Indo-Israeli Friendship Society in August 1964 annoyed the Arabs. In October of the same year, the presence of an office bearer (Miss Romila Thapar) of the Indo-Israeli Friendship Society at a dinner given by the Ministry of External Affairs (in honour of a Lebanese newspaper editor) led to a walkout of the Ambassadors of Lebanon, Iraq and Morocco, and the Arab League representative. The Lebanese Ambassador was later summoned by the Ministry of External Affairs and questioned about his undiplomatic action in leading the walkout.[70]

In May 1966, the Food and Agriculture Minister, Mr. C. Subramaniam, told the Lok Sabha that Israel had offered to supply fertilizers to India but India declined the offer because of "political considerations". On being asked whether people should be allowed to starve because of the government's politics, he replied "We had to take into account other reactions. In the judgement of the Government, we thought we need not accept it."[71]

Reacting sharply to the above incident, *The Times of India* editorially commented that India's handling of the Israeli offer showed "a deplorable lack of finesse". "In fairness to Arab countries, it must be mentioned that there is no reason to believe that they would have attributed sinister motives to such an innocent and marginal contact with Israel." It advised the government that its policy should be based on "mature considerations and not on inhibitory fears".[72]

Again in 1966, the Calcutta police permitted Arab demonstrations to come close to Israeli President Shazar, who was passing through India on an official visit to Nepal. The Indian government refused to let President Shazar rest overnight in New Delhi, and sent no official to greet him at the airport when his plane stopped for refuelling.[73] There was an outcry both in the Lok Sabha and in the Indian press over the "curt and uncivil treatment" meted out to the Israeli President by the Indian government.[74]

It is difficult to imagine the possible motives behind the actions of the Indian government in the series of incidents narrated above. It could not possibly be attributed to India's abhorrence of Israeli policies, for India always had a working private relationship with Israel. If it was meant to please the Arabs, then it was an insult to Arab intelligence, for the Arab states themselves always weighed their actions in terms of their concrete national interests and not in terms of petty and frivolous considerations. Perhaps the more probable explanation for these indefensible, inexplicable and almost laughable actions of the Indian government was its extreme self-consciousness and timidity in its dealings with the region in general and with the Arab–Israeli dispute in particular.

The Arab–Israeli War, 1967

The uneasy and fragile peace that obtained in the Middle East after the Suez Crisis could not have been maintained indefinitely. It needed but a mere spark to set off the powder keg which the region had become on account of the Arab–Israeli dispute.

The recurring Syrian commando raids into Israel provoked an Israeli threat of retaliation in May 1966. This, in turn, led to Damascus invoking the military pact it had signed with Egypt in 1966. Nasser responded by saying that the UAR would fight if Israel attacked Syria.

Meanwhile, the UN Secretary-General, U Thant, flew to Cairo for discussions with the leaders of the UAR on 21 May. Then came the UAR's decision to close the Gulf of Aqaba to Israeli shipping and to other shipping carrying strategic goods for Israel. And the die was cast.

On 6 June the Israeli Air Force, in a pre-emptive strike, more or less destroyed the UAR Air Force in a couple of hours. This was followed by a rout of the Arab armies by the Israeli forces. In the six days that the war lasted, the Israelis seized the Sinai, Gaza, the Golan Heights, the West Bank and East Jerusalem from the Arabs.

The way the Indian government handled this crisis generated much heat and controversy within the government, in the Parliament and in the national press. On 25 May 1967, the Minister of External Affairs, Mr. Chagla, made a statement in both Houses of Parliament. The first sentence he uttered - "The creation of Israel has given rise to tension between Israel and the Arab countries"[75] - caused much resentment. Some members interpreted it to mean that he was questioning the very existence of Israel.

Regarding the closure of the Gulf of Aqaba, he said that the Indian government had accepted that "the Gulf of Aqaba is an inland sea and that the entry to the Gulf lies within the territorial waters of UAR and Saudi Arabia".[76] Mr. Chagla seemed to acknowledge implicitly and justify the UAR's right to close the Gulf of Aqaba to Israel.

Addressing the Lok Sabha again in July 1967, Mr. Chagla justified his statement about the creation of Israel by saying that it was a "factual statement", and reminded the members that India had recognized Israel.[77]

Regarding the Gulf of Aqaba (i.e. whether it was in the territorial waters of the UAR or whether it was an international waterway), Mr. Chagla quoted statements made by Mr. Dulles in 1957 and by the British Foreign Secretary, Mr. George Brown, in 1967 to justify the Indian government's stand.[78]

What Mr. Chagla seemed conveniently to forget was the fact that the issue, by then, had gone beyond legal semantics, and that the closing of the Gulf of Aqaba could have meant cutting off Israel's lifeline. How long could Israel have tolerated such a situation to continue while waiting for international mediation to solve the problem is anybody's guess. There could be very little doubt that it was Nasser's rash action of closing the Gulf of Aqaba that precipitated the crisis which resulted in another Arab military debacle. However, Mrs. Gandhi seemed completely impervious to this reality when she told the Lok Sabha on 6 June 1967,

> I do not wish to utter harsh words or use strong language. But on
> the basis of information available there can be no doubt that Israel
> has escalated the situation into an armed conflict, which has now
> acquired the proportions of a full-scale war.[79]

The attitude of the Indian government to the conflict predictably came
under severe attack from the opposition. These opposition parties had
their own reasons for being critical of the government's blatantly pro-
Arab policy.[80] What did come as a surprise, though, was the fact that

> Dissatisfaction with the West Asia policy is as widespread as it is
> strong. It is by no means confined to the ranks of the opposition
> … . Even within the Cabinet's Foreign Affairs Committee, serious
> doubts were expressed by some of the most senior Ministers before
> they agreed to the policy statement eventually made by Mrs. Gandhi
> in Parliament … . The angularities, excesses and distortions of the
> West Asia policy have apparently become the enemy of its pith and
> substance.[81]

On 20 July, it was reported that there were sharp exchanges between Mrs.
Gandhi and the members of the Congress Party Parliamentary Executive
over the government's Middle Eastern policy. The issue became so
contentious that Mrs. Gandhi felt compelled to threaten a General Election
to demonstrate popular support for her government's Middle Eastern
policy. A couple of days later, amid rumours of opposition to her Middle
Eastern policy from Morarji Desai and Swaran Singh, Mrs. Gandhi denied
that there was a rift in the Cabinet over the issue.[82] Nevertheless, "enough
had happened to indicate that opposition to the Government's Middle
East policy was sufficiently widespread to bring its very existence into
jeopardy".[83]

Moreover, this was the first time that there was such extensive criticism
both by the press and the public about the Indian government's attitude
to the Arab-Israeli dispute. All the major newspapers were critical of India's
unqualified and unwarranted support of reckless Arab actions, such as
ordering the withdrawal of the UNEF and the closing of the Gulf of Aqaba
which precipitated the crisis and made conflict inevitable.[84]

To cap it all, India chose to play a partisan role in the UN in favour of
the Arabs in spite of the fact that it was one of the non-permanent members

of the Security Council at that time. India's Permanent Representative, Mr. G. Parthasarathy, more or less endorsed the Arab and particularly the UAR's position in the dispute,[85] and placed the responsibility for the "grave situation" prevailing in the Middle East "squarely on Israel".[86] India also introduced a draft resolution[87] along with Mali and Nigeria. It envisaged Israeli withdrawal from occupied territories, the right of every state to live in peace and security, a just settlement of the question of Palestine refugees, and freedom of navigation in accordance with international law in the area.

The Israeli Foreign Minister, Mr. Abba Eban, predictably rejected the Indian resolution on the grounds that it was formulated without consulting Israel, and that it prejudiced Israel's negotiating position in advance. "The suggestion that Israel should move from the ceasefire lines without a peace treaty defining permanent and secure frontiers is unacceptable," he said.[88]

It is difficult to believe that India expected Israel to take this resolution seriously, as a possible basis for solving its dispute with the Arabs. To expect Israel to withdraw from occupied lands without an overall settlement is rather naive. In fact, this is in complete contrast to India's own approach to regaining the territory it lost to China during the Sino–Indian war of 1962. It is possible that the resolution was intended more as a demonstration of India's support for the Arab cause than as a fair and realistic basis for negotiation.

Incidentally, it may be of interest to note that Syria off-handedly rejected the Indian resolution on the Middle East, together with that of the USA. Both these drafts were unacceptable to Syria because they subjected Israeli withdrawal to conditions.[89]

India was much more directly involved in the six-day war than in any other Middle Eastern conflict. Apart from the fact that India was one of the non-permanent members of the Security Council at the time of the conflict, an Indian, Major-General Inder Jit Rikhye, commanded the UN Emergency Force in the Gaza and Sinai, and a battalion of the Indian Army was a part of that force. When the fighting broke out on 5 June, the Indian contingent came under artillery fire and strafing from the Israelis (in all probability, by mistake).[90] 14 Indian soldiers were killed, 21 wounded and 19 reported missing. Mrs. Gandhi described these attacks as "deliberate and without provocation", and asked the House to "unreservedly condemn this cowardly attack".[91]

There can be little doubt that this incident cost Israel considerable sympathy in India. However, there was opposition to a move in Parliament to condemn this attack on the ground that Indian troops should have been withdrawn from the battle zone earlier. Later, the Israeli government expressed condolence and offered to pay compensation, but the Indian government rejected both offers.

Purely from a military point of view, though, Israeli achievements in the brief war seemed to have impressed quite a few Indians. The Indian Defence Minister, Swaran Singh, told the Lok Sabha that

> India is deeply impressed by the achievements of the Israeli armed forces and particularly their tactic of speedy mobilization at extremely short notice. It was, therefore, keen to find out how Israel had been able to mobilize her entire force in less than 24 hours and in such a manner that it ensured positive results.[92]

Major Ranjit Singh, a member of Lok Sabha and founder member of the Indian Parliamentary Defence Council, visited Israel for an on-the-spot study of the six-day war. He recommended a defence system similar to that of Israel, against China and Pakistan.[93]

The Arab military debacle only reinforced Arab intransigence and hostility towards Israel. The Arab summit in Khartoum in August 1967 passed a resolution which contained three "Nos": No recognition, No negotiation, and No peace with Israel. Politically, the Arab-Israeli dispute was back to square one.

Notwithstanding the publicly partisan attitude of the Indian government during the 1967 Arab-Israeli war, India maintained cordial but low-key contacts with Israel thereafter. Though India always maintained that its support for the Arabs was based on the merits of their case and was independent of other considerations, the fact of the matter was that India always expected a *quid pro quo* from the Arabs in terms of their support for Pakistan (in relation to its dispute with India).

After the Rabat fiasco in 1969, the Indian Foreign Minister, Dinesh Singh, had a half-hour meeting with the Israeli Foreign Minister, Abba Eban, at the latter's request in New York on 3 October 1969. The meeting was primarily intended to underscore the point that friendship implied "reciprocity" to those Arab countries which sided with Pakistan to keep India out of the Islamic Summit in Rabat.[94] However, the fact that India's insistence on Arab "reciprocity" found no takers in the Arab world was clearly demonstrated within a couple of years, during the crisis in the eastern wing of Pakistan.

The Bangladesh crisis, as it came to be known later, and the lack of understanding shown by the Middle Eastern countries to the influx of millions of refugees into India (following the military crackdown in East Pakistan) once again brought under the microscope India's policy towards the region, especially India's relations with Israel.

Israel's response to the crisis was prompt and predictable for obvious reasons. Dr. Dov B. Schmorak, the Director of Foreign Publicity of the government of Israel, said at a news conference in New Delhi that Israel had great sympathy for the sufferings of the people of Bangladesh. He also pointed out that Israel had already announced its decision to extend aid for the relief fund. He added for good measure that Israel would welcome the establishment of diplomatic relations with India.[95]

Amid reports that the Indian government was reconsidering her Middle East policy on account of the attitude of the countries of that region towards the Bangladesh issue, the Indian Foreign Minister, Swaran Singh, told the Rajya Sabha in July that there was no change in India's support for the Palestinian cause, because India's stand on the issue was in consonance with "justice and the facts of the situation".[96]

During the war, India received some military hardware and logistical support from Israel. According to Dr. Swamy, D.P. Dhar "organised a certain crucial weapons" import from Israel.[97]

In January 1972, India scotched all rumours that it was going to establish diplomatic relations with Israel. An official spokesman described the rumours as "totally false and baseless". However, one cannot help wondering why the Indian government chose not to upgrade its relations with Israel during the Bangladesh crisis. This would have been a diplomatic slap in the face for the Arabs not to take India's support for granted. Public opinion in India, generally speaking, would have welcomed such a move.

The press was certainly critical of the treatment meted out to Israel. One newspaper commented that India's policy reflected "neither the realities of power in the area nor the civilities of customary diplomatic behaviour" but only the "myopia of a lobby in South Block".[98] Another opined that

> India will benefit more through opening up its options in West Asia. It is an overdue move and if in making it our relations with some of the Arab states suffer a temporary setback well then, isn't India strong enough to take that in her stride?[99]

Obviously, the Indian government considered discretion to be the better part of valour and chose not to take the plunge. Looking back, it looks as though it was a good opportunity that India let go. Consequently, India was hardly in any position to do anything positive or constructive when the Arab-Israeli stalemate was shattered in October 1973 by the booming Arab guns.

The Yom Kippur War, 1973
When Egypt and Syria launched a simultaneous and surprise attack on Israel on 7 October 1973, the Indian government reacted in a way which had almost become customary by now.

> The Government have consistently declared that the cause of the tension in the area is due to Israeli aggression and refusal to vacate territories occupied by armed force. This intransigence on the part of Israel is clearly the basic cause leading to the present outbreak of hostilities. Our sympathies are entirely with the Arabs whose sufferings have long reached a point of explosion.[100]

India's Permanent Representative at the UN, Samar Sen, demanding the withdrawal of Israel from occupied territories, stated that "it will be both unfair and unjust for the Council to ask for a ceasefire, which will leave vast territories of Egypt, Jordan and Syria in the illegal occupation of Israel".[101]

India's stand once again reflected total support for the Arabs and conveniently ignored certain unpleasant facts in relation to the conflict. While Israeli intransigence was berated, no reference was made to the Arab refusal to negotiate. The fact that the Arabs had initiated the hostilities was by-passed. Moreover, India's stand at the UN seemed to justify the Arab use of force to regain the lost territory.

Suffice to say that India's stand on the issue was neither constructive nor realistic. It once again betrayed a desire to curry favour with the Arabs by assuming a vociferously pro-Arab stand with little regard to the facts of the situation; a tendency which it displayed again when it chose to side with the Arabs in branding Zionism a form of racism at the UN a couple of years later.

It goes without saying that India made a major blunder in 1975 by voting for the UN General Assembly resolution No. 3379 which determined that "Zionism is a form of racism and racial discrimination"[102] at the 2400th Plenary meeting on 10 November 1975. India always maintained that the Arab-Israeli dispute was a political one, which was consistent with her own secular approach to politics. It also de-emphasized the importance of religion in Middle Eastern politics, which again was in her own enlightened self-interest.

Hence, it would have been more prudent and more consistent with her own stand if India had either abstained or even absented itself from voting. By voting for the resolution, India had diluted her own principled stand on the issue, and made a mockery of her own long-term interests. The explanation of India's Ambassador to the USA, T.N. Kaul, that Indian support for the resolution was not an act against Israel or the Jews but a protest against what he termed "anti-Arabism",[103] sounds rather unconvincing and simplistic.

The Janata government and Israel

When the first non-Congress government was formed in New Delhi in 1977 following Mrs. Gandhi's electoral debacle, hopes were raised of a fresh look at the successive Congress governments' foreign policy. The fact that the Janata Party, during its election campaign, promised to subscribe to "genuine nonalignment" gave rise to such speculation. When a former Jana Sanghite and vocal critic of traditional Indian policy towards the Middle East, Mr. A.B. Vajpayee, took over as Foreign Minister, expectations rose even further. However, the Janata Party's foreign policy initiatives, such as they were, proved to be "much ado about nothing".

The Israeli Foreign Minister, Moshe Dayan, paid a secret visit to India in August 1977.[104] Dayan met both Morarji and Vajpayee. Morarji reiterated India's traditional stand on the Middle East, saying that Israel should withdraw from occupied territories, which should be proclaimed a Palestinian state. Regarding diplomatic relations, he said that it should have been done at the time of recognition and he could not do it now. He further said that he would be out of office if Dayan's visit became public but he took the risk for the sake of peace. Then Moshe Dayan raised a very pertinent point.

Now, when his [Morarji's] help was needed on behalf of peace, he could do nothing, since he had no diplomatic relations with Israel; and once peace was attained, and India were to establish such relations, its help would no longer be necessary.[105]

However, it must be admitted that the Janata government was in no position to take such a momentous decision, for it was a weak coalition government. Only a strong, cohesive and confident government could have made such a major foreign policy decision. Besides, the Foreign Minister, Vajpayee, was a former member of the Jana Sang and, as a member of the opposition, was a vocal critic of the Congress Party's Middle East policy. When he took over as Foreign Minister, he was very much on the defensive in relation to the Middle East, and bent over backwards to assure the Arabs of continued Indian support. More importantly, India's economic stake in the region had increased substantially after the oil boom, and the Janata government was understandably loth to do anything that might jeopardize it.

When Sadat's initiative broke the decades of diplomatic silence between the Arabs and Israel, and led to the signing of the Camp David Accord, the Janata government's reaction was extremely cautious and muted. Vajpayee stated at a press conference that India did not welcome it because Palestine was the hard core of the Middle Eastern problem, and there could be no peace unless the rights of the Palestinians were restored.[106] A few weeks later, the Janata government extended qualified support to Camp David, saying that it "cannot but commend the efforts to bring about a peaceful solution to the problems of an area which has seen dangerous conflicts".[107]

However, the proof of India's real appreciation of the signing of the Camp David Accord came later when India firmly opposed the move by some Arab countries to expel Egypt from the NAM for signing a separate peace treaty with Israel. Morarji told Cuba that he would stay away from the Havana Summit if any effort was made to exclude Egypt from the conference.[108]

The Janata government's contacts with Israel continued even after Dayan's visit to India. When Morarji went to London to attend the Commonwealth Conference, he met the Israeli Defence Minister, Weizman, who urged closer contacts between the two countries. The Israelis offered their military technology to India, including the Mirage III, the Kaffir jet fighters and the Merkevah tanks, through third countries. V. Shankar, the Principal Private Secretary to the Prime Minister, visited Israel for four days in early 1979 to explore this offer. But no deal could be struck because the Janata government fell in July 1979.[109]

But Dayan's visit to India remained a secret till Mrs. Gandhi made it public in early 1980, after she returned to power following the collapse of the Janata government. At a press conference[110] Vajpayee said that he had earlier denied the visit in the "national interest". "I am also constrained to say that the closest relationship between the two countries was in 1962, 1965 and 1971 and not during my tenure in the external affairs Ministry," he added. However, according to Dr. Swamy, Mrs. Gandhi's government did not snap the links with Israel established by the Janata government.

Defence deals worth about Rs 60 crores were negotiated with Israel through third-party contacts.

Israeli invasion of Lebanon, 1982

The Israeli invasion of Lebanon in June 1982 brought about a strong condemnation from India. Mrs. Gandhi minced no words when she told the Lok Sabha on 9 July 1982: "This Israeli action is a flagrant violation of all canons of international law and behaviour. It is indicative of an arrogance which has shown callous disregard for the rights of other nations and peoples." She called upon "nations who are in a position to influence Israel to take immediate steps to lift the siege of West Beirut and withdraw its troops to its own territory".[111] India also rushed medicines, medical equipment and foodstuffs to Lebanon. Two medical teams were sent to Damascus to render aid to the injured.

The Pakistani bomb and Indo-Israeli cooperation

Even before India's virulent criticism of Israel's invasion of Lebanon had died down, there were reports in the international press that India and Israel were in touch with each other, because of their mutual concern about Pakistan's nuclear programme. It was reported that Israel was worried that Pakistan might pass on its nuclear technology to its Arab friends.

Mrs. Gandhi, the report said, seriously considered a pre-emptive strike against Pakistan's nuclear targets in 1982, but decided against it because of the fear that Pakistan would inflict equal damage to Indian nuclear installations. Indian officials were quite dismissive about such speculation, but reports persisted that India and Israel had held secret discussions about Pakistan's nuclear progress.[112]

It is difficult to vouch for the authenticity or otherwise of these rumours. However, going by past experience, it is fairly likely that there could have been some sort of cooperation between the two countries in monitoring Pakistan's nuclear programme, and in coordinating their security policies to counter this potential and mutual threat. It is plausible that this was one of the reasons why Mrs. Gandhi's government resisted strong pressures, both from the Arab ambassadors and in the Parliament, to close down the Israeli Consulate in Bombay in 1981.[113]

Indo-Israeli relations: a reappraisal

India's lack-lustre and low-key policy towards Israel ever since its creation is just an element of India's generally timid and passive posture towards the Middle East as a whole, and is not a result of any unfriendly feelings towards the Jewish state. The creation of Pakistan and its efforts to cultivate its co-religionists in the Middle East in the name of Islamic solidarity put Indian policy-makers on the defensive from the word go.

The fact that the Muslims constitute the predominant section of the inhabitants in the region led to the belief that supporting the Muslim Arab states against the Jewish state of Israel *per se* would be sufficient to promote India's interests. Implicit in it was the assumption that conflicts in West Asia were virtually coterminous with the Arab-Israeli conflict.[114]

Consequently, India's policy towards Israel tended to become more and more of a by-product of such an attitude. India, having recognized Israel, refused to establish diplomatic relations with it, ostensibly in deference to Arab sentiments. Thus India, consciously or unconsciously, started using Indo-Israeli relations to balance Pakistani-Arab relations, and as a result India's policy towards Israel was cast in a very rigid mould. This is very obvious from the way the Indian government, over the years, made subtle threats to upgrade its relations with Israel whenever it felt slighted by the Arabs.

However, it cannot be "reasonably argued that India obtained a *quid pro quo* from the Arab countries in her disputes with Pakistan. As a matter of fact, none of the Arab countries, including Egypt, ever supported India on the issue of Kashmir."[115] On the other hand, "It is also entirely possible that if Indian policy had been more flexible and imaginative at certain crucial stages ... India might have been instrumental in bridging the gap between the Arabs and the Israelis."[116]

It is highly doubtful that the Arabs would have reacted harshly and concertedly if India had exchanged ambassadors with Israel at the time of recognition. After all, the Arabs have been doing business with scores of other countries that have had diplomatic relations with Israel. Nor was India an insignificant and nondescript country for the Arabs just to brush her aside. On the whole, however, Indians were aware of the importance and usefulness of contacts with Israel. Hence, they followed a dual policy towards it: private contact with and public denunciation of Israel.

Whatever little balance India had displayed in its relations with Israel simply disappeared with the emergence of Mrs. Gandhi on the Indian political scene. Her domestic electoral strategy of cultivating the depressed classes and minorities, particularly Muslims, as her "vote-banks" contributed in no small measure to this development. Mrs. Gandhi, instead of addressing the real problems and fears that haunted the Indian Muslims and trying to solve them on a long-term basis, adopted a vociferously pro-Palestinian and overtly anti-Israeli stance in order to gain the support of the Indian Muslims on the cheap. According to one scholar, "The first five months of Mrs. Gandhi's Premiership were marked by an unmistakable hardening of this [anti-Israeli] attitude in comparison not only with the Nehru era but even with the immediately preceding Shastri regime."[117]

The verbal excesses that India has committed in criticizing Israel and supporting the Arabs helped neither. Supporting the Arabs against Israel is a negative way of earning their goodwill. Moreover, it cannot go on for ever. India can and should base her relationships with the Middle Eastern countries on a more positive and concrete basis. Nor should India allow the Arab-Israeli dispute to dominate its thinking towards the Middle East. An overtly anti-Israeli stance in no way benefits the Indian Muslims. The policies pursued by successive governments have made India irrelevant in the region - ignored by Israel and taken for granted by the Arabs.

Whatever may have been the compulsions of such a policy in the 1950s and 60s, it cannot be justified in the 1970s and 80s, when the strategic environment in subcontinental, regional and global terms has undergone radical changes.

After the Bangladesh war in 1971, the balance of power shifted decisively in favour of India in the subcontinent, and Pakistan's pretensions to parity with India were finally laid to rest. India has been in a much more confident frame of mind in relation to its security concerns regarding Pakistan ever since.

Pakistan itself has moved closer to the Middle Eastern countries, particularly Iran and Saudi Arabia, since its dismemberment. The Soviet invasion of Afghanistan in 1979 made Pakistan a frontline state and a recipient of massive American military and economic aid. With the threat of an Islamic bomb looming large over the horizon, India cannot but consider Israel as a potential ally in any future dealings with the Middle East.

The attitude of the Arab countries themselves towards Israel has undergone changes in the 1970s. After the Camp David Accord in 1978, Egypt normalized its relations with Israel. Without Egypt, the Arab military option against Israel is non-existent. Saudi Arabia, along with Israel, has been part of the American strategic consensus against the USSR. The Fahd Plan has implicitly acknowledged the existence of Israel as a state too. With its enormous wealth, Saudi Arabia will wield considerable influence in the region for a long time to come, and, given its political preferences, it is most likely to use this influence on the side of moderation and reconciliation. Iran's relations with Israel under the Shah were good though not publicized. Khomeini's Iran even bought arms from Israel for its war with Iraq.

There have been reports that China has been importing arms and technology from Israel.[118] The USSR, too, softened its attitude towards Israel in the 1980s.[119] It exchanged consular delegations with Israel, and also adopted a liberal policy in relation to Jewish emigration from the USSR.

Even the Palestine Liberation Organization's attitude to Israel has undergone a remarkable change over the last two decades. Under Arafat's charismatic, moderate and pragmatic leadership, the PLO's approach to Israel has softened over the years, and is now much more conciliatory and realistic.[120]

Besides, Israel has been one of the most powerful and stable countries in the region over the last two decades or so. Any policy which fails to take cognizance of this simple truth is doomed to failure. In short, the power realities in the region by themselves necessitate a reorientation of India's policy towards the region in general and Israel in particular.

Given the nature of the American political system, the Jewish lobby in the USA will continue to wield political influence which will be out of all proportion to its numbers. India would be well advised to take advantage of this peculiarly American phenomenon and have the Jewish lobby on its side.[121] This would facilitate India's dealings with the USA, and also counter whatever influence Pakistan has built up in the US Congress and outside over the years. Apart from increased trade, India can also benefit from Israel's experience in drip irrigation, desalination, horticulture, poultry farming, solar energy and medicine. Indian policy-makers over the years have shown a remarkable lack of sensitivity to the changing scenario in the region, and seem to have been obsessed with playing it safe all the time. By and large, India has failed to develop a well-thought-out, balanced and integrated approach to the Middle East. Its approach to the region has been piecemeal in nature, smacking of ad hocism, and suffering from inexplicable political diffidence and self-consciousness.

This is nowhere better demonstrated than in India's relations with Israel over the decades. It is nothing less than scandalous that India failed to include Israel as an integral part of its policy towards a region which has been of the utmost importance to her from the beginning. India's claims to regional preponderance will sound rather hollow if it fails to act with confidence and imagination in a region where it has so much at stake.

This is not to advocate that India should immediately upgrade its relations with Israel. The change should be gradual and incremental, and can be done, perhaps, even with the prior consultation of India's Arab friends. That way, India would regain its leverage with Israel, and serve its own enlightened interests as well as those of the Arabs in general and the Palestinians in particular, much more positively and effectively than she was able to in the past.

6. India and the Palestine Liberation Organization

India's policy towards the Palestine Liberation Organization (the PLO) has been one of the least understood but more sensible aspects of India's policy towards the Middle East. India, of course, has been closely following and concerned with the Palestinian issue from the very beginning.[1] In this chapter, an attempt will be made to study in two parts the Indian attitude to the Palestinian question, the first part dealing with the Indian approach to the issue after the creation of the state of Israel in 1948 till the assumption of the leadership of the PLO in 1969 by Yasser Arafat, and the second with the Indian attitude to the PLO thereafter.

In doing so, the emphasis will be on examining and analysing the motives and calculations behind India's consistent support for the Palestinian cause. It will be argued that India's support for the Palestinians was, of necessity, rather unspectacular and less than substantial in material terms. Since India was in no position to extend anything more than diplomatic support for the Palestinian cause, it needs to be examined whether India used this option with dexterity and imagination. It will also be discussed whether India's non-relationship with Israel, which was deliberately cultivated to keep the Arab states in good humour, got in the way of India making a more effective contribution to furthering the Palestinian cause. Finally, it will be argued that the mere extension of vocal support to Arab causes in general or to the Palestinian issue in particular is a totally inadequate basis for promoting Indian interests in a region which has been undergoing tremendous changes in the last decade.

India and the Palestinian question till 1969
Though India's political elite consistently and firmly upheld the cause of the Palestinian Arabs even before India won independence, one could discern a subtle change in its attitude to the issue after India became free

in 1947, and particularly after the creation of the state of Israel in 1948, in spite of India's steadfast opposition to partition.

India did vote against the partition of Palestine and subsequently against the admission of Israel to the UN in the General Assembly. However, the Indian attitude to the issue, at this stage, was governed by two important factors. Firstly, Israel was, by then, a reality which simply could not be wished away. India could not but take cognizance of this basic facts regardless of how the Arabs felt or thought about it. Secondly, India was now an independent country and as such could not get carried away by its emotional pre-independence sentiments towards the Palestinian issue. It now had to weigh the issue in terms of its concrete national interests in the sense that principle had to yield some place to pragmatism.

Differences between the Indian and Arab approaches

The Indian attitude to the Palestinian issue, from this point onwards, was characterized by the recognition of the reality of the state of Israel, a firm belief in the necessity and possibility of solving the Palestinian issue through negotiations and a deep concern for the fate of the Palestinian refugees who were uprooted from their homes as a result of the Arab-Jewish conflict over Palestine.

In view of India's vociferous support for the Palestinian Arabs in the latter years, it is not often realized that India was one of the earliest countries to recognize the state of Israel. India, in fact, extended formal recognition to Israel on 17 September 1950 in spite of considerable opposition from the Arab countries. According to the official communiqué, "... India's decision to recognise Israel is the recognition of an established fact".[2] However, there seems to be so little awareness even in India with regard to India's recognition of the state of Israel, that even a Minister of State of External Affairs, as recently as the 1980s, having been asked if India recognized Israel *de jure*, could only mumble, "I don't know," after a lot of dithering.[3]

India also thought that it was both necessary and feasible to solve the Palestinian issue through negotiations. It was, of course, in India's interest to settle the issue amicably and through negotiations which would ensure peace and stability in a region which was so close and important to her. The official communiqué, in fact, makes a direct reference to this when it states that continuing non-recognition "limits the effectiveness of the Government of India's role as a possible intermediary between Israel and the Arab states".[4]

India, at this stage, recognized the problem of displaced Palestinians only as a "refugee" problem. Hence, the accent of India's approach was on the early return and rehabilitation of the displaced Palestinian Arabs and the need to look after them till then. Though India abstained from voting on the UN General Assembly resolution No. 194 (III) of 11 December 1948, its basic stand, thereafter, was in consonance with it.

The resolution, *inter alia*, states that

> the refugees wishing to return to their homes and live at peace with their neighbours should be permitted to do so at the earliest practicable date and that compensation should be paid for the property of those choosing not to return ... [and efforts should be made to] facilitate the repatriation, resettlement and economic and social rehabilitation of the refugees and the payment of compensation ... .[5]

It is absolutely crucial to emphasize these three elements in India's approach to the Palestinian question in order to demonstrate that there have been fundamental differences between the Indian approach and that of the more extremist elements among the Arabs and the Palestinians to the issue from the very beginning, though these differences have been somewhat obscured by India's loud and consistent support for the Palestinian cause over the years.

Firstly, it is often overlooked that India never associated itself in any way with the extreme Arab demand for the liquidation of the state of Israel. Once India recognized the existence of Israel as an established fact, it implicitly accepted the position that any solution put forward for solving the Palestinian refugee problem should address and take care of the legitimate security interests of the Jewish state.

To cite just one instance, in one of the preparatory meetings in Colombo for the Afro-Asian Conference in Bandung in 1955, the Pakistani Prime Minister, Muhammad Ali, introduced a draft resolution which, *inter alia*, described the creation of Israel as a violation of international law. Nehru took serious exception to this and pointed out that since India recognized Israel, he could not condemn it as a violation of international law.[6] India has maintained this position firmly and consistently over the years, which is certainly a major departure from the traditional Arab/Palestinian position of not accepting the existence of the state of Israel and having an open commitment to its destruction.

Secondly, India never endorsed the Arab position of refusing to negotiate with Israel. India, over the years, stuck to the position that only direct negotiations between the Arabs and Israel would provide a way out of the Arab–Israeli stalemate. Nehru himself, time and again, "probed in his talks with Arab leaders, especially Nasser, into whether there was an opening for reconciliation with Israel, but he had always come up against a wall of steel".[7]

However, Nehru refused to give up. At the Bandung Conference, he took exception to Mr. Ahmad Shukairy, a Palestinian and a member of the Syrian delegation, who, in the course of his speech said that a negotiated settlement was not possible in the case of the Arab-Israeli conflict. Nehru maintained that "sometime or other, whether you are enemies or whether you have fought a war, there must be negotiations. There is always some kind of settlement .... After all, one can settle things either by compulsion, that is by pressure, or by negotiation."[8] Thus, India, from the beginning, desired and supported a negotiated settlement to the Arab-Israeli dispute despite the fact that such a stand was not entirely to the liking of the Arabs.

Thirdly, India was genuinely concerned about the plight of the displaced Palestinians, though at this stage India merely considered them as "refugees" and even thought it possible that some of them, at least, could be absorbed by various Arab countries. Hence, India extended consistent support to all efforts aimed at providing immediate relief as well as long-term rehabilitation of the Palestinian refugees. This can be seen from the stand taken by Indian representatives and delegations at the UN over the years.

Indian support at the UN for the Palestinian refugees
A member of the Indian delegation, Mr. Akbar Ali Khan, making a statement[9] at the United Nations Special Political Committee in November 1958 argued that

> The responsibility for relief and rehabilitation of the refugees is the responsibility of the United Nations because the refugees would not have become a homeless people had it not been for a political decision taken by the United Nations, and in spite of their opposition and supported the continuation of the United Nations Relief and Works Agency (UNRWA) activities with stress on vocational and educational needs, and appeal to all governments to contribute to the funds of the agency.

India's Permanent Representative, C.S. Jha, making a statement[10] on the report of UNRWA in November 1959, stated that

> the problem of Palestine refugees is not merely an intensely human problem; it is also one of great political importance and indeed affects the entire complex of political relations in the Middle East. It cannot be treated in isolation and purely in terms of economic rehabilitation.

The 1967 Arab-Israeli War and the Palestinian issue

The six-day Arab-Israeli war of June 1967 was a watershed in the history of the Middle East. The rout of the Arab armies and the Israeli occupation of the West Bank, Gaza, the Golan Heights and East Jerusalem changed the whole complexion of Middle Eastern politics. *Inter alia*, it disabused the Palestinians of any hope that the Arab countries on their own would be able to deliver them from their physical misery and uncertain political future. This realization prompted the Palestinians to think in terms of self-reliance and self-help and a determination to shape their own destiny. Moreover, the Israeli occupation of new territories not only brought millions of Palestinian Arabs under direct Israeli rule, but also compounded the refugee problem by displacing thousands of Palestinian Arabs afresh.

The Indian response to these developments was both prompt and profound. The India-UAR joint statement[11] issued during Mrs. Gandhi's visit to Cairo in October 1967 expressed "support for the just rights of the Palestinian people". The term "Palestinian people" was significant because this was the first time that such an expression was officially used and was, perhaps, meant to acknowledge and approve the moves made by the Palestinians to steer their future as they deemed fit.

Mr. D.P. Dhar, a member of the Indian delegation, making a statement[12] at the UN Special Political Committee in December 1967 reiterated the new Indian position which recognized the Palestinians as a people and not merely refugees when he said:

> It cannot be over-emphasised that the conflict of June 1967 and the consequent occupation of vast Arab territories has greatly complicated the situation in West Asia. It is our firm belief that lasting solutions of the many problems existing at present can be worked out only when the key issue of the refugees is dealt with and steps are taken to ensure the just rights of the Arab people of Palestine on the basis of paragraph 11 of resolution 194 (III).

India and the PLO

India, as has already been pointed out, both welcomed and supported the moves made by various Palestinian factions to come together in order to present a united front to Israel and enable them to pursue their interests without being too dependent on external help. India also could not but have welcomed the removal of Mr. Ahmed Shukairy from the Chairmanship of the PLO in 1968 as a direct consequence of the six-day war which spelt disaster for the Arabs. Many in the Arab world felt that it was his inflammatory utterances which made Israel fear that an Arab attack was imminent and resort to a pre-emptive strike. Another sore point was his insistence that he should be accepted as the head of a government in exile. Not surprisingly, he became a source of discord among Arabs, and Tunisia reportedly refused to attend some top-level Arab meetings because of Mr. Shukairy's participation in them as the head of a Palestinian delegation.[13]

It was at about this time that the Indian government plumped for the largest of the various Palestinian factions that came under the umbrella of the PLO, namely Al Fatah and its leader, Yasser Arafat. India's preference for Al Fatah and Arafat is understandable. Firstly, Al Fatah was essentially nationalistic in its approach and shunned the ideological militancy of some of the other PLO factions, and that was to India's liking. Secondly, it also tried to steer clear of mixing religion with politics by characterizing its struggle with Israel as political rather than religious. Its secular credentials could not but endear it to the Indian leadership which was so concerned about religious resurgence in the region and the Pakistani ability to exploit it to India's discomfiture. Thirdly and lastly, India saw in Arafat a pragmatic and charismatic leader who, more than anyone else, could carry the various factions of the PLO along with him and who, when the time came for eventual settlement, would be able to deliver it from the Palestinian side.

An Al Fatah delegation visited India in September 1969 at the invitation of the Indian Association for Afro-Asian Solidarity. During the visit, the delegation called on the Indian Foreign Minister, Mr. Dinesh Singh, and requested permission to open an office in India. Mr. Singh assured the delegation that the government of India would consider its request sympathetically.[14] Besides, the Al Fatah delegation collected Rs 80,000 for its cause. The money was left in a trust as no permission was sought to take it out of India.[15]

In August 1970, the Indian Foreign Minister, Mr. Swaran Singh, assured the three Al Fatah delegates, Abu Ghassan, Abu Bashar and Abu Javad, that he would consider favourably their request for opening an information centre in New Delhi.[16] However, when fighting broke out between Jordanian troops and Palestinian commandos in Jordan in September 1970, India maintained a neutral stance by taking the view that it was an internal affair of Jordan.[17]

However, the Bangladesh crisis and the lack of understanding shown by the Arab countries to the influx of millions of refugees into India, and the economic burden and the social tensions that the influx generated, made some people in India call into question the wisdom of continuing India's strong and unwavering support for the Palestinian refugees.

A Member of Parliament, Mr. Kishan Kant, pointedly asked the Indian government whether it would consider the possibility of treating the Arab refugee problem as an internal problem of the Arab countries, in view of the Arab stand that the crisis in the then East Pakistan was an internal affair of Pakistan. The Indian Foreign Minister, Mr. Swaran Singh, wisely ruled out any such possibility, saying that India's stand on the Palestinian refugees was in consonance with "justice and the facts of the situation". The government did not think that it should reverse its policy because "certain Arab countries are not in complete accord with our stand" (in relation to Bangladesh).[18]

However, the Indian representative making a statement[19] at the special Political Committee at the UN on 26 November 1971 shrewdly drew a parallel between the problem of the Palestinian refugees imposed on the Arab states by Israel and the intolerable burden of refugees that Pakistan's inhuman policies in the then East Pakistan imposed on India's fragile economy and delicate social fabric. *Inter alia*, he said:

> The very fact that a section of a population is obliged to take refuge in a neighbouring state or states is indicative of the gross violations of human rights.
>
> The only solution to the problem of refugees is that they go back to their hearths and homes.
>
> Refugees are a direct responsibility of the state which has forced them to flee and not of the state who has come forward to their succour.
>
> We maintain that Israeli responsibility towards its refugees is independent of her relations with her neighbours. Arab neighbours of Israel are not bound either legally or morally to negotiate, cooperate or discuss the subject of refugees with Israel. Israel must take back its refugees. It is her duty to create a climate of confidence in which these refugees go back to their homes in safety with dignity

and honour enjoying full right of self-determination.

By drawing a close parallel to the refugee situation in the Middle East and in the Indian subcontinent, the Indian representative implicitly but pointedly warned the Arab states against adopting double standards in relation to the refugee situation in the subcontinent.

Thus, while the Indian government refused to use its support for the Palestinian people as a bargaining chip to persuade the Arab states to support the Indian stand in relation to the Bangladesh crisis, it did not hesitate to make clear to Arab states the untenability and unacceptability of their stand that the crisis in the then East Pakistan was an internal affair of Pakistan. India also chose to express its solidarity with and commitment to the Palestinian cause by resisting pressures to establish diplomatic relations with Israel in reaction to the unsympathetic attitude adopted by most of the Arab countries in relation to the Bangladesh issue.[20] Nevertheless, the Indian government reacted sharply to the slaying of 11 Israeli athletes by Palestinian commandos in the Olympic village in Munich on 6 September 1972. A statement of the Ministry of External Affairs said:

> The act resulting in this tragedy was senseless and condemnable. It remains so whatever the dissatisfaction and frustration leading to it. There is no justification for dragging terrorism into the arena of sports. Terrorist activities of this type are deplorable and damage the very cause which is sought to be advanced.[21]

The Indian Prime Minister, Mrs. Gandhi, too was quick to condemn the Munich massacre. She said: "This shocking and senseless violence cannot but be condemned in the strongest terms. Such a dastardly act of hatred can never solve any problem."[22]

The Yom Kippur War and the Palestinian issue

When the uneasy peace in the Middle East was broken by the surprise attack launched by Egypt and Syria on 7 October 1973, the Ministry of External Affairs issued a statement[23] which was totally supportive of the Arabs. It said:

> The Government have consistently declared that the cause of the tension in the area is due to Israeli aggression and refusal to vacate territories occupied by armed force. This intransigence on the part

of Israel is clearly the basic cause leading to the present outbreak of hostilities.

Meanwhile, India's Deputy Permanent Representative at the UN, Mr. N.P. Jain, addressing the Ad Hoc Committee of the General Assembly for the announcement of voluntary contributions to UNRWA on 30 November 1973, announced a contribution of Rs 100,000 in kind. He also mentioned that India had been awarding scholarships directly to the Palestinians, which would continue the following year as well.[24]

India strengthens the PLO's diplomatic option
Though India has always been in favour of a political and diplomatic solution to the Palestinian problem, it threw its entire weight behind the PLO's quest for diplomatic recognition in the post-1973 period primarily for three reasons. Firstly, India realized that the PLO was much more amenable to pursue its diplomatic option at that critical juncture because it began to appreciate both its necessity and efficacy. Secondly, India was also aware that such a course would strengthen the hands of Arafat and Al Fatah within the PLO, whose ideological moderation suited India's political preferences in the region admirably. Thirdly and lastly, India was worried that, unless the momentum for peace and a negotiated settlement that the Yom Kippur war had generated all round was carefully nurtured, there was always the possibility that it might lead to a new political stalemate in the Middle East in which Palestinians would be the worst sufferers.

Consequently, India sought to help the PLO gain international political acceptance as a reasonable and moderate organization and live down its image as a terrorist outfit by canvassing its case in the UN and outside, so that when the time for the final settlement came, the PLO would have gained sufficient respectability and credibility to participate in the negotiations as an independent organization, genuinely representative of the Palestinian people.

The Algiers Declaration, March 1974
The qualitative upgrading of the Third World's diplomatic support to the PLO came in March 1974 when the Bureau of IV Conference of Nonaligned Countries adopted a declaration[25] in Algiers on the Middle East and the question of Palestine. It emphasized that just and durable peace in the region could be obtained only on the basis of "two indispensable fundamental prerequisites":

Restoration of the Palestine people's national rights, foremost among which is the right to return to its homeland and exercise its right of self-determination ... [and] ... Ensuring global recognition of the Palestine Liberation Organization as the legitimate and sole representative of the Palestinian people.

The recognition of the right of the Palestinian people to self-determination and the acceptance of the PLO as the legitimate and sole representative of the Palestinian people by the international community became the underlying theme of the Third World's diplomatic offensive from this point onwards. India played a key role in this process, both in the UN and outside.

On 8 October 1974, India co-sponsored a draft resolution in the UN General Assembly calling for the PLO's participation in the deliberations of the General Assembly on the Palestinian question. The draft resolution[26] was as follows:

The General Assembly, considering that the Palestinian people is the principal party to the question of Palestine, invites the Palestine Liberation Organization, the representative of the Palestinian people, to participate in the deliberations of the General Assembly on the question of Palestine, in plenary meetings.

Explaining and justifying India's sponsoring of the aforementioned draft resolution, India's Permanent Representative, R. Jaipal,[27] contended that

The draft resolution ... seeks to invite the Palestine Liberation Organization to participate in our deliberations because that organization represents the people of Palestine ... whether or not the PLO has been elected by the Palestinian people is neither material nor relevant at this stage. The fact is that the PLO is recognized by all the Arab states and many others as the political organization, representing the Palestine people.

Commending the adoption of the draft resolution, Mr. Jaipal was careful to point out that

in adopting it, we are not in any sense threatening the security or the existence of the state of Israel. We shall, in fact, only be granting the Palestinian people the right to be heard before their future is decided.

Resolution of the Rabat Arab Summit, 28 October 1974

In the meantime, the Seventh Arab Summit in Rabat in October 1974 passed a resolution[28] which formally recognized the PLO as the legitimate representative of the Palestinian people. This further reinforced and strengthened the diplomatic process set in motion by the Algiers Nonaligned Summit to confer legitimacy and acceptance on the PLO by the international community. The Rabat Arab resolution, *inter alia*, recognized the right of the Palestinian people "to return to their homeland and to self-determination" and "to establish an independent national authority under the leadership of the PLO in its capacity as the sole legitimate representative of the Palestine people, over all liberated territory".

Acknowledging India's positive and purposeful contribution to the Palestinian cause at the UN, the PLO Chairman, Yasser Arafat, conveyed his "deep gratitude" and "appreciation" for the attitude of the Indian delegation at the UN in calling for the participation of the PLO delegation in the General Assembly discussion of the Palestinian issue.[29]

Arafat's address to the UN, 13 November 1974

As a consequence of the sustained and persistent diplomatic effort made by various Third World organizations and movements, Mr. Yasser Arafat was invited to address the UN General Assembly on 13 November 1974. In his historic address,[30] Mr. Arafat traced the origins of the Palestinian problem, the sufferings of the Palestinian people and the great injustice done to them over the years. Implicitly stressing the PLO's willingness and preference for a peaceful solution to the issue, Arafat warned the world body, "Today, I have come bearing an olive branch and a freedom fighter's gun. Do not let the olive branch fall from my hand."

India's Foreign Secretary, Mr. Kewal Singh, while making a statement[31] at the UN General Assembly on 19 November 1974, seized on the opportunity to emphasize and endorse the moderation and reasonableness that permeated Arafat's address to the UN.

> In Mr. Arafat's speech, we found echoes of the same values to which we are also dedicated, i.e. democracy, secularism, human dignity and common nationhood for multi-racial, multi-religious groups.

He also tried to explain the desperation and frustration that prompted some Palestinians to violence and terrorism.

Why should we be surprised if a people who have been deprived of their homes and normal existence were reduced to such frustrations that they did not look upon the international community to restore to them their legitimate rights to return and resettlement?

Encouraged by the response and emboldened by the success of its labours at the UN in favour of the Palestinian cause, India introduced another draft resolution[32] on 21 November 1974 in relation to the Palestinian issue. It, *inter alia*, reaffirmed

the inalienable rights of the Palestinian people in Palestine to self-determination without external interference ... [and] ... to national independence and sovereignty.

India recognizes the PLO, 10 January 1975

As a logical corollary to India's sustained effort to help the PLO gain diplomatic recognition in the comity of nations, India extended formal recognition to the PLO by granting diplomatic status to the PLO's representatives in New Delhi on 10 January 1975. India was the first non-Arab country to extend such recognition. Reacting to India's decision to extend diplomatic status to the PLO, Arafat said that the move would give the struggle of the Palestinian people "a very big push forward".[33]

The Annual Report (1974–75) of the Ministry of External Affairs, displaying a mood of self-congratulation, said that

The [Indian] Government ... sponsored/supported resolutions in the General Assembly of the United Nations which accepted the status of the Palestine Liberation Organization and accorded her an Observer Status.[34]

Explaining India's decision to extend diplomatic recognition to the PLO, the report said that

In view of the widening relationship and recognition achieved by the PLO in other parts of the world and in the UNO ... the Government of India agreed to the request of the PLO to open a separate office in New Delhi.[35]

At the UN

India's Permanent Representative, Mr. R. Jaipal, making a statement[36] at the UN, said:

They [the Palestinians] have now come to the United Nations with an olive branch, for the gun is out of place here.

We consider this to be a good and healthy development. It represents the desire to turn away from paths of violence to ways of non-violence and negotiation.

It is vital that the United Nations should therefore adopt decisions that give hope to the Palestinian Arabs, because to do otherwise would be callous and cruel.

Mr. Jaipal, again making a statement[37] in the UN General Assembly on 4 December 1975 on the situation in the Middle East, referred to the plight of the stateless Palestinians being at a disadvantage to pursue their interests in an effective way and the need for the UN to come to their rescue.

The sovereign Arab states, using the attributes of their sovereignty, are in a position to take care of themselves, but the Palestinian Arabs are not yet in a similar situation.

He also tried to allay Israeli fears in relation to its security.

A fallacy is being deliberately propagated that the rights of the Palestinian Arabs conflict with the right of Israel to exist. The purpose of this fallacy could only be to deny the Palestinian Arabs their inalienable rights. It is entirely absurd even to contemplate the extinction of the State of Israel, which has asserted its right to exist in no uncertain manner.

As can be seen from the foregoing analysis, India, ever since the Yom Kippur war, sought to strengthen the diplomatic option of the PLO by canvassing its case in various international forums. In doing so, it sought to soften the PLO's image as a terrorist organization and tried to project its image as a moderate and reasonable organization which, in the past, was driven to violence and terrorism in desperation and frustration.

Thus, the PLO's endeavours for international diplomatic recognition and legitimacy started bearing fruit in the mid-70s. After acquiring an Observer Status in the UN in 1974, the PLO's diplomatic march proceeded without a hitch. It became a member of the NAM in 1975 and of the "Group of 77" in 1976.

India, at this stage, seemed to be urging moderation on the part of the PLO, a sense of urgency and purposefulness on the part of the UN, and flexibility and reasonableness on the part of Israel, as essential for a negotiated settlement.

The Janata government and the PLO

When the Janata Party came to power in March 1977, and particularly when a former Jana Sangh member and a vocal critic of the Congress Party's traditional policy of friendship to Arab countries, Vajpayee, took over as the Foreign Minister, speculation became rife that India's policy towards the Middle East might come under review and even revision. However, there was very little difference, in terms of substance, between the foreign policy approaches of the Janata Party and its predecessor. The Janata government lost no time in reaffirming and reiterating India's strong support of the Arabs in general and the Palestinians in particular.[38]

Nevertheless, the Israeli Foreign Minister, Mr. Moshe Dayan, visited India secretly on 14 August 1977 at the invitation of the Janata Prime Minister, Mr. Morarji Desai. In his talks with Mr. Dayan, Morarji insisted that Israel must make peace with the Arabs. While he wanted the Arabs to guarantee the existence of Israel, the solution to the Palestinian problem, according to him, was "to establish a Palestinian State in the Arab territories which you [Israel] will evacuate". He refused to accept Dayan's argument that a Palestinian state would endanger Israel, and that the Palestinian refugees should be absorbed by the Arab countries in which they lived just as Israel absorbed almost a million Jews who came to Israel from various Arab countries. Nor did Morarji consent to an exchange of ambassadors between the two countries, nor a visit by his Foreign Minister to Israel, even in secret.[39]

However, the Janata government reacted sharply to the regularization of Israeli settlements in the occupied territories in August 1977. The Ministry of External Affairs said in an official release on 27 August 1977:

> ... India has always been against acquisition of territory by any country by the use of force ... . India, therefore, strongly deplores the action taken to regularize existing Israeli settlements in occupied areas and to authorize new ones.[40]

Nevertheless, the Janata government felt it necessary to reassure the Arab countries of the continued Indian support of the Arabs. Hence, the Annual Report (1977-78) of the Ministry of External Affairs was quick to point out that "The Minister of External Affairs [Mr. Vajpayee] lost no time in allaying the misapprehensions among Arab countries about India's support to the Arab cause."[41] However, the report made no effort to conceal India's positive response to Sadat's bold initiative in the Middle East. "India has been watching developments taking place in West Asia since the visit of President Anwar Sadat to Israel which has resulted in a tremendous change in the West Asian scene."[42]

However, when the Camp David Accord was signed on 17 September 1978, the Arab world including the PLO denounced Egypt for betraying the Arab cause. Sadat was accused of destroying Arab solidarity by signing a separate peace treaty with Israel. India had to take into account the strong and negative reaction of the Arab world to the Camp David Accord. The Indian Foreign Minister, Mr. Vajpayee, said at a press conference that India did not welcome the Camp David Accord because it suffered from three major shortcomings. Firstly, Palestine was the hard core of the Middle Eastern problem. There could be no lasting peace until the inalienable rights of the Palestinian people were restored. Secondly, the PLO had not been accepted as the representative body of the Palestinians. Thirdly, the Camp David Accord was silent on the status of Jerusalem.[43] Nevertheless, when the Arab states made a concerted effort to expel Egypt from the NAM in 1979 for signing a peace treaty with Israel, India stood by Egypt and firmly opposed any such move.[44]

The then Foreign Minister of India, Mr. S.N. Mishra, leading the Indian delegation to the Havana Summit of the Nonaligned Countries in September 1979, expressed his misgivings about the Camp David Accord much more explicitly in his speech[45] at the conference. He said that "The Egypt-Israeli treaties have caused fears and misgivings which have led to the exacerbation of the situation particularly by dividing the Arab world. It is for Egypt to remove these misgivings." Later, elaborating India's position on the Camp David Accord at the UN on 28 November 1979, India's Permanent Representative, Mr. B.C. Mishra, said that India did not dispute the sovereign right of any state to enter into treaties and agreements on bilateral matters. However, such agreements could not presume to settle matters affecting others who were not contracting parties. India could not agree that any agreement to which the PLO was not a party should seek to impose on the Palestinian people a pre-determined settlement.[46]

A special function to observe the "International Day of Solidarity with the Palestinian People", jointly organized by the Indian Council for Cultural Relations and the PLO, was held in New Delhi on 29 November 1979. Presiding over the function, the Minister of State for External Affairs, Mr. B. Barua, said:

Today, when an increasing number of people all over the world are coming to see and understand the justice of Palestinian demands, we Indians not only feel a sense of gratification but also a sense of vindication for our own long-standing and consistent policies.[47]

India extends full diplomatic status to the PLO, March 1980

The 1980s saw the intensification of India's efforts to further strengthen the PLO diplomatically and politically in order to wean it away from violence and terrorism and to build up its image as a responsible organization which was amenable to reason and negotiation. As a part of this ongoing process, the Indian Foreign Minister, Mr. P.V. Narasimha Rao, announced in Parliament on 26 March 1980 that India had decided to accord full diplomatic recognition to the office of the PLO in New Delhi. Mr. Rao also announced that the Indian Prime Minister, Mrs. Gandhi, had invited Mr. Arafat "to pay us an official visit".[48]

Consequently, Mr. Arafat paid a three-day official visit to India between 28 and 30 March 1980. Mrs. Gandhi, speaking at a dinner given in his honour, said that sympathy for the Palestinians "has been a part of independent India's foreign policy from its very inception".[49]

Mr. Arafat, in his speech, described India as an "eternal friend". However, he strongly denounced the Camp David Accord as "a new conspiracy against our national liberation, against our national rights". He also expressed the PLO's determination to "continue the just struggle by all means, including armed struggle", which his hosts might have found a little uncomfortable to explain away.[50] In a TV interview in New Delhi, Mr. Arafat said that with a "great country" like India steadfastly supporting the Palestinian cause, "I am sure of our success".[51]

The first ever Indo–PLO joint statement[52] issued in New Delhi on 20 March 1980 reflected the close political understanding that the two leaders were able to achieve in relation to issues which were of importance to them. Mrs. Gandhi reiterated that "a just peace and a comprehensive solution to the Middle East crisis" can be found only with the "full participation of the Palestine Liberation Organization as an equal partner in any settlement". Both leaders, in an implicit reference to the Soviet invasion of Afghanistan, agreed that "the de-escalation of tensions could only be achieved through political and diplomatic measures and not by military confrontation through induction of arms".

Though India's full diplomatic recognition of the PLO was, in general, meant to strengthen the PLO's diplomatic option, there were at least three immediate considerations that weighed with the Indian government in taking such a step. Firstly, India considered it in her interest to strengthen the radical elements in the Arab world to "counterbalance the resurgence of Islamic fundamentalists" who were trying to give a "religious twist" to what was essentially a political crusade against Israeli domination. Secondly, India was also impressed by the "refreshing moderation" that Arafat himself had been displaying in promoting the Palestinian cause.[53] Thirdly, India perhaps also thought it wise to clear the "misunderstanding" created in the Islamic world about the initial Indian posture with regard to the Soviet intervention in Afghanistan by reaffirming her support to the Palestinian cause.[54]

India supports the Fahd Plan, 20 November 1981

The official spokesman of the Ministry of External Affairs welcomed the Fahd Plan[55] as "a declaration of the basic principles of peace in West Asia". He said that

> The Saudi initiative has rightly included the recognition of the Palestinian issue as one of the important elements of any comprehensive and durable West Asian settlement. The Saudi initiative is in line with India's general position, consistently stated in various national and international forums. India, therefore, welcomes the Fahd Plan ... .[56]

India supported the Fahd Plan primarily because it was in line with her general position on the Arab-Israeli dispute. Nevertheless, there were at least two other important considerations which must have weighed with the Indian government in supporting it. Firstly, the post-1973 period saw the emergence of Saudi Arabia as an important actor in Middle Eastern politics because of its oil reserves and subsequent petro-dollar wealth. The PLO itself became quite dependent on the Saudis for financial as well as diplomatic assistance. Given Saudi Arabia's political preferences in the region, it was likely to use its newly acquired leverage with the PLO only to moderate its stance towards Israel. Hence, India thought it wise to extend its support to the Fahd Plan. Secondly, the move was, at least partly, aimed at improving India's bilateral relations with Saudi Arabia which were, at this stage, not as good as they might have been, given Saudi misgivings about India's initial response to the Soviet intervention in Afghanistan and the Indian attitude to Pakistan. By supporting the Fahd Plan, India was not only acknowledging the importance of the Saudi role in the region but also emphasizing the similarity of views of India and Saudi Arabia with regard to the Palestinian issue. Meanwhile, Arafat made his second visit to India as a head of state in exile in May 1982. The visit was important, for it took place against the background of Israeli threats to invade Lebanon and the resurgence of Islamic fervour in the region as a consequence of the Iranian revolution and the Soviet invasion of Afghanistan.

Mrs. Gandhi, speaking at a dinner given in honour of Mr. Arafat, described him as "the symbol of a people afire with the spirit of freedom".[57] Mr. Arafat, in his reply, expressed his gratitude for "the strong and very important support which you extend to our just cause and national struggle".[58] In the Indo–PLO joint communiqué[59] issued on 23 May 1982, the two leaders expressed their concern over the "Israeli acts of violence and aggression against the Palestinian people in the occupied territories and their continuous aggressive acts and threats of invasion of South Lebanon, aided by the regular flow of highly sophisticated imported weapons". The statement implicitly criticized the USA for supplying sophisticated arms to Israel. It also seemed to betray a sense of frustration and helplessness in view of the strong American support for the Jewish state.

Israeli invasion of Lebanon, 6 June 1982
India reacted very harshly to the Israeli invasion of Lebanon in June 1982. The Indian Foreign Minister, Mr. P.V. Narasimha Rao, speaking at a function in New Delhi on 19 June, referred to the "enactment of a savage drama involving the butchery of our Palestinian brothers and sisters".[60] India also rushed medicines, medical equipment and foodstuffs to Lebanon. Mrs. Gandhi, making a statement in the Lok Sabha on 25 July 1982, came out strongly in favour of the Palestinian people. She asserted that "Israeli attempts to wipe out the Palestinian Movement cannot succeed in the long run."[61]

Later, speaking at a public reception in Calcutta in August 1982, the PLO Ambassador to New Delhi, Mr. Faisal Ahudaha, acknowledged the support extended by India at a critical stage to the PLO. He said: "I can say that India has come to our aid even more than some of our closer neighbours."[62]

Mrs. Gandhi sent a message to Arafat in September 1982 in which she praised the PLO's spirited resistance to the Israeli invasion of Lebanon.[63] The Indians seemed to be particularly appalled by the savagery of the Israeli invasion of Lebanon and the innumerable civilian casualties that accompanied it.

In a broader context, the timing of the Israeli invasion raised doubts in

Indian minds whether Israel was really serious about a negotiated settlement with the PLO or whether it entertained any secret hope of settling the issue militarily with the willing support of the USA. India was also worried that the Israeli invasion might also bring the extremist elements in the PLO to the forefront and reverse the process of moderation and accommodation that the PLO had been pursuing under Arafat's leadership.

The 7th Nonaligned Summit and the Palestinian question

The 7th Nonaligned Summit, held in New Delhi in March 1983, took special interest in the Palestinian issue and India, as the Chairperson of the NAM, played no mean role in it. "The New Delhi Message",[64] issued by the nonaligned countries on the occasion, expressed customary support for the Palestinian cause. They also sent a message of solidarity to the Palestinian people which, *inter alia*, strongly condemned the Israeli "attempt to quell legitimate opposition by the Palestinians in the occupied territories".[65]

The summit also resolved to set up a NAM Committee on Palestine in order to monitor closely the developments in relation to the Palestine issue and initiate "some action" in the face of a rapidly deteriorating situation in the Middle East.

Inaugurating the first meeting of the NAM Committee on Palestine on 30 October 1983, the Indian Foreign Minister, Mr. Narasimha Rao, emphasized "the need for a comprehensive rather than a piecemeal approach to the question".[66] The first meeting[67] of the committee was held in New Delhi on 30-31 October 1983. The meeting was attended by Algeria, Bangladesh, Cuba, India, the PLO, Senegal, Yugoslavia and Zambia. The committee urged that a process of negotiation should be launched without delay. At the request of the PLO, the committee discussed the question of securing a separate seat for the Palestine Arab state at the UN to be occupied temporarily by the PLO with the status of Observer.

Factional fights within the PLO, November 1983

Reacting to the internal squabbles within the various factions of the PLO, a spokesman of the Ministry of External Affairs urged the Palestinians to remain united and to devote all their efforts and energies towards the attainment of their common goal. "Any divisions among the ranks of the valiant Palestinian people will only give comfort to their enemies," he said.

Meanwhile, the Chargé d'Affaires of the PLO in New Delhi, Mr. Jamil

Hajaj, appealed to Mrs. Gandhi to intervene in the PLO crisis in her capacity as Chairperson of NAM. He accused the Syrian President Assad of masterminding the conflict within the various PLO factions in Tripoli. Mr. Jamil said that Assad was trying to convert the PLO into a "Syrian puppet organization and use it as a bargaining chip to wrest the Golan Heights from Israel".[68] However, India's capacity to intervene in the dispute was limited, and it was no surprise that India chose not to get too actively involved in any mediation effort.

The serious differences within the various factions of the PLO over Arafat's responses to the Israeli invasion of Lebanon and the subsequent evacuation of the PLO fighters from Lebanon threatened the continuation of Arafat's leadership of the PLO. However, both India and the NAM were in favour of Arafat continuing at the helm of the PLO and strengthening the PLO as a united body of the Palestinians.

Arafat's moderation and the need for unity within the ranks of the PLO were the reasons behind India's support of Arafat's leadership. The new Indian Prime Minister, Mr. Rajiv Gandhi, sent Mr. S.L. Yadav, the Deputy Chairman of the Rajya Sabha (the upper House of the Indian Parliament), to attend the crucial 17th Session of the Palestine National Council (PNC) in Amman in November 1984, which was to decide the fate of Arafat's leadership of the PLO. It was a matter of satisfaction to India when Arafat's leadership was confirmed by the PNC.[69]

India was also instrumental in the convening of a meeting of the Nonaligned Committee on Palestine in New Delhi in April 1985. The committee recommended the convening of an international conference under the aegis of the United Nations in order to obtain "a comprehensive, just and durable peace in West Asia".[70] India also strongly condemned the Israeli bombing of the PLO headquarters in Tunis in October 1985. Rajiv Gandhi sent messages of solidarity and support to Arafat and the Prime Minister of Tunisia.[71]

Evaluation of India's support of the PLO

At this stage, it is essential to take a critical look at India's support of the PLO over the years, its nature and content and its efficacy in promoting the Palestinian cause.

India vehemently opposed the partition of Palestine and the creation of the Jewish state till the very end. However, once the partition became an accomplished fact, India recognized the state of Israel despite its earlier reservations. Concomitantly, India never subscribed to the maximalist demands of the PLO, calling for the liquidation of the state of Israel. Nor did India accept the PLO's view that armed struggle was the only way to liberate Palestine. India, from the beginning, urged a negotiated settlement as both possible and desirable. In consonance with this position, India extended strong diplomatic support to the PLO in order to wean it away from terrorism and strengthen its diplomatic option. Hence, India urged ideological and methodological moderation on the part of the PLO and stressed the importance of unity within PLO ranks in order to present a united front to Israel.

Though India treated the Palestinians as "refugees" till 1967 and supported their cause in the UN, it recognized the Palestinians as a "people" thereafter and extended its support to their right to self-determination and a state of their own. Over the years, India extended consistent diplomatic, moral and material support to the Palestinians. Though there were reports of India's military assistance to the PLO,[72] the former Indian Foreign Secretary, Mr. A.P. Venkateswaran, was quite emphatic that India's support of the PLO was strictly "humanitarian".[73]

If one were to prepare a balance sheet on India's support of the PLO, it appears to be a mixed blessing. On the credit side, India's support of the PLO enabled it to encourage and nurture secular forces in the region. It helped prevent the Arab-Israeli dispute from degenerating into a religious conflict between the Arabs and the Jews and enabled the majority of Arabs to see it as a political struggle between Arab nationalism and Israeli domination. This, in turn, kept in check any tendencies towards Islamic resurgence in the region, which Pakistan could have taken advantage of to the detriment of India.

India also tried to use its support of the Palestinian cause as an instrument to improve its bilateral relations with a number of Arab countries. To cite just one instance, Arafat "is generally believed to have played a not unimportant role in bringing New Delhi and Riyadh closer together ...".[74] It goes without saying that India's firm support to the PLO enhanced India's general standing in the region and was a positive factor in improving India's bilateral relations with the Arab states.

As a consequence of India's consistent support to the PLO, India was probably spared the terrorist attacks and threats which seriously affected many Western and even Arab states.

Given the presence of a substantial Muslim minority in India, the Indian support of the Palestinians also acted as a sop to the domestic Muslim constituency, which all political parties in India have been only too eager to exploit.

On the debit side, in the absence of diplomatic relations and consequent lack of leverage with Israel, India could not play a positive and purposeful role in bridging the gap between the two adversaries and pave the way for an eventual settlement. India's support of the Palestinians was seen as one-sided in Israel, and hence Israel paid no heed to what India had to say on the subject. This impression needs to be dispelled if India is to be taken seriously by Israel.

India's total and unqualified support of Yasser Arafat and Al Fatah made it difficult for her to see the Palestinian issue in its entirety and true complexity.

> For years, New Delhi has gone headlong into a policy of support for Mr. Yasser Arafat, without comprehending the constantly shifting sands in the region. Indications are that New Delhi's policy may be under review, to take in the nuances of developments in West Asia.[75]

India's total identification with Arafat and Al Fatah left it with no leverage whatsoever with other major factions of the PLO.

More importantly, Jordan remains a crucial link in any possible solution of the Palestinian issue on account of both the history and geography of the region.[76] And India's relations with Jordan over the years have been rather cold and distant. Consequently, India has to overcome these impediments if it is to play any sort of role in relation to the Palestinian issue, let alone help to solve it.

India's attempt to use its support of the PLO to improve its bilateral relations with the Arab countries, though successful to some extent, has its limitations in the long run. The PLO's relations with Arab countries are uneven and variable. Many Arab governments are suspicious and even scared of the PLO and its radical rhetoric. Therefore, India would be well advised to base its relations with the Arab states on mutuality of interests, which is more enduring and solid in the long run.

India's vociferous support of the PLO also put it on the diplomatic spot whenever there were terrorist attacks on soft targets. Hence, India adopted a rather ambivalent attitude towards the PLO's terrorist methods. It opposed terrorism in principle and condemned specific acts of terrorism. But in the same breath, it tried to explain away the PLO's terror tactics as acts of desperation and frustration, caused by Israeli intransigence and oppression.

It goes without saying that India's firm and consistent support of the Palestinian cause has been just and can be justified on moral as well as practical grounds. India's stand in relation to the Palestinian issue has been in consonance with the norms that governed India's foreign policy endeavours and objectives in general. As such, there was no way India could have taken a different stand on the Palestinian issue without jeopardizing its general standing in the international community.

Critics of Indian policy towards the Middle East often make the mistake of questioning India's support to the Palestinians as an example, thereby undermining the credibility of such criticism. Instead, they should take a critical look at India's bilateral relations with the Arab states, independently of the Palestinian issue. It would have been cynical and extremely shortsighted of India to have used the Palestinian issue as a bargaining tool. The issue was never whether or not India should have supported the Palestinian cause, but whether there were alternative strategies which India could have adopted and utilized to serve the just cause of the Palestinians much more effectively and successfully than it actually did.

Conclusion

It is no exaggeration to say that beyond the Indian subcontinent the Middle East constitutes the most important region for India in political, security and economic terms. At this juncture, it is necessary to examine in some detail the circumstances and personalities that went into the making of India's Middle Eastern policy at the time of India's independence, if only to show that such a policy was not axiomatic, and that it could have been considerably different in a different political context and under different political personalities.

Independent India's foreign policy, for one thing, could not have begun with a clean slate. The ideological and emotional baggage of the pre-independence days did have an impact on free India's foreign policy orientation. It was in this context that one needs to take a second look at Nehru's role as the formulator of India's foreign policy. Nehru, like many other leaders of his generation, was essentially a product of India's freedom struggle and was Gandhi's personal choice to lead the newly independent India. It was Gandhi's intervention, time and again, that prevented others in the Congress Party like Sardar Patel from successfully challenging Nehru's dominance. However, Nehru's position as the principal spokesman of the Congress on foreign affairs was firmly established even before independence, primarily because other prominent leaders in the Congress hardly evinced any interest in the subject. As Michael Brecher points out, "No one in the Congress or the Government, not even Sardar Patel, ever challenged his control in this sphere."[1] Besides, Nehru remained his own Foreign Minister until his death.

Another possible reason for Nehru's near total control over foreign policy could have been that, at the time of independence, there was no established foreign policy bureaucracy nor institutional memory to serve the new political elite, who were novices in the art of conducting foreign affairs in the modern age. This was so primarily because Indian foreign policy was completely subordinated to that of the British, to subserve the latter's colonial interests under the colonial dispensation. It was run from London to all intents and purposes and remained so to the very end of British rule in India. With no established traditions and practices to act as precedents, it was not surprising that Nehru had a field day in conducting India's external affairs immediately after independence.

Nehru himself disclaimed any personal credit for formulating India's foreign policy and said that it was "completely incorrect" to call it "Nehru's policy". In his own words

> Looking back, India's policy has not been some sudden bright inspiration of an individual, but a gradual growth evolving from even before independence. The inevitable line that we took subsequently has followed that thinking as a matter of course.[2]

Nevertheless, while India's foreign policy stance, in a broad sense, would have remained very much the same even under a different leader, it is quite possible that some nuances and details in its orientation could have been considerably different.

At this juncture, it is worth pondering the question of how Sardar Patel would have handled India's foreign relations, even within the broad parameters that India's immediate historical experience and geography had determined at the time of India's independence. The value of such an exercise, of necessity, will remain academic and even speculative, but it could throw some light on the fallacies and weaknesses that crept into India's foreign relations under Nehru, particularly in relation to the Middle East. For instance, Patel seemed to have made a very realistic and clinical assessment of the Chinese occupation of Tibet in 1950, and appeared to have had a better appreciation than Nehru of its implications for India and the measures and steps that India needed to take to meet the changed situation on her north-eastern borders.[3] Nehru's policy to China was, at least partly, influenced by considerations of anti-imperialism, Asian solidarity and empathy with a socialist line of thinking, all of which precluded him from exercising the sort of cold and ruthless logic that permeated Patel's outlook.

The issue of Kashmir has been one of the principal preoccupations of India's foreign policy and had implications for India's Middle Eastern policy as well. A thoroughgoing realist like Patel "would probably have dealt with the Kashmir question rather differently from the very

202 INDIA AND THE MIDDLE EAST

beginning".[4] It is unlikely that he would have made the sort of unilateral declaration that Nehru made in relation to holding a plebiscite in Kashmir regarding its final accession to India. Patel, who kept away from the Kashmir issue by agreement with Nehru, is reported to have once remarked:

> If only Jawaharlal would let me handle Kashmir, I could settle it quickly. Instead, he is fumbling all over the place.[5]

It goes without saying that India's Middle Eastern policy, in addition to the objective conditions that existed at that time, bore the imprint of Nehru's ideological predilections and intellectual preferences, which did not necessarily serve India's long-term interests in the region. It is quite possible that a realist and an ideologically less fussy person like Patel would have avoided these pitfalls and defined India's interests in the region with much more clarity and pursued them with vigour. Nehru failed to give a concrete definition of India's interests in the region, and as such India's policy towards the Middle East remained rather incoherent and vague.

It is very clear, at least in retrospect, that Nehru entertained exaggerated fears about the emergence of an Islamic bloc which could have posed a threat to India's security and secularism. Consequently, the Pakistani-factor was given much more weight than it should have had in India's dealings with the Middle East. As a result, India expended most of her time and energies trying to counter a threat which was almost non-existent.

> While Pakistan could, at times, gain some marginal advantage over India on relatively unimportant issues by playing its "Islamic" card, these instances were so few and far between that they did not require the expenditure of Indian diplomatic and political energies far disproportionate to the actual threat they posed to Indian interests.[6]

Nehru's penchant for nonalignment was also a factor in India's rather rigid and doctrinaire approach to the region. While a country of India's size, location and population was justified in adopting a nonaligned policy, Nehru's prescription of it for all the Third World countries was unrealistic and uncalled for. While India's nonaligned stance was primarily in relation to the superpowers in the context of the Cold War, it still had to cultivate individual countries which were of importance to her on a bilateral basis. This was so because the projection of nonalignment was not an adequate basis to evolve bilateral relations with individual states in the Middle East.

Nehru's "self-righteous" stance against aligned countries in the region precluded any such possibility. Nehru also made a somewhat artificial and unnecessary distinction between conservative and radical states in the region, which prompted him to adopt a Cairo-centric policy which needlessly alienated some Middle Eastern states opposed to Nasser but otherwise well-disposed to India.

India's policy to the region more or less reduced Middle Eastern politics to the Arab-Israeli dispute, thereby pushing India into a political and diplomatic straitjacket. India sought to win the support of the Middle Eastern states or at least neutralize their support to Pakistan by extending vociferous support to Arab and Palestinian causes and by ignoring Israel after formally recognizing the Jewish state in 1950. However, neither support to the Arab causes nor a reflexive anti-Israeli stance are a reliable and realistic basis in the long run to promote India's interests in the region.

In view of the changing Arab perspective in relation to Israel in the late 1970s and 80s and the moderation and accommodation displayed by the PLO, India needs to take a fresh look at the problem instead of sticking to its traditional and somewhat outworn stand on the issue. India's changing defence perspective in relation to the Middle East, in the context of Pakistan's "Islamic bomb" and its closely evolving security relationship with Saudi Arabia and other Gulf states, does not permit it to persist with its customary policy of totally ignoring Israel.

India's rather timid and diffident approach to the Middle East also led to a serious distortion in her domestic policy in relation to her emergence as a modern and secular state. Though Nehru set store by secularism, the fear of a conservative Muslim bloc ganging up against India externally, and obscurantist mullahs inciting the Indian Muslims with the slogan that Islam was in danger internally, dissuaded Nehru from attempting basic reforms in relation to the Indian Muslim community.

As such, India lost a golden opportunity to project herself as a modern, progressive and secular country by clearly identifying herself with and promoting such forces both in the domestic and international context. This would have created a positive interaction between the domestic milieu and international environment, and established a creative link between foreign and domestic policies. However, Nehru faltered because of his unfounded fears and left a hiatus between India's foreign and domestic policies.

The resultant impression was that the government was trying to appease the Muslims in India and not integrate them. Such a policy did not serve the long-term interests of the Indian Muslims either. As one writer commented on India's banning of Salman Rushdie's controversial book *The Satanic Verses*

> Pre-emptive measures such as the ban on *The Satanic Verses* serve the limited purpose of satisfying sectional interests, but in the long run a policy of appeasement does not help even those who are sought to be appeased. For there is always the danger that those who benefit from such a policy today can also get hurt the next time around when other sectional interests assert themselves.[7]

In fact, it was "our failure to make our secular policy work internally that made us support the Arabs more and more",[8] a hangover of pre-independence days.

India, it seems, has failed to develop a coherent and integrated policy towards the Middle East and her policy responses to the region smack of ad hocism. It has abounded in inconsistencies, contradictions and angularities which appear to be largely self-inflicted. As a result, it has become rigid and self-conscious and has tended to be reactive rather than active, passive rather than positive. The most serious indictment of India's Middle Eastern interaction came from the former Foreign Secretary of India, Mr. A.P. Venkateswaran.

> It is a relationship without a *quid pro quo*. Any relationship that does not involve a *quid pro quo* is indicative of bad diplomacy since the first principle of diplomacy is reciprocity.[9]

Consistency of policy in a rapidly changing region ceases to be a virtue beyond a point. The Indian political leadership and the foreign policy bureaucracy need to cultivate more finesse, sophistication and sensitivity in dealing with the Middle East in order that India is not caught napping or overtaken by new developments there in the troubled days ahead.

Notes

Introduction

1 For a detailed account of India's political, commercial and cultural contacts with the Arab world from ancient up to modern times see Maqbul Ahmad, *Indo-Arab Relations*, Popular Prakashan, Bombay, 1969.

2 Howard Wriggins, "Changing Power Relations Between the Middle East and South Asia", *ORBIS*, Vol.20, no.3, Fall 1976, p.787.

3 M.S. Agwani, "India and the Arab World" in B.R. Nanda ed., *Indian Foreign Policy: The Nehru Years*, Vikas, New Delhi, 1976, p.63.

4 Ibid.

5 J. Nehru, *Glimpses of World History*, Oxford University Press, New Delhi, 1982, pp.735-736.

6 For the complete text of Nehru's report to the Congress see Bimla Prasad, *The Origins Of Indian Foreign Policy*, Bookland, Calcutta, 2nd edition, 1962, Appendix 1.

7 Bimal Prasad, "Foreign Policy in the Making" in B.N.Pande ed., *History of Indian National Congress - (1885-1985)*, Vikas, New Delhi, 1985, Vol.3, pp.814-815.

8 For a detailed study of Sir Syed's life and work see Shan Muhammad's *Sir Syed Ahmad Khan: A Political Biography*, Meenakshi Prakashan, Meerut, 1969.

9 See B.N. Pandey ed., *The Indian Nationalist Movement 1885-1947, Select Documents*, Macmillan, London, 1979, p.15.

10 Ibid., p.14.

11 Ibid., p.16.

12 For a very stimulating study of the Khilafat movement and its implications for the Indian freedom struggle see A.C. Neimeijer, *The Khilafat Movement in India - 1919-1924*, Martinus Nijhoff, The Hague, 1972.

13 Ibid., p.96.

14 Bimal Prasad, "Foreign Policy in the Making", op.cit., p.809.

15 Ibid.

16 B.N. Pandey ed., *The Indian Nationalist Movement 1885-1947*, op.cit., p.53.

17 For the full text of the Non-Cooperation Resolution see Girija K. Mookerjee, *History of Indian National Congress*, Meenakshi Prakashan, Meerut, 1974,

pp.209-210.
18   A.C. Neimeijer, op.cit., p.170.
19   J. Nehru, *Glimpses of World History*, op.cit., p.720.
20   Cited by Bruce Maynard Borthwick, *Comparative Politics of the Middle East*, Prentice Hall, New Jersey, 1980, p.92.
21   J. Nehru, *Glimpses of World History*, op.cit., p.763.
22   Ibid., p.767.
23   Ibid., p.762.
24   Ibid., p.767.
25   Gandhi's *Harijan*, November 26, 1938 cited by G.H. Jansen, *Zionism, Israel and Asian Nationalism*, The Institute for Palestine Studies, Beirut, 1971, p.172.
26   A. Main Zaidi ed., *Congress and the Minorities*, Indian Institute of Applied Political Research, New Delhi, 1984, p.40.
27   Cited by G.H. Jansen, op.cit., p.181.
28   Bimal Prasad, *Foreign Policy in the Making*, op.cit., p. 814.
29   Ibid.
30   Ibid.
31   G.H. Jansen, op.cit., p.181.
32   Ibid., p.182.
33   Cited by Subramaniam Swamy, "The Secret Friendship between India and Israel", *Sunday*, November 28-December 4, 1982, p.19. For a critical account of Gandhi's attitude to the Jewish question see Gideon Shimoni, *Gandhi, Satyagraha and the Jews: A Formative Factor in India's policy Towards Israel*, Jerusalem Papers on Peace Problems, The Hebrew University of Jerusalem, Jerusalem, 1977. On another occasion Gandhi, reacting to the criticism that his attitude to Palestine was influenced by his sensitivity to Indian Muslim feelings, said, "I have said often that I would not sell truth for India's deliverance. Much less would I do so for winning Muslim friendship." G.H. Jansen, op.cit., p.181.
34   Cited by Keith Callard, *Pakistan: A Political Study*, Allen and Unwin, London, 1957, p.11.
35   Sisir Gupta, "Indo-Pakistan Relations" in M.S. Rajan and S. Ganguly eds., *India and the International System*, Vikas, New Delhi, (Year not given), p.226.
36   Callard, op.cit., pp.63-65.
37   Ironically, Jinnah - whose demand for Pakistan was solely based on the premise that Hindus and Muslims constituted two separate nations - made a political *volte face* when he addressed the Pakistan Constituent Assembly on 11th August, 1947. He declared: "You are free to go to your temples, you are free to go to your mosques or to any other place of worship in this state of Pakistan ... . You may belong to any religion or caste or creed - that has nothing to do with the business of the state ... . We are starting with this fundamental principle that we are all citizens and equal citizens of one State." However, it was not long before Pakistan became "Islamic" for a variety of reasons. See Ayesha Jalal, *The State of Martial Rule*, Cambridge University Press, Cambridge, 1990, Chapter 6. Also S.S. Bindra, *Politics of Islamisation*, Deep and Deep, New Delhi, 1990, Chapters 2,3 and 4.
38   For a comprehensive study of the origins of the Kashmir problem see Josef

Korbel, *Danger in Kashmir*, Princeton University Press, New Jersey, 1954. Korbel was a member of the UN Commission on India and Pakistan (UNCIP) and had first-hand knowledge of the problem. Also, Michael Brecher, *The Struggle for Kashmir*, Oxford University Press, New York, 1953. A. Campbell-Johnson, *Mission with Mountbatten*, Greenwood Press, Westport, Connecticut, 1977.

39 For further elaboration of this point see M.J. Akbar, *The Siege Within*, London, Penguin, 1985.

40 S. Gopal, *Jawaharlal Nehru*, Vol. II, Jonathan Cape, London, 1979, p.18.

41 For a detailed account of the military operations in Kashmir see, Lt. Gen. L.P. Sen, *Slender was the Thread*, Orient Longmans, New Delhi, 1969. Major S.K. Sinha, *Operation Rescue*, Vision Books, New Delhi, 1977. For Pakistani viewpoint see Maj. Gen. Akbar Khan, *Raiders in Kashmir*, Pak Publishers, Karachi, 1970.

42 Josef Korbel, op.cit., p.25. See also Brecher, *The Struggle for Kashmir*, op.cit., pp.51-54.

43 S. Gopal, *Jawaharlal Nehru*, Vol.II, op.cit., p.20.

44 Ibid., p.28.

45 Ibid., pp.27,33.

46 See Werner Levi, *Free India in Asia*, University of Minnesota Press, Minneapolis, 1952, pp.31-32. Jawaharlal Nehru, *The Discovery of India*, Meridian, London, 1946, pp.460-461.

47 *The Times of India*, 10 October 1954.

48 Chester Bowles, *Ambassador's Report*, Harper and Row, New York, 1954, p.104.

49 Ibid., p.66.

50 M.S. Rajan, *Non-Alignment: India and the Future*, University of Mysore, Mysore, 1970, p.14.

51 Selig S. Harrison, "Foreword" in Surjit Mansingh's *India's Search for Power*, Sage, New Delhi, 1984, p.ix.

52 Ashok Kapur, *India's Nuclear Option*, New York, Praeger, 1976, p.58.

53 E.F. Penrose, *The Revolution in International Relations: A Study in the Changing Nature of Balance of Power*, Cass and Co., London, 1965, p.67.

54 Cited by M.M. Rahman, *The Politics of Nonalignment*, Associated Publishing House, New Delhi, 1969, pp.75-76.

55 Ibid., p.76.

56 Ashok Kapur, op.cit., p.48.

57 Surjit Mansingh and Charles H. Heimsath, *A Diplomatic History of Modern India*, Allied Publishers, New Delhi, 1971, p.59.

58 Cited by M.M. Rahman, op.cit., p.52.

59 Chester Bowles, *Promises to Keep: My Years in Public Life, 1941-1969*, Harper and Row, New York, 1971, p.490.

60 J. Nehru, *Indian Foreign Policy, Selected Speeches, September 1946 - April 1961*, The Publications Division, The Government of India, New Delhi, 1961, p.79.

61 Mansingh and Heimsath, op.cit., pp.61-62.

62 Cited by Sisir Gupta, "National Interest and World Reform", in Paul F. Power ed., *India's Nonalignment Policy*, Heath and Co., Boston, 1967, p.9.

63   Bimal Prasad, *The Origins of Indian Foreign Policy*, op.cit., Appendix 1.
64   K.P.S. Menon, *Many Worlds: An Autobiography*, Oxford University Press, London, 1965, pp.229-230.
65   R.K. Karanjia, *The Philosophy of Mr. Nehru*, Allen and Unwin, London, 1966, p.58.
66   R.K. Karanjia, *The Mind of Mr. Nehru*, Allen and Unwin, London, 1960, p.101.
67   M.M. Rahman, op.cit., p.53.
68   Sisir Gupta, "Great Power Relations, World Order and the Third World" in M.S. Rajan and S. Ganguly eds., *India and the International System*, op.cit., p.57.
69   Stephen P. Cohen and Richard L. Park, *India: Emergent Power?*, Crane Russak, New York, 1978, p. XIII.
70   Cited by Ashok Kapur, op.cit., p.137.
71   Ibid., p.229.
72   Ibid.
73   Onkar Marwah, "National Security and Military Policy in India" in L. Ziring ed., *The Subcontinent in World Politics*, Praeger, New York, 1982, p.91.
74   Jawaharlal Nehru, *The Defence of India*, Appendix II, in Bimal Prasad's *The Origins of Indian Foreign Policy*, op.cit., pp.306-307.
75   See S. Gopal, *Jawaharlal Nehru*, op.cit., Vol. III, pp.89-91.
76   Lorne J. Kavic, *India's Quest for Security*, University of California Press, Berkeley, 1967, p.61.
77   Cited by Mansingh, *A Diplomatic History of Modern India*, op.cit., p.192.
78   See S. Gopal, *Jawaharlal Nehru*, Vol. III, op.cit., pp.34-37.
79   Michael Brecher, *India and World Politics*, Oxford University Press, London, 1968, p.166.
80   Yaacob Y.I. Vertzberger, *Misperceptions in Policymaking: The Sino-Indian Conflict 1959-62*, Westview Press, Boulder, Colorado, 1984, p.91.
81   Ibid.
82   See P.V.R. Rao, *Defence without Drift*, Popular Prakashan, Bombay, 1970, pp.8-17. Also Brecher, *India and World Politics*, op.cit., p.151.
83   Vertzberger, op.cit., pp.88-96.
84   S. Gopal, *Jawaharlal Nehru*, Vol. III, op.cit., p.131.
85   See R.K. Karanjia, *The Mind of Mr. Nehru*, op.cit., pp.109,111,118, 119.
86   "India as a World Power", *Foreign Affairs*, Vol. 27, no.4, July 1949, p.550.

1:   India's Politico-diplomatic Interests in the Middle East: Egypt and Iraq

1   The countries are Egypt, Iran, Iraq, Saudi Arabia, Syria, Lebanon, Kuwait, UAE, Qatar, Oman and North and South Yemen.
2   Charles H. Heimsath and Surjit Mansingh, *A Diplomatic History of Modern India*, Allied Publishers, New Delhi, 1971, p.275.
3   K.M. Panikkar, *An Autobiography*, Oxford University Press, Madras, 1977, pp.284-285.
4   Durga Das, *India from Curzon to Nehru and after*, Collins, London, 1969,

p.384.

5   M.S. Agwani, "India, Pakistan and West Asia", *International Studies*, Vol.8, nos. 1-2, July–October. 1966, p.159.

6   Ibid.

7   S.M. Burke, *Pakistan's Foreign Policy*, Oxford University Press, London, 1973, p.66.

8   Ibid. See also M.S. Agwani, "India, Pakistan and West Asia", op.cit., pp.158-159.

9   S.M. Burke, *Mainsprings of Indian and Pakistani Foreign Policies*, University of Minnesota Press, Minneapolis, 1974, p.133.

10 Ibid., p.138.

11 Keith Callard, *Pakistan: A Political Study*, Allen and Unwin, London, 1957, p.314.

12 See Mushtaq Ahmad, *Pakistan's Foreign Policy*, Space Publishers, Karachi, 1968, p.69.

13 A.P. Venkateswaran, former Foreign Secretary of India, agrees with this assessment. Personal Interview, New Delhi, 23-9-88.

14 M.S. Agwani, "India and the Arab World" in B.R. Nanda ed., *Indian Foreign Policy: The Nehru Years*, Vikas, New Delhi, 1976, p.76.

15 Charles H. Heimsath and Surjit Mansingh, op.cit., p.275.

16 V.P. Dutt, *India's Foreign Policy*, Vikas, New Delhi, 1984, p.331.

17 Ibid.

18 Girilal Jain, Personal Interview, New Delhi, 9-12-88.

19 Arif Hussain, *Pakistan: Its Ideology and Foreign Policy*, Frank Cass, London, 1966, p.149.

20 See the article "Saudi Arabia and India" in *The Indian Express*, 24 October 1969.

21 V.P. Dutt, op.cit., p.331.

22 M.S. Agwani, "India and the Arab World", op.cit., p.77.

23 Arif Hussain, op.cit., p.160.

24 Sudha V. Rao, *The Arab-Israeli Conflict: The Indian View*, Orient Longman, New Delhi, 1972, pp.59-60.

25 See Bharat Karnard's article in *The Hindustan Times*, 9 October 1982.

26 Ibid.

27 *Security Council Official Records (SCOR)*, 7th Year, 570th Meeting, 17 January 1952, pp.14-15.

28 *SCOR*, 12th Year, 770th Meeting, 18 February 1957, p.38.

29 M.S. Agwani, "India and the Arab World", op.cit., p.67.

30 A.P. Venkateswaran, Personal Interview, New Delhi, 23-9-88.

31 Charles H. Heimsath and Surjit Mansingh, op.cit., p.291.

32 M.S. Agwani, "India and the Arab World", op.cit., p.72.

33 Ibid., p.304.

34 Gamal Abdal Nasser, "My Revolutionary Life", *The Sunday Times*, London, 24 June 1962, pp.21-22.

35 Charles H. Heimsath and Surjit Mansingh, op.cit., p.291.

36 *The Indian Express*, 21 July 1966.

37 Ibid.

38 *The Times of India*, 25 October 1966.

39   *Foreign Affairs Record*, no.4, April 1970, p.74.
40   See Girilal Jain's article "Israeli-Arab Stalemate", in *The Times of India*, 28 November 1967.
41   Mushtaq Ahmad, op.cit., p.74.
42   S.M. Burke, *Pakistan's Foreign Policy*, op.cit., p.202.
43   Ibid., p.203.
44   Ibid., p.204.
45   V.P. Dutt, op.cit., p.304.
46   Ibid., p.305.
47   For the details of the proposals see Krishan Gopal and Kokila Krishan Gopal, *West Asia and North Africa*, V.I. Publications, New Delhi, 1981, p.361.
48   See G.H. Jansen, *Afro-Asia and Non-Alignment*, Faber and Faber, London, 1966, pp.378-379. Also M.S. Agwani, "The Reactions of West Asia and the UAR", in *International Studies*, Vol.V, nos.1-2, July-December 1963, pp.75-79.
49   For the text of the resolution see *UAR News*, New Delhi, September 1965.
50   Krishan Gopal, op.cit., p.391.
51   See G.S. Bhargava's article in *The Tribune*, 12 June 1980.
52   *India: Lok Sabha Debates*, Part II, Vol. VI, Col.1561, 31 July 1956.
53   Durga Das, op.cit., p.326.
54   Jawaharlal Nehru, *India's Foreign Policy: Selected Speeches, September 1946-April 1961*, The Publications Division, The Government of India, New Delhi, 1961, p.530.
55   Ibid., p.531.
56   For the full text of the proposals see Krishan Gopal, op.cit., pp.310-314.
57   Jawaharlal Nehru, *Selected Speeches, September 1946 - April 1961*, op.cit., p.535.
58   *The Hindustan Times*, 7 October 1964.
59   *The Hindu*, 8 October 1964.
60   *Bharat Jyoti*, 10 April 1966.
61   *The Statesman*, 14 May 1966.
62   See Krishan Bhatia's article in *The Hindustan Times* 15 July, 1966.
63   *The Statesman*, 4 July 1971.
64   *The Hindustan Times*, 3 June 1971.
65   *The Hindustan Times*, 31 January 1973.
66   For details see V.P. Dutt, op.cit., pp.310-314.
67   *The Hindustan Times*, 17 September 1972.
68   V.P. Dutt, op.cit., p.314.
69   See G.K. Reddy's article in *The Hindu*, 2 September 1972.
70   See Inder Malhotra's article in *The Times of India*, 1 January 1981.
71   Ibid.
72   For full text of the document see *Foreign Policy of India, Texts of Documents: 1947-64*, Lok Sabha Secretariat, 1966, New Delhi, pp.44-45.
73   Edith and E.F. Penrose, *Iraq: International Relations and National Development*, Westview Press, Boulder, Colorado, 1978, p.123.
74   M.S. Agwani, "India, Pakistan and West Asia", op.cit., p.164.
75   Jawaharlal Nehru, *India's Foreign Policy: Selected Speeches, September 1946-April 1961*, op.cit., p.94.

76 Ibid.
77 Cited by Krishna Menon, *SCOR*, 12th Year, 799th Meeting, 5 November 1957, p.34.
78 *SCOR*, 12th Year, 769th Meeting, 15 February 1957, p.6.
79 *SCOR*, 12th Year, 797th Meeting, 25 October 1957, p.16.
80 Jawaharlal Nehru, *India's Foreign Policy: Selected Speeches, September 1946-April 1961*, op.cit., p.95.
81 V.P. Dutt, op.cit., p.322.
82 Edith and E.F. Penrose, op.cit., pp.214-215.
83 V.P. Dutt, op.cit., p.322.
84 Krishan Gopal, op.cit., pp.362-363.
85 Ibid., p.365.
86 Ibid.
87 *Asian Recorder*, 8-14 January 1963, p.4983.
88 For the full text of the document see *Foreign Policy of India, Texts of Documents: 1947-64*, op.cit., pp.316-318.
89 *Official Records of the General Assembly (ORGA)*, 20th Session, 1354th Plenary Meeting, 8 October 1965, p.7.
90 Krishan Gopal, op.cit., p.392.
91 *Asian Recorder*, 26 March-1 April 1966, p.7002.
92 *The Hindustan Times*, 7 March 1967.
93 *The Statesman*, 9 March 1967.
94 *Patriot*, 11 February 1968.
95 For the full text of the document see *Foreign Affairs Record*, no.1, January 1970, pp.15-16.
96 V.P. Dutt, op.cit., p.323.
97 *Foreign Affairs Record*, no.6, June 1972, p.170.
98 See the editorial in *The Tribune*, 29 August 1972.
99 *The Times of India*, 6 October 1972.
100 *The Hindu*, 7 April 1973.
101 *Foreign Affairs Record*, no.3, March 1974, pp.104-107.
102 *The Hindu*, 28 March 1974.
103 See the editorial in *The Patriot*, 29 March 1974.
104 *Foreign Affairs Record*, no.1, January 1975, pp.6-7.
105 Ibid.
106 Ibid.
107 *The National Herald*, 3 November 1975.
108 *The Statesman*, 7 July 1978.
109 *The Times of India*, 7 February 1980.
110 See the editorial in *The Times of India*, 9 February 1980.
111 *The Times of India*, 24 September 1980.
112 *Foreign Affairs Record*, no.11, November 1980, p.254.
113 *Foreign Affairs Record*, no.7, July 1981, p.204.
114 *The Times of India*, 10 November 1984.

2: India's Politico-diplomatic Interests in the Middle East: Iran and Saudi Arabia

1   For the text of the document see *Foreign Policy of India, Texts of Documents: 1947-1964*, Lok Sabha Secretariat, 1966, New Delhi, pp.42-43.
2   See *India: Parliamentary Debates*, Vol.8, no.9, part 1. 24 March 1950, Col.1042.
3   See Bimla Prasad, *Origins of India's Foreign Policy*, Bookland, Calcutta, 1960, pp.264-265.
4   L.P. Elwell-Sutton cited by Sushma Gupta, *Pakistan as a Factor in Indo-Iranian Relations 1947-1978*, Chand, New Delhi, 1988, p.46.
5   For a more detailed account of Iran's initial posture of neutralism see Sushma Gupta, op.cit, pp.46-47.
6   Ibid., p.59.
7   Abbas Amirie, "Iran's Regional Foreign Policy Posture", *India Quarterly*, Vol.XXXIV, no.4, 1978, p.457.
8   See *The Hindu*, 24 June 1968. See also V.P. Dutt, *India's Foreign Policy*, Vikas, Delhi, 1984, pp.314-315.
9   See Sushma Gupta, op.cit., p.84.
10 See the editorial in *The Times of India*, 3 May 1974.
11 For the full text of the joint statement see *Foreign Policy of India, Texts of Documents: 1947-64*, op.cit., p.315.
12 See K.V. Padmanabhan, "Indo-Iranian Relations", *Swarajya*, Vol.19, no.30, 25 January 1975, p.4.
13 K.R. Singh, "Iran - The Quest for Security: An Overview", *India Quarterly*, Vol.XXX, no.2, 1974, p.127.
14 The Shah detested Nasser so intensely that the former President of Pakistan Ayub Khan's complimentary references to Nasser in his autobiography *Friends Not Masters* were said to have irked him no end. See Dilip Mukerjee's article in *The Statesman*, 1 November 1968.
15 Sushma Gupta, op.cit., p.82.
16 Ibid.
17 *India: Lok Sabha Debates*, Vol.I, no.7, 25 March 1957, p.654.
18 See *Pakistan: National Assembly Debates*, Vol.I, no.15, February 1957, p.1069.
19 *India: Lok Sabha Debates*, Vol.3, no.32, 29 March 1956, p.3735.
20 *Dawn*, 7 June 1956.
21 K.R. Singh, op.cit., p.128.
22 Sushma Gupta, op.cit., p.73.
23 K.R. Singh, op.cit., p.128.
24 Cited by Sushma Gupta, op.cit., p.83.
25 See Kuldip Nayar's article in *The Statesman*, 15 January 1974.
26 Sushma Gupta, op.cit., p.93.
27 *Official Records of the General Assembly (ORGA)*, 20th Session, 1362nd Plenary Meeting, 14 October 1965.
28 S.M. Burke, *Pakistan's Foreign Policy*, Oxford University Press, London, 1973, p.354. Also Khalida Qureshi, "Pakistan and Iran: A Study in Neighbourly Diplomacy", *Pakistan Horizon*, Vol.21, no.1, 1968, p.39.
29 See former Indian Ambassador to Iran M.R.A. Baig's article in *The Hindustan*

Times, 26 October 1966.

30 K.R. Singh, op.cit., p.128.
31 Ibid., p.129.
32 See Dilip Mukerjee's article in *The Statesman*, 1 November 1968.
33 Sushma Gupta, op.cit., p.103.
34 Ibid., p.104.
35 See Dilip Mukerjee's article in *The Statesman*, 1 November 1968.
36 Sushma Gupta, op.cit., p.187.
37 Shirin Tahir-Kheli, "Iran and Pakistan: Cooperation in an area of Conflict", *Asian Survey*, Vol.XVII, no.5, May 1977, p.477.
38 Ibid.
39 Sushma Gupta, op.cit., p.110.
40 See Peter Avery, "Iran 1964-68: The Mood of Growing Confidence", *The World Today*, London, Vol.24, no.11, November 1968, pp.453-465.
41 *The National Herald*, 4 January 1969.
42 *Amrit Bazar Patrika*, 4 January 1969.
43 *The Hindustan Times*, 5 January 1969.
44 *The National Herald*, 4 January 1969.
45 For the full text of the joint communiqué see *The Indian Express*, 14 January 1969.
46 *Dawn*, 30 March 1971.
47 *Blitz*, 26 June 1971.
48 *ORGA*, 26th Session, 2003rd Plenary Meetings, 7 December 1971, pp.5-6.
49 See G.K. Reddy's article in *The Hindu*, 18 August 1971.
50 *The New York Times*, 30 November 1971.
51 Cited by Sushma Gupta, op.cit., p.129.
52 *Motherland*, 3 November 1971.
53 See Girilal Jain's article in *The Times of India*, 4 July 1973.
54 See G.K. Reddy's article in *The Hindu*, 19 July 1973. See also Sushma Gupta, op.cit., p.130.
55 Sushma Gupta, op.cit., p.137.
56 *The New York Times*, 22 April 1973.
57 K.R. Singh, op.cit., p.131.
58 Mohammed Ayoob, "Indo-Iranian Relations: Strategic, Political and Economic Dimensions", *India Quarterly*, Vol.XXXIII, no.1, 1977, p.2.
59 Ibid., p.3.
60 Ibid., p.2.
61 Ibid., p.3.
62 Alexander MacLeod, "Shah of the Indian Ocean?", *Pacific Community*, Vol.7, no.3, April 1976, p.426.
63 Mohammed Ayoob, op.cit., pp.6-7.
64 Shirin Tahir-Kheli, op.cit., p.478.
65 Ibid.
66 K.R. Singh, op.cit., p.131.
67 See Girilal Jain's article in *The Times of India*, 4 July 1973.
68 Mohammed Ayoob, op.cit., p.11.
69 See India's then Defence Minister Jagjivan Ram's statements in *The National Herald*, 27 July 1973, and *The Hindustan Times*, 21 August 1973.

70   K.R. Singh, "Indo-Iranian Relations" in *Assam Tribune*, 4 July 1973.
71   See the editorial in *The Times of India*, 3 May 1974.
72   For the full text of the communiqué see *Foreign Affairs Record*, no.5, May 1974, pp.168-170.
73   See the editorial in *The Hindustan Times*, 6 May 1974.
74   *The Hindustan Times*, 5 October 1974.
75   *The National Herald*, 27 September 1974.
76   *The Statesman*, 28 September 1974.
77   See Sushma Gupta, op.cit., pp.174-175.
78   For the full text see *Foreign Affairs Record*, no.2, February 1978, pp.81-83.
79   *The Tribune*, 3 February 1978.
80   See the editorial in *The Tribune*, 7 February 1978.
81   Shirin Tahir-Kheli, op.cit., p.477.
82   Ibid., p.481.
83   See Sushma Gupta, op.cit., p.173.
84   Ibid.
85   *The Statesman*, 7 February 1978.
86   *The Times of India*, 27 May 1978.
87   *The Hindustan Times*, 11 June 1978.
88   Sushma Gupta, op.cit., p.182.
89   *The Hindustan Times*, 23 February 1979.
90   *Annual Report*, Ministry of External Affairs, 1979-80, New Delhi, p.22.
91   *The Hindu*, 26 April 1980.
92   *The Hindu*, 5 May 1980.
93   *The Hindu*, 21 March 1981.
94   G.S. Bhargava, "India's Security in the 1980s", *Adelphi Paper 125*, London, 1976, p.26.
95   See the editorial in *The Hindu*, 22 April 1982.
96   S.M. Burke, *Pakistan's Foreign Policy*, op.cit., p.204.
97   For the full text of the statement see *Foreign Policy of India, Texts of Documents: 1947-1964*, op.cit., p.435.
98   *The Hindu*, 11 December 1955.
99   *Foreign Policy of India, Texts of Documents: 1947-64*, op.cit., p.436.
100 S.M. Burke, *Pakistan's Foreign Policy*, op.cit., p.205.
101 See Joseph Abboud's article in *The Hindustan Times*, 16 December 1969.
102 See the article by a special correspondent "Saudi Arabia and India" in *The Indian Express*, 24 October 1969. See also William B. Quandt, *Saudi Arabia in the 1980s*, The Brookings Institution, Washington D.C., 1981, p.7.
103 Abdullah M. Sindi, "King Faisal and Pan-Islamism" in *King Faisal and the Modernization of Saudi Arabia*, ed., Willard A. Beling, Croom Helm, London, 1980, p.184.
104 Ibid., p.185.
105 Naveed Ahmad, "Pakistan-Saudi Relations" in *Pakistan Horizon*, Vol.XXXV, no.4, 1982, pp.52-53.
106 *The Indian Express*, 16 February 1967.
107 Ibid.
108 Ibid.
109 *The Indian Express*, 24 October 1969.

110 Ibid.
111 Ibid.
112 Ibid.
113 Ibid.
114 Ibid.
115 Naveed Ahmad, op.cit., p.53.
116 *The Hindu*, 24 April 1972.
117 *Motherland*, 23 May 1973.
118 *Motherland*, 6 November 1973.
119 *The Indian Express*, 10 November 1973.
120 *The Statesman*, 9 February 1975.
121 *The Sunday Standard*, 9 February 1975.
122 See the editorial in *The Statesman*, 12 February 1975.
123 Bhabani Sen Gupta, *The Afghan Syndrome*, Croom Helm, London, 1982, pp.13-17.
124 See G.K. Reddy's article in *The Hindu*, 13 April 1981.
125 Ibid.
126 *The National Herald*, 14 April 1981.
127 *The Hindustan Times*, 14 April 1981.
128 *The Statesman*, 15 April 1981.
129 See the editorial in *The Times of India*, 22 April 1982.
130 For the full text of the joint communiqué see *Foreign Affairs Record*, no.4, April 1982, pp.133-136.
131 *The Hindustan Times*, 21 April 1982.
132 See the editorial in *The Hindu*, 22 April 1982.
133 See the editorial in *The Statesman*, 22 April 1982.

3: India's Security and Strategic Interests in the Middle East

1   M.S. Agwani, "India and the Arab World", in B.R. Nanda ed., *Indian Foreign Policy: The Nehru Years*, Vikas, New Delhi, 1976, p.61.
2   Ibid., p.64.
3   Ibid., p.63.
4   See Sisir Gupta, "Islam as a factor in Pakistani Foreign Relations", in M.S. Rajan and S. Ganguly eds., *India and the International System*, Vikas, New Delhi, (Year not given), pp.88-110.
5   Durga Das, *India from Curzon to Nehru and after*, Collins, London, 1969, p.384.
6   For details see chapter 2, pp.2-4.
7   M.S. Agwani, "India and the Arab World", op.cit., p.66.
8   Jawaharlal Nehru, *India's Foreign Policy: Selected Speeches, September1946-April 1961*, The Publications Division, The Government of India, New Delhi, 1961, pp.94-95.
9   *Dawn*, 7 June 1956.
10   Jawaharlal Nehru, *India's Foreign Policy: Selected Speeches, September 1946-April 1961*, op.cit., p.282.
11   M.S. Agwani, "India and the Arab World", op.cit., p.64.

12Ibid.
13Jawaharlal Nehru, *India's Foreign Policy: Selected Speeches, September1946-April 1961*, op.cit., p.531.
14Krishan Gopal and Kokila Krishan Gopal, *West Asia and North Africa*, V.I. Publications, New Delhi, 1981, p.4.
15*The Hindu*, 28 July 1967.
16*Northern India Patrika*, 10 August 1967.
17*The Statesman*, 28 October 1970.
18Khalida Qureshi, "Pakistan and Iran: A Study in Neighbourly Diplomacy", *Pakistan Horizon*, Vol. 21, no.1, January-March 1968, p.39. Also S.M. Burke, *Pakistan's Foreign Policy*, Oxford University Press, London, 1973, p.354.
19Sushma Gupta, *Pakistan as a Factor in Indo-Iranian Relations 1947-1978*, Chand, New Delhi, 1988, p.129.
20*Motherland*, 3 November 1971.
21*The Hindu*, 19 July 1973.
22Syed Sikander Mehdi, "The New Pakistan and the Asia-Pacific Region", *Pakistan Horizon*, Vol.XXVII, no.4, 1974, p.21.
23N.A. Mughal, "Inching Together or a Mile Apart: India and Pakistan Towards Detente", *Pakistan Horizon*, Vol.XXIX, no.3, 1976, p.23.
24Syed Sikander Mehdi, op.cit., p.22.
25N.A. Mughal, op.cit., pp.26-28.
26Raju G.C. Thomas, *Indian Security Policy*, Princeton University Press, Princeton, 1986, p.36.
27Zubeida Mustafa, "Recent Trends in Pakistan's Policy Towards the Middle East", *Pakistan Horizon*, Vol.XXVIII, no.4, 1975, p.1.
28Zubeida Mustafa, "Pakistan and the Middle East", *Pacific Community*, Vol.7, no.4, July 1976, p.608.
29Howard Wriggins, "Changing Power Relations between the Middle East and South Asia", *ORBIS*, Vol.20, no.3, Fall 1976, pp.790-791.
30Raju G.C. Thomas, op.cit., p.37.
31M.G. Weinbaum and Gautam Sen, "Pakistan Enters the Middle East", *ORBIS*, Vol.22, no.3, Fall 1978, pp.595-596.
32Amir Tahiri, "Policies of Iran in the Persian Gulf Region", in Abbas Ameri ed., *The Persian Gulf and the Indian Ocean in International Politics*, Institute for International Political and Economic Studies, Tehran, 1975, pp.265-270.
33Raju G.C. Thomas, op.cit., p.38.
34*The Guardian*, 16 March 1973.
35Bhabani Sen Gupta, "The View from India" in Abbas Ameri ed., *The Persian Gulf and the Indian Ocean in International Politics*, op.cit., p.210.
36*The Times of India*, 29 June 1973.
37Bhabani Sen Gupta, "India's relations with Gulf Countries", in Alvin Z. Rubinstein ed., *The Great Game*, Praeger, New York, 1983, p.151.
38R.K. Karanjia, *The Mind of a Monarch*, Allen and Unwin, London, 1977, pp.232-242.
39Ibid., p.247.
40Bhabani Sen Gupta, "India's Relations with Gulf Countries", op.cit., p.151.
41Raju G.C. Thomas, op.cit., p.40.
42Naveed Ahmad, "Pakistan-Saudi Relations", *Pakistan Horizon*, Vol.XXXV,

no.4, 1982, pp.52-53.

43   Shirin Tahir-Kheli and William O. Staudenmaier, "The Saudi-Pakistani Military Relationship: Implications for US Policy", *ORBIS*, Vol.26, no.1, Spring 1982, p.156.

44   Ibid., p.157.

45   Ibid., p.159.

46   Bhabani Sen Gupta, "India's Relations with Gulf Countries", op.cit., p.165.

47   Raju G.C. Thomas, op.cit., pp.38-39.

48   For an account of Pakistan's nuclear activities before Bhutto see Shyam Bhatia, *Nuclear Rivals in the Middle East*, Routledge, London, 1988, pp.88-91.

49   Z.A. Bhutto, *If I am assassinated...*, Vikas, New Delhi, 1979, p.137.

50   *Dawn*, 21 November 1965.

51   Z.A. Bhutto, *The Myth of Independence*, Oxford University Press, London, 1969, p.153.

52   Shyam Bhatia, op.cit., pp.94-95.

53   Sreedhar ed., *Dr. A.Q. Khan on Pakistan Bomb*, ABC Publishing House, New Delhi, 1987, pp.9-13.

54   *Dawn*, 20 May 1974.

55   *Dawn*, 25 June 1974.

56   Z.A. Bhutto, *If I am assassinated...*, op.cit., p.138.

57   *The Sunday Times*, 25 November 1979.

58   Sreedhar, *Pakistan's Bomb: A Documentary Study*, ABC Publishing House, New Delhi, 1987, pp.xiii-xv.

59   *The Daily Telegraph*, 12 July 1985.

60   *The Financial Times*, 29 October 1986.

61   Shyam Bhatia, op.cit., p.105.

62   For the text of the interview see Sreedhar, *Dr. A.Q. Khan on Pakistan Bomb*, op.cit., pp.151-155.

63   Ibid., p.151.

64   Ibid., p.155.

65   Ibid., p.154.

66   *India: Constituent Assembly Debates*, Vol.15, 2nd Session, 6 April 1948, pp.3326-38.

67   For a detailed study of India's nuclear and space programmes, see *India 1985: A Reference Annual*, Ministry of Information and Broadcasting, Government of India, New Delhi, 1986, pp.106-116.

68   Dorothy Norman ed., *Nehru: The First 60 Years*, Bodley Head, London, 1965, p.186.

69   *India: Constituent Assembly Debates*, op.cit., pp.3326-38.

70   See Mohammed B. Alam, *India's Nuclear Policy*, Mittal Publications, New Delhi, 1988, pp.7-48.

71   M.J. Sullivan, "Indian Attitudes on International Atomic Energy Controls", *Pacific Affairs*, Vol.43, no.3, Fall 1970, p.354.

72   Stephen P. Cohen and Richard L. Park, *India: Emergent Power?*, Crane Russak, New York, 1978, p.5.

73   *Asian Recorder*, 30 July-5 August 1967, p.7833.

74   *The Hindu*, 6 May 1967. For a detailed discussion of India's rather futile

search for a nuclear guarantee following the Chinese nuclear explosion see A.G. Noorani, "India's Quest for a Nuclear Guarantee" *Asian Survey*, Vol.VII, no.7, July 1967, pp.490-502.

75   Rodney W. Jones, *Nuclear Proliferation: Islam, the Bomb and South Asia*, Sage Publications, Beverly Hills, 1981, p.53.

76   For a general discussion of Islamic fundamentalism in the Middle East see Dilip Hiro, *Islamic Fundamentalism*, Paladin, London, 1988. Also Youssef M. Choueiri, *Islamic Fundamentalism*, Pinter, London, 1990; W. Montgomery Watt, *Islamic Fundamentalism and Modernity*, Routledge, London, 1989.

77   For a general discussion of the subject see Daniel Pipes, "The Islamic Revival of the Seventies", *ORBIS*, Vol.24, no.1, Spring 1980, pp.9-41.

78   Dilip Hiro, op.cit., pp.1-2.

79   Cited by S. Gopal, *Jawaharlal Nehru*, Vol.II, Jonathan Cape, London, 1979, p.206.

80   S. Gopal, *Jawaharlal Nehru*, Vol.III, op.cit., p.281.

81   Cited by G.S. Bhargava, *South Asian Security after Afghanistan*, Heath and Company, Lexington, 1983, p.116.

82   See G.K. Reddy's article in *The Hindu*, 1 August 1973.

83   See the editorial in *The Tribune*, 10 December 1979.

84   See Kuldip Nayar's article in *The Tribune*, 29 April 1982.

85   *The Statesman*, 19 March 1988.

86   M.S. Agwani, Personal Interview, 11-8-88, New Delhi.

87   A.K. Damodaran, Personal Interview, 9-12-88, New Delhi.

88   Ibid.

89   For details of the case see Nicholas Nugent, *Rajiv Gandhi*, BBC Books, London, 1990, pp.182-185.

90   Ibid., p.185.

91   Bhabani Sen Gupta, "India's Relations with Gulf Countries", op.cit., p.161.

92   Cited by Gary Sick, "The Evolution of US Strategy Toward the Indian Ocean and Persian Gulf Regions", in Alvin Rubinstein ed., *The Great Game*, op.cit., pp.73-74.

93   Ibid., pp.74-75.

94   Ibid., p.76.

95   B.A. Robertson, "South Asia and the Gulf Complex", in Barry Buzan and Gowher Rizvi eds., *South Asian Insecurity and the Great Powers*, Macmillan, London, 1986, p.170.

96   Robert W. Bradnock, *India's Foreign Policy since 1971*, Pinter Publishers, London, 1990, p.103.

97   Bhabani Sen Gupta, "India's Relations with Gulf Countries", op.cit., p.151.

98   For a detailed account of India's stance on Afghanistan see Bimal Prasad, "India and the Afghan Crisis", in K.P. Misra ed., *Afghanistan in Crisis*, Croom Helm, London, 1981, pp.77-83.

99   Ibid., p.161.

100 Barry Buzan and Gowher Rizvi "The Future of the South Asian Security Complex", in *South Asian Insecurity and the Great Powers*, op.cit., p.247.

4: India's Economic Interests in the Middle East

1 Girijesh C. Pant, "Indo-Gulf Economic Relations: A Profile", *International Studies*, Vol.24, no.3, July-September 1987, p.177.
2 Cited by Anoop Babani, "The Gulf in the Trade Gap", *South* March, 1988, p.33.
3 Marcus Franda, "India, Iran and the Gulf", *American Universities Field Staff Reports*, No.17, Hanover, NH, 1978, p.6.
4 Deepak Nayyar, "International Labour Migration from India: A Macro-Economic Analysis", Working Paper No.3, *Asian Regional Programme on International Labour Migration*, UN Development Programme, New Delhi, 1988, p.5.
5 Deepak Nayyar, op.cit., p.50.
6 Girijesh C. Pant, Personal Interview, 12-8-88, New Delhi.
7 Girijesh C. Pant, "Indo-Gulf Economic Relations: A Profile", op.cit., p.198.
8 *Economic Survey*, 1984-85, Ministry of Finance, Government of India, New Delhi, pp.20-21.
9 *Economic Survey*, 1985-86, Ministry of Finance, Government of India, New Delhi, p.24.
10 See *Report on Currency and Finance*, 1985-86, The Reserve Bank of India, pp.158-159.
11 Girijesh C. Pant, "Indo-Gulf Economic Relations: A Profile", op.cit., p.205.
12 Ibid.
13 Ibid.
14 Ibid.

5: Indo-Israeli Relations

1 *The Israel Economist*, November 1987, p.6.
2 This has been discussed in some detail in the first chapter.
3 The other members of the Committee were: Australia, Canada, Czechoslovakia, Guatemala, Iran, the Netherlands, Peru, Sweden, Uruguay and Yugoslavia.
4 *ORGA*, First Special Session, vol.II, 29 April-7 May 1947, pp.38,42,95.
5 *ORGA*, First Special Session, U.N. Document A/364: Report of UNSCOP, Supplement no.11, Vol.I.
6 *ORGA*, Second Session, Ad Hoc Committee on the Palestinian Question, 25 September-25 November 1947, Summary Records of Meetings, p.62.
7 *ORGA*, Second Special Session, vol.II, 16 April-14 May 1948, pp. 63-64. The Pakistani representative, Sir Zafrullah Khan, while justifying the partition of India and opposing it in Palestine stated that Pakistan did not "regard partition as inadmissible in principle but each problem had to be studied on its own merits". Ibid., pp.201-202.
8 G.H. Jansen, *Zionism, Israel and Asian Nationalism*, The Institute of Palestine Studies, Beirut, 1971, p.210.
9 Cited in *India and Palestine: The Evolution of a Policy*, Ministry of External Affairs, New Delhi, 1968, pp.69-70.

10   Richard J. Koziciki, *India and Israel: A Problem in Asian Politics*, Middle Eastern Affairs, New York, 1958, p.164.
11   *Constituent Assembly of India: Legislative Debates*, Vol.VI, no.9, Part I, 20 August 1949, p.380.
12   Ibid., p.381.
13   Ibid.
14   Ibid.
15   *Constituent Assembly of India: Legislative Debates*, Vol.VI, Part 1, 19-31 August 1948, p.381.
16   Ibid.
17   *Constituent Assembly of India: Legislative Debates*, Vol.IV, no.7, Part 1, 6 December 1949, p.233.
18   The official communiqué issued by the government of India in *The Hindu*, 18 September 1950.
19   Ibid.
20   Ibid.
21   Ibid.
22   Ibid.
23   Ibid.
24   See Krishna Menon's speech in the Lok Sabha, 26 March 1957, explaining the delay in recognizing Israel. Krishan Gopal and Kokila Krishan Gopal, *West Asia and North Africa*, V.I. Publications, New Delhi, 1981, pp.4-5.
25   K.P. Mishra, *India's Policy of Recognition of States and Governments*, Allied Publishers, New Delhi, 1966, p.59.
26   Ibid., p.60. See also B.N. Mehrish, *India's Recognition Policy Towards the New States*, Oriental Publishers, Delhi, 1972, p.80.
27   Walter Eytan, *The First Ten Years: A Diplomatic History of Israel*, Weidenfeld and Nicolson, London, 1958, pp.169-170.
28   Michael Brecher, *The New States of Asia*, Oxford University Press, London, 1963, p.130.
29   Ibid., p.131.
30   Gideon Rafael, *Destination Peace: Three Decades of Israeli Foreign Policy*, Weidenfeld and Nicolson, London, 1981, p.89.
31   Michael Brecher, *India and World Politics*, Oxford University Press, London, 1968, p.79.
32   Cited by Charles H. Heimsath and Surjit Mansingh, *A Diplomatic History of Modern India*, Allied Publishers, New Delhi, 1971, p.277.
33   G.H. Jansen, op.cit., pp.169-181.
34   Michael Brecher, *The New States of Asia*, op.cit., p.129.
35   G.H. Jansen, op.cit., p.184.
36   Subramaniam Swamy, "The Secret Friendship Between India and Israel", *Sunday*, 28 November-4 December 1982, p.22.
37   Meron Medzini, "Reflections on Israel's Asian Policy", in M. Curtis and S.A. Gitelson eds., *Israel in the Third World*, Transaction Books, New Jersey, 1976, p.203.
38   Ibid. See also Samuel Decalo, "Israeli Foreign Policy and the Third World", *ORBIS*, Vol.XI, no.3, Fall 1967, pp.724-725.
39   Uri Bialer, *"Our Place in the World", Mapai and Israel's Foreign Policy*

Orientation 1947-1952, Jerusalem Papers on Peace Problems 33, The Magnes Press, The Hebrew University, Jerusalem, 1981, pp.5-6.

40   Ibid., p.202.
41   Brecher, *The New States of Asia*, op.cit., p.129.
42   See G.S. Bhargava's article in *The Tribune* 12 June 1980. Also Meron Medzini, op.cit., p.203.
43   Ibid.
44   Sudha V. Rao, *The Arab Israeli Conflict: The Indian View*, Orient Longman, New Delhi, 1972, p.59. See also Walter Eytan, op.cit., pp.170-171.
45   Pakistan and Indonesia did not recognize Israel.
46   G.H. Jansen, op.cit., pp.250-253.
47   Ibid., p.256.
48   Ibid., p.257.
49   Ibid., p.258.
50   Brecher, *The New States of Asia*, op.cit., p.134.
51   G.H. Jansen, op.cit., p.259.
52   Samuel Decalo, op.cit., p.737.
53   Brecher, *India and World Politics*, op.cit., pp.210-211.
54   Samuel Decalo, op.cit., p.729.
55   Ibid., p.731.
56   Ibid., p.729.
57   Other aspects of this issue are discussed later in the study.
58   *Foreign Affairs Record*, no.10, October 1956, p.150.
59   *The Hindu*, 2 November 1956.
60   Sudha V. Rao, op.cit., p.60.
61   Gideon Rafael, op.cit., p.87.
62   *The Times*, London, 13 November 1959.
63   "Israel's Security and Her International Position", *Government Year Book*, Jerusalem, 1959-1960, p.75. See also Moshe Pearlman, *Ben Gurion Looks Back*, Weidenfeld and Nicolson, London, 1965, pp.178-179.
64   Walter Eytan, op.cit., p.169. See also G.H. Jansen, op.cit., p.213.
65   *Indo-Israel Relations: A Study of India's Posture on Arab-Israel Conflict*, 1971, pp.17-18. Library of Congress Cat. No. DS 450 I7I54.
66   *The Statesman*, 7 April 1970.
67   Neville Maxwell, *India's China War*, Penguin, Harmondsworth, 1972, pp.419-420. See also Subramaniam Swamy, op.cit., p.20.
68   *The Tribune*, 27 May 1980.
69   Yaakov Morris's interview in *The Statesman*, 28 October 1970. Also Arun Kumar Banerji, "India and West Asia: Changing Images Reflect Shifts in the Regional Balance of Power", *The Round Table*, no.305, January 1988, p.28.
70   *The Times of India*, 17 January 1965.
71   *The Hindustan Times*, 11 May 1966.
72   *The Times of India*, 24 May 1966.
73   Meron Medzini, op.cit., p.210.
74   B. Schechtman, "India and Israel", *Midstream*, August-September 1966, pp.48-61.
75   Krishan Gopal, op.cit., p.27.

76 Ibid., p.30.
77 Ibid., p.42.
78 Ibid., pp.42-43.
79 Ibid., p.31.
80 G.H. Jansen, op.cit., p.303. Also see Girilal Jain, "Disillusionment with the Arabs: A Shift in Indian Opinion", *The Round Table*, July 1967. Reproduced in Krishan Gopal, op.cit., pp.48-49.
81 Inder Malhotra in *The Statesman*, 9 June 1967.
82 G.H. Jansen, op.cit., p.304.
83 Ibid.
84 See major English newspapers such as *The Times of India*, *The Hindustan Times* and *The Statesman*, for the period May-July 1967.
85 Krishan Gopal, op.cit., pp.193-195.
86 Ibid., p.199.
87 Ibid., pp.216-217.
88 *The Times of India*, 14 November 1967.
89 *The Times of India*, 16 November 1967.
90 See Indar Jit Rikhye, *The Sinai blunder: the withdrawal of the UNEF leading to the Six-Day War of June 1967*, Cass, London, 1980, pp.150-155.
91 Krishan Gopal, op.cit., p.32.
92 *Pakistan Times*, 22 July 1967.
93 *The Times of India*, 13 September 1967.
94 *The Times of India*, 5 October 1969.
95 *The Hindustan Times*, 30 June 1971.
96 *The Hindu*, 22 July 1971.
97 Dr. Swamy, op.cit., p.20. See also *Motherland*, 26 April 1972.
98 *The Statesman*, 4 January 1972.
99 *The Indian Express*, 6 October 1972.
100 Krishan Gopal, op.cit., pp.145-146.
101 *The Hindu*, 11 October 1973.
102 *ORGA*, Thirtieth Session, Supplement no.34, 1976, pp.83-84.
103 *The Patriot*, 14 November 1975.
104 For the details of the strange circumstances in which the trip came about see Moshe Dayan, *Breakthrough*, Vikas, New Delhi, 1981, pp.26-27.
105 Ibid., pp.28-29.
106 *The Hindu*, 7 October 1978.
107 *The Hindu*, 25 October 1978.
108 *The Tribune*, 10 November 1979.
109 Dr. Swamy, op.cit., p.21.
110 *The Hindu*, 17 May 1980.
111 Ibid., pp.183-184.
112 *The Observer*, London, 29 December 1982.
113 *The Hindustan Times*, 3 February 1981.
114 Arun Kumar Banerji, op.cit., pp.26-27.
115 Sudha V. Rao, op.cit., pp.59-60.
116 Ibid., p.59.
117 G.H. Jansen, op.cit., p.302.
118 *The Israel Economist*, November 1987, p.5.

119 Efrain Karsh, "Soviet-Israeli relations: a new phase?", *The World Today*, London, December 1985.
120 See Alan Hart, *Arafat: Terrorist or Peacemaker?*, Sidgwick and Jackson, London, 1987. Also the unpublished M.Phil. thesis of Prithvi Ram Mudiam, *The Evolution of the Palestinian National Movement: 1969-82. Internal and External Dynamics*, University of Hyderabad, Hyderabad, India, 1985.
121 See F.J. Khergamvala's article in *The Hindu*, 21 September 1989.

6: India and the Palestine Liberation Organization

1 For a fairly detailed discussion of the Indian attitude to the Palestinian issue before the emergence of the PLO, see chapters 1 and 5.
2 *The Hindu*, 18 September 1950.
3 Subramaniam Swamy, "The Secret Friendship between India and Israel", *Sunday*, 28 November-4 December 1982, p.20.
4 *The Hindu*, 18 September 1950.
5 For the text of the resolution see Sami Hadawi ed., *United Nations Resolutions on Palestine 1947-66*, The Institute for Palestine Studies, Beirut, 1967, pp.39-43.
6 G.H. Jansen, *Zionism, Israel and Asian Nationalism*, The Institute of Palestine Studies, Beirut, 1971, pp.250-253.
7 Gideon Rafael, *Destination Peace: Three Decades of Israeli Foreign Policy*, Weidenfeld and Nicolson, London, 1981, p.88.
8 G.H. Jansen, op.cit., p.257.
9 Krishan Gopal and Kokila Krishan Gopal, *West Asia and North Africa*, V.I. Publications, New Delhi, 1981, pp.272-274.
10 Ibid., pp.274-277.
11 *The Times of India*, 22 October 1967.
12 Krishan Gopal, op.cit., pp.278-279.
13 *The Indian Express*, 17 January 1968.
14 *The Hindu*, 24 September 1969.
15 *The Hindustan Times*, 12 March 1970.
16 *Patriot*, 29 August 1970.
17 *The Statesman*, 22 September 1970.
18 *The Hindu*, 22 July 1971.
19 *Foreign Affairs Record*, no.11, November 1971, pp.286-287.
20 *The Egyptian Gazette*, 28 December 1971.
21 *The Statesman*, 7 September 1972.
22 *The Times of India*, 7 September 1972.
23 Krishan Gopal, op.cit., pp.145-146.
24 *Foreign Affairs Record*, no.11, November 1973, p.409.
25 For the text of the declaration see *Foreign Affairs Record*, no.3, March 1974, pp.121-123.
26 Ibid., p.291.
27 Ibid., pp.291-292.
28 For the text of the resolution see *Journal of Palestine Studies*, Vol.IV, no.2, Winter 1975, pp.177-178.

29   *The Statesman*, 1 November 1974.
30   For the text of Arafat's address see *Journal of Palestine Studies*, Vol.IV, no.2, Winter 1975, pp.180-192.
31   Krishan Gopal, op.cit., pp.292-294.
32   Ibid., pp.295-296.
33   *International Herald Tribune*, 11 January 1975.
34   Ibid., p.44.
35   Ibid.
36   Krishan Gopal, op.cit., pp.296-297.
37   *Foreign Affairs Record*, no.12, December 1975, pp.331-332.
38   *Foreign Affairs Record*, no.4, April 1977, p.59.
39   Moshe Dayan, *Breakthrough*, Vikas, New Delhi, 1981, pp.26-29.
40   *Foreign Affairs Record*, no.8, August 1977, p.138.
41   *Annual Report*, Ministry of External Affairs, 1977-78, New Delhi, p.12.
42   Ibid.
43   *The Hindu*, 7 October 1978.
44   *The Hindu*, 6 June 1979.
45   *Foreign Affairs Record*, no.9, September 1979, pp.173-180.
46   *Foreign Affairs Record*, no.11, November 1979, p.215.
47   Ibid., p.213.
48   *The Hindustan Times*, 27 March 1980.
49   *Foreign Affairs Record*, no.3, March 1980, pp.75-76.
50   Ibid., pp.76-77.
51   *The Hindustan Times*, 29 March 1980.
52   *Foreign Affairs Record*, no.3, March 1980, pp.77-79.
53   See G.K. Reddy's article in *The Hindu*, 29 March 1980.
54   See the editorial in *Tribune*, 31 March 1980.
55   For the text of the Fahd Plan see *Journal of Palestine Studies*, Vol.XI, no.1, Autumn 1981, pp.241-243.
56   *Foreign Affairs Record*, no.11, November 1981, p.310.
57   *Foreign Affairs Record*, no.5, May 1982, pp.152-154.
58   Ibid., pp.154-156.
59   Ibid., pp.156-158.
60   *Foreign Affairs Record*, no.6, June 1982, pp.163-164.
61   *Foreign Affairs Record*, no.7, July 1982, pp.183-184.
62   *Amrita Bazar Patrika*, 12 August 1982.
63   *Foreign Affairs Record*, no.9, September 1982, p.227.
64   *Foreign Affairs Record*, no.3, March 1983, pp.54-56.
65   Ibid., p.60.
66   *Foreign Affairs Record*, no.10, October 1983, pp.213-215.
67   Ibid., pp.215-216.
68   *The Times of India*, 10 November 1983.
69   *Amrita Bazar Patrika*, 27 November 1984.
70   *Annual Report*, Ministry of External Affairs, 1985-86, New Delhi, p.20.
71   Ibid.
72   *The Observer*, 4 May 1980.
73   Personal interview, Mr. A.P. Venkateswaran, New Delhi, 23-9-88.
74   See the editorial in *The Times of India*, 27 May 1982.

75   See F.J. Khergamvala's article in *The Hindu*, 6 October 1986.
76   To appreciate the importance of Jordan in solving the Palestinian problem
     see Avi Shlaim, *Collusion Across the Jordan*, Clarendon Press, Oxford, 1988.

Conclusion

1   Michael Brecher, *Nehru: A Political Biography*, Oxford University Press,
     London, 1959, pp.564-565.
2   J. Nehru, *India's Foreign Policy*, Delhi, 1961, pp.80,83.
3   See Sardar Patel's letter to Nehru on 7 November 1950 in Durga Das, *India
     from Curzon to Nehru and After*, Collins, London, 1969, Appendix II.
4   J. Bandyopadhyaya, *The Making of India's Foreign Policy*, Allied Publishers,
     New Delhi, 1984, p.298.
5   Michael Brecher, op.cit., p.428.
6   Mohammed Ayoob, *India and Southeast Asia*, Routledge, London, 1990, p.25.
7   Hasan Suroor, "Behind the ban", *Frontline*, 29 October-11 November 1988,
     p.94.
8   A.K. Damodaran, Personal Interview, 9-12-88, New Delhi.
9   A.P. Venkateswaran, Personal Interview, 23-9-88, New Delhi.

Bibliography

I. Primary sources

Documents

a) Records
Asian Recorder.
Foreign Affairs Record, Ministry of External Affairs, New Delhi.
Foreign Policy of India, Texts of Documents: 1947-64, Lok Sabha Secretariat, 1966, New Delhi.
India: Constituent Assembly Debates.
India: Lok Sabha Debates.
India: Rajya Sabha Debates.
Kessing's Contemporary Archives.
Pakistan: National Assembly Debates.
UN: Official Records of the General Assembly (ORGA).
UN: Security Council Official Records (SCOR).

b) Books
Chakrabarty, D. and Bhattacharya, C., *Congress in Evolution: Resolutions 1885-1934*, The Book Company Ltd., Calcutta, 1935.
Gopal, Krishan, *West Asia and North Africa: A Documentary Study of Major Crises 1947-78*, V.I. Publications, New Delhi, 1981.
Gupta, N.L., ed., *Nehru on Communalism*, Sampradayikta Virodhi Committee, New Delhi, 1965.
Hadawi, Sami, ed., *United Nations Resolutions on Palestine 1947-66*, The Institute for Palestine Studies, Beirut, 1971.
Nehru, Jawaharlal, *Indian Foreign Policy, Selected Speeches, September 1946 - April 1961*, The Publications Division, The Government of India, New Delhi, 1961.
Nehru, Jawaharlal, *Jawaharlal Nehru's Speeches, September 1946 - May 1947*, Delhi, 1967.
Pandey, B.N. ed., *The Indian Nationalist Movement 1885-1947, Select Documents*, Macmillan, London, 1979.
Prasad, Bimal, *Indo-Soviet Relations, 1947-72: A Documentary Study*, Allied Publishers, New Delhi, 1973.

Sreedhar ed., *Dr. A.Q. Khan on Pakistan Bomb*, ABC Publishing House, New Delhi, 1987.

Sreedhar, *Pakistan's Bomb: A Documentary Study*, ABC Publishing House, New Delhi, 1987.

c) Reports and Surveys

American Universities Field Staff Reports.

Annual Reports, Ministry of External Affairs, New Delhi.

Economic Survey, Ministry of Finance, New Delhi.

Handbook of Export Statistics, Project Export Supplement, Engineering Export Promotion Council, Calcutta.

Report on Currency and Finance, The Reserve Bank of India, New Delhi.

d) Interviews

Agwani, M.S., Vice-Chancellor, Jawaharlal Nehru University, 11-8-88, New Delhi.

Damodaran, A.K., Veteran diplomat and writer, 9-12-88, New Delhi.

Dua, H.K., Editor, *The Hindustan Times*, 9-12-88, New Delhi.

Jain, Girilal, The then Editor, *The Times of India*, 9-12-88, New Delhi.

Pant, Girijesh C., Centre for West Asian Studies, School of International Studies, Jawaharlal Nehru University, 12-8-88, New Delhi.

Venkateswaran, A.P., former Foreign Secretary of India, 23-9-88, New Delhi.

II. Secondary sources

a) Books

Agwani, M.S., *Politics in the Gulf*, Vikas Publishing House, New Delhi, 1978.

Ahmad, Maqbul, *Indo-Arab Relations*, Popular Prakashan, Bombay, 1969.

Akbar, M.J., *The Siege Within*, Penguin, London, 1985.

Alam, Mohammed B., *India's Nuclear Policy*, Mittal Publications, New Delhi, 1988.

Ameri, Abbas ed., *The Persian Gulf and the Indian Ocean in International Politics*, Institute for International Political and Economic Studies, Tehran, 1975.

Appadorai, A. and Arora V.K., *India in World Affairs*, Sterling, New Delhi, 1975.

Bandyopadhyaya, J., *The Making of India's Foreign Policy*, Allied Publishers, New Delhi, 1984.

Barnds, William J., *India, Pakistan and the Great Powers*, Praeger, New York, 1972.

Beling, Willard A. ed., *King Faisal and the Modernization of Saudi Arabia*, Croom Helm, London, 1980.

Bhargava, G.S., *South Asian Security After Afghanistan*, Heath and Company, Lexington, 1983.

Bhargava, G.S., *India's Security in the 1980s*, Adelphi Paper 125, London, 1975.

Bhatia, Shyam, *Nuclear Rivals in the Middle East*, Routledge, London, 1988.

Bhatia, Shyam, *India's Nuclear Bomb*, Vikas, New Delhi, 1979.

Bhutto, Z.A., *If I am assassinated ...*, Vikas, New Delhi, 1979.

Bialer, Uri, *"Our Place in the World", Mapai and Israel's Foreign Policy Orientation 1947-1952*, Jerusalem Papers on Peace Problems 33, The Magnes Press, The Hebrew University, Jerusalem, 1981.

Bowles, Chester, *Promises to Keep: My Years in Public Life, 1941-1969*, Harper and Row, New York, 1971.

Bradnock, Robert W., *India's Foreign Policy Since 1971*, Pinter Publishers, London, 1990.

Brecher, Michael, *The New States of Asia*, Oxford University Press, London, 1963.

Brecher, Michael, *Nehru: A Political Biography*, Oxford University Press, London, 1959.

Brecher, Michael, *India and World Politics: Krishna Menon's View of the World*, Oxford University Press, London, 1968.

Brecher, Michael, *The Struggle for Kashmir*, Oxford University Press, New York, 1953.

Burke, S.M., *Mainsprings of Indian and Pakistani Foreign Policies*, University of Minnesota Press, Minneapolis, 1974.

Callard, Keith, *Pakistan: A Political Study*, Allen and Unwin, London, 1957.

Campbell-Johnson, A., *Mission with Mountbatten*, Greenwood Press, Westport, Connecticut, 1977.

Choudhury, G.W., *India, Pakistan, Bangladesh and the Major Powers*, Free Press, New York, 1975.

Cohen, Stephen P. and Park, Richard L., *India: Emergent Power?*, Crane Russak, New York, 1978.

Curtis, M. and Gitelson, S.A. eds., *Israel in the Third World*, Transaction Books, New Jersey, 1976.

Das, Durga, *India from Curzon to Nehru and After*, Collins, London, 1969.

Dayan, Moshe, *Breakthrough*, Vikas, New Delhi, 1981.

Dutt, V.P., *India's Foreign Policy*, Vikas, New Delhi, 1984.

Eytan, Walter, *The First Ten Years: A Diplomatic History of Israel*, Weidenfeld and Nicolson, London, 1958.

Freedman, Robert O., *Soviet Policy Towards the Middle East Since 1970*, Praeger, New York, 1975.

Gopal, S., *Jawaharlal Nehru*, Jonathan Cape, London, 1979.

Gupta, Sushma, *Pakistan as a Factor in Indo-Iranian Relations 1947-1978*, Chand, New Delhi, 1988.

Heimsath, Charles H. and Mansingh, S., *A Diplomatic History of Modern India*, Allied Publishers, New Delhi, 1971.

Hiro, Dilip, *Islamic Fundamentalism*, Paladin, London, 1988.

India and Palestine: The Evolution of a Policy, Ministry of External Affairs, New Delhi, 1968.

Indo-Israel Relations: A Study of India's Posture on Arab-Israel Conflict, 1971, Library of Congress Cat. No. DS 450 I7I54.

Jansen, G.H., *Zionism, Israel and Asian Nationalism*, The Institute for Palestine Studies, Beirut, 1971.

Jansen, G.H., *Afro-Asia and Non-Alignment*, Faber and Faber, London, 1966.

Jha, Ajay N., *India's Economic Diplomacy in the Gulf*, ABC Publishing House, New Delhi, 1988.

Jones, Rodney W., *Nuclear Proliferation: Islam, the Bomb, and South Asia*, Sage Publications, Beverly Hills, 1981.

Kapur, Ashok, *India's Nuclear Option*, New York, Praeger, 1976.

Karanjia, R.K., *The Philosophy of Mr. Nehru*, Allen and Unwin, London, 1966.

Karanjia, R.K., *The Mind of Mr. Nehru*, Allen and Unwin, London, 1960.

Kavic, Lorne J., *India's Quest for Security*, University of California Press, Berkeley, 1967.

Korbel, Josef, *Danger in Kashmir*, Princeton University Press, New Jersey, 1954.

Lamb, Alistair, *Crisis in Kashmir 1947 to 1966*, Routledge and Kegan Paul, London, 1966.

Levi, Werner, *Free India in Asia*, University of Minnesota Press, Minneapolis, 1952.

Mansingh, Surjit, *India's Search for Power*, Sage, New Delhi, 1984.

Mehrish, B.N., *India's Recognition Policy Towards the New States*, Oriental Publishers, Delhi, 1972.

Mellor, John W. ed., *India: A Rising Middle Power*, Westview Press, Boulder, Colorado, 1979.

Miller, J.D.B., *The Politics of the Third World*, Oxford University Press, London, 1966.

Misra, K.P., *India's Policy of Recognition of States and Governments*, Allied Publishers, New Delhi, 1966.

Misra K.P. ed., *Afghanistan in Crisis*, Croom Helm, London, 1981.

Mookerjee, Girija K., *History of Indian National Congress*, Meenakshi Prakashan, Meerut, 1974.

Mortimer, Robert A., *The Third World Coalition in International Politics*, Praeger, New York, 1980.

Nanda B.R. ed., *Indian Foreign Policy: The Nehru Years*, Vikas, New Delhi, 1976.

Nayar, Kuldip, *Distant Neighbours*, Vikas, New Delhi, 1972.

Nayar, Baldev Raj, *American Geopolitics and India*, Manohar, New Delhi, 1976.

Nayyar, Deepak, *International Labour Migration from India: A Macro-Economic Analysis*, Working Paper No.3, Asian Regional Programme on International Labour Migration, UN Development Programme, New Delhi, 1988.

Nehru, Jawaharlal, *Glimpses of World History*, Oxford University Press, New Delhi, 1982.

Nehru, Jawaharlal, *The Discovery of India*, Meridian, London, 1946.

Nehru, Jawaharlal, *Eighteen Months in India, 1936-37: Being Further Essays and Writings*, Allahabad, 1938.

Neimeijer, A.C., *The Khilafat Movement in India, 1919-1924*, Martinus Nijhoff, The Hague, 1972.

Pande, B.N., ed. *A Centenary History of the Indian National Congress, 1885-1985*, Vikas, New Delhi, 1985.

Pearlman, Moshe, *Ben Gurion Looks Back*, Weidenfeld and Nicolson, London, 1965.

Penrose E.F., *The Revolution in International Relations: A Study in the Changing Nature of Balance of Power*, Cass and Co., London, 1965.

Penrose, Edith and E.F. *Iraq: International Relations and National Development*, Westview Press, Boulder, 1978.

Power, Paul F., ed., *India's Non-alignment Policy*, Heath and Co., Boston, 1967.

Prasad, Bimla, *The Origins of Indian Foreign Policy*, Bookland, Calcutta, 1962.

Rafael, Gideon, *Destination Peace: Three Decades of Israeli Foreign Policy*, Weidenfeld and Nicolson, London, 1981.

Rahman M.M., *The Politics of Non-alignment*, Associated Publishing House, New Delhi, 1969.

Rajan, M.S. and Ganguly, S. eds., *India and the International System*, Vikas, New Delhi, (Year not given).

Rajan, M.S. ed., *India's Foreign Relations During the Nehru Era*, Asia Publishing House, New Delhi, 1976.

Rajan, M.S., *Non-Alignment: India and the Future*, University of Mysore, Mysore, 1970.

Rajkumar, N.V. ed., *The Background of India's Foreign Policy*, New Delhi, 1952.

Rao, V. Sudha, *The Arab-Israeli Conflict: The Indian View*, Orient Longman, New Delhi, 1972.

Rikhye, Indar Jit, *The Sinai Blunder: the Withdrawal of the UNEF Leading to the Six-day War of June 1967*, Cass, London, 1980.

Rizvi, Gowher and Buzan, Barry eds., *South Asian Insecurity and the Great Powers*, Macmillan, London, 1986.

Rubinstein, Alvin Z. ed., *The Great Game*, Praeger, New York, 1983.

Shimoni, Gideon, *Gandhi, Satyagraha and the Jews: A Formative Factor in India's Policy Towards Israel*, Jerusalem Papers on Peace Problems, The Hebrew University of Jerusalem, Jerusalem, 1977.

Thomas, Raju G.C., *Indian Security Policy*, Princeton University Press, Princeton, 1986.

Vertzberger, Yaacob Y.I., *Misperceptions in Policymaking: The Sino-Indian Conflict, 1959-62*, Westview Press, Boulder, Colorado, 1984.

Williams, Shelton L., *The U.S., India and the Bomb*, Johns Hopkins Press, Baltimore, 1969.

Zaidi, A.M. ed., *Congress and the Minorities*, Indian Institute of Applied Political Research, New Delhi, 1984.

b) Articles

Agwani, M.S., "The Reactions of West Asia and the UAR", *International Studies*, Vol.5, nos.1-2, July-December 1963.

Agwani, M.S., "India, Pakistan and West Asia", *International Studies*, Vol.8, nos.1-2, July-October 1966.

Ahmad, Naveed, "Pakistan-Saudi Relations", *Pakistan Horizon*, Vol. XXXV, no.4, 1982.

Amirie, Abbas, "Iran's Regional Foreign Policy Posture", *India Quarterly*, Vol.XXXIV, no.4, 1978.

An Indian Official, "India as a World Power", *Foreign Affairs*, Vol.27, no.4, July 1949.

Avery, Peter, "Iran 1964-68: The Mood of Growing Confidence", *The World Today*, Vol.24 no.11. 1968.

Ayoob, Mohammed, "Indo-Iranian Relations: Strategic, Political and Economic Dimensions", *India Quarterly*, Vol.XXXIII, no.1, 1977.

Babani, Anoop, "The Gulf in the Trade Gap", *South*, March 1988.

Karsh, Efrain, "Soviet-Israeli Relations: A New Phase?", *The World Today*, December 1985.

McLeod, Alexander, "Shah of the Indian Ocean?", *Pacific Community*, Vol.7, no.3, April 1976.

Mehdi, Syed Sikander, "The New Pakistan and the Asia-Pacific Region", *Pakistan Horizon*, Vol.XXVII, no.4, 1974.

Mughal, N.A., "Inching Together or a Mile Apart: India and Pakistan Towards Détente", *Pakistan Horizon*, Vol. XXIX, no.3, 1976.

Mustafa, Zubeida, "Pakistan and the Middle East", *Pacific Community*, Vol.7, no.4, July 1976.

Mustafa, Zubeida, "Recent Trends in Pakistan's Policy Towards the Middle East", *Pakistan Horizon*, Vol. XXVIII, no.4, 1975.

Padmanabhan, K.V., "Indo-Iranian Relations", *Swarajya*, Vol.19, no.30, January 1975.

Pant, Girijesh C., "Indo-Gulf Economic Relations: A Profile", *International Studies*, (Vol. no. not given), April 1987.

Pipes, Daniel, "The Islamic Revival of the Seventies", *ORBIS*, Vol.24, no.1, Spring 1980.

Qureshi, Khalida, "Pakistan and Iran: A Study in Neighbourly Diplomacy", *Pakistan Horizon*, Vol.XXI, no.1, 1968.

Ramazani, R.K., "Emerging Patterns of Regional Relations in Iranian Foreign Policy", *ORBIS*, Vol.18, no.4, Winter 1975.

Saddy, Fehmy, "OPEC Capital Surplus Funds and Third World Indebtedness: the Recycling Strategy Reconsidered", *Third World Quarterly*, Vol.4, no.4, October 1982.

Shihata, Ibrahim, "The OPEC Special Fund and the North-South Dialogue", *Third World Quarterly*, Vol.1, no.4, October 1979.

Shihata, Ibrahim, "The OPEC Fund for International Development", *Third World Quarterly*, Vol.3, no.2, April 1981.

Singh, K.R., "Iran - The Quest for Security: An Overview", *India Quarterly*, Vol.XXX, no.2, 1974.

Sobhan, Rehman, "Institutional Mechanisms for Channelling OPEC Surpluses within the Third World", *Third World Quarterly*, Vol.2, no.4, October 1980.

Srivastava, R.K., "India's West Asian Policy in Perspective", *Afro-Asian and World Affairs*, Vol.5, no.1, Spring 1968.

Sullivan, M.J., "Indian Attitudes on International Atomic Energy Controls", *Pacific Affairs*, Vol.43, no.3, Fall 1970.

Suroor, Hasan, "Behind the Ban", *Frontline*, 29 October-11 November, 1988.

Swamy, Subramaniam, "The Secret Friendship Between India and Israel", *Sunday*, 28 November-4 December 1982.

Tahir-Kheli, Shirin and Staudemaier, William O., "The Saudi-Pakistani Military Relationship: Implications for U.S. Policy", *ORBIS*, Vol.26, no.1, Spring 1982.

Tahir-Kheli, Shirin, "Iran and Pakistan: Cooperation in an Area of Conflict", *Asian Survey*, Vol.XVII, no.5, May 1977.

Weinbaum, M.G. and Sen, Gautam, "Pakistan Enters the Middle East", *ORBIS*, Vol.22, no.3, Fall 1978.

Wriggins, Howard, "Changing Power Relations Between the Middle East and South Asia", *ORBIS*, Vol.20, no.3, Fall 1976.